Vilcabamba
and the Archaeology of Inca Resistance

UCLA COTSEN INSTITUTE OF ARCHAEOLOGY PRESS

MONOGRAPHS

Monograph 80

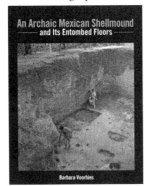

*An Archaic Mexican Shellmound
and Its Entombed Floors*
Barbara Voorhies (ed.)

Monograph 79

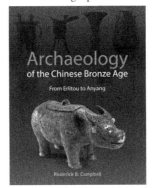

*Archaeology of the Chinese Bronze Age:
From Erlitou to Anyang*
Roderick B. Campbell

Monograph 78

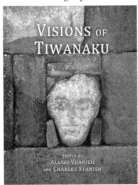

Visions of Tiwanaku
Alexei Vranich and Charles Stanish (eds.)

Monograph 77

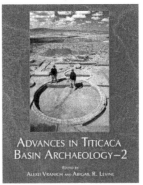

Advances in Titicaca Basin Archaeology–2
Alexei Vranich and Abigail R. Levine (eds.)

Monograph 76

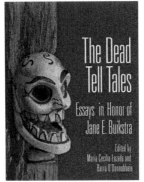

The Dead Tell Tales
María Cecilia Lozada and Barra O'Donnabhain (eds.)

Monograph 75

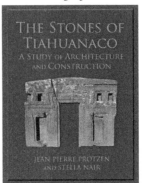

The Stones of Tiahuanaco
Jean-Pierre Protzen and Stella Nair

See page 181 for a complete list of Cotsen Institute of Archaeology Monographs.

Vilcabamba
and the Archaeology of Inca Resistance

Brian S. Bauer

Javier Fonseca Santa Cruz

Miriam Aráoz Silva

The Cotsen Institute of Archaeology Press is the publishing unit of the Cotsen Institute of Archaeology at UCLA. The Cotsen Institute is a premier research organization dedicated to the creation, dissemination, and conservation of archaeological knowledge and heritage. It is home to both the Interdepartmental Archaeology Graduate Program and the UCLA/Getty Master's Program in the Conservation of Archaeological and Ethnographic Materials. The Cotsen Institute provides a forum for innovative faculty research, graduate education, and public programs at UCLA in an effort to impact positively the academic, local, and global communities. Established in 1973, the Cotsen Institute is at the forefront of archaeological research, education, conservation, and publication, and is an active contributor to interdisciplinary research at UCLA.

The Cotsen Institute Press specializes in producing high-quality academic volumes in several different series, including *Monographs*, *World Heritage* and *Monuments*, Cotsen Advanced Seminars, and Ideas, Debates, and Perspectives. The Press is committed to making the fruits of archaeological research accessible to professionals, scholars, students, and the general public. We are able to do this through the generosity of Lloyd E. Cotsen, longtime Institute volunteer and benefactor, who has provided an endowment that allows us to subsidize our publishing program and produce superb volumes at an affordable price. Publishing in nine different series, our award-winning archaeological publications receive critical acclaim in both the academic and popular communities.

Edited by Peg Goldstein
Designed by Doug Brotherton
Index by Brian S. Bauer

Library of Congress Cataloging-in-Publication Data

Bauer, Brian S.
Vilcabamba and the archaeology of Inca resistance / Brian S. Bauer, Javier Fonseca Santa Cruz, and Miriam Aráoz Silva.
    pages cm. -- (Cotsen Institute of Archaeology Press monographs; Monograph 81)

ISBN 978-1-938770-03-6
1. Incas--Peru--Vilcabamba Mountains Region--Antiquities. 2. Excavations (Archaeology)--Peru--Vilcabamba Mountains Region. 3. Vilcabamba Mountains Region (Peru)--Antiquities. 4. Incas--Wars--Peru--Vilcabamba Mountains Region.
5. Vilcabamba Mountains Region (Peru)--History, Military--16th century. 6. Vilcabamba Mountains Region (Peru)--Ethnic relations--History--16th century. I. Fonseca Santa Cruz, Javier. II. Silva, Miriam Aráoz. III. Title.

F3429.1.V48B28 2015
985'.37--dc23

2015011160

Epigraphs

The town [of Vilcabamba] covers or, better said, used to cover, an area half a league wide, similar in plan to Cusco, and a great stretch in length, where parrots, chickens, ducks, local rabbits, turkeys, pheasants, curassows, guans, macaws, and a thousand other types of birds of diverse and beautiful plumages. The houses and huts were covered with good straw. . . . The house of the Inca had upper and lower floors covered in tiles, and the whole palace was painted with great variety of paintings in their style, which was quite a sight to see. There was a plaza that could hold many people, where they celebrated and even raced horses. The doors of the houses were of very fragrant cedar, which is plentiful in that land. . . . In this way, the Incas did not miss the pleasures, grandeur, or the opulence of Cusco, in that distant land or, better said, in that land of exile, because the Indians brought them anything they could want from the outside for their joy and pleasure.

—Martín de Murúa, *Historia General del Perú*, 1616

[On] June 24, 1572, the entire army marched into the town of Vilcabamba at ten o'clock in the morning. . . . They found the entire town sacked, such that if the Spaniards and Indian allies had done it, it would have been no worse because all the Indian men and women fled and went into mountains, taking as much as they could with them. . . . They burned and destroyed the city such that it was still smoldering when the army arrived. The House of the Sun where they kept their major idol was also burned. The Indians believed that if the Spaniards did not find food or any sustenance quickly, they would soon turn around and leave the region. . . . It was with this intention that the Indians fled, setting fire to everything they could not take.

—Martín de Murúa, *Historia General del Perú*, 1616

Contents

List of Figures

Contributors

Miriam Aráoz Silva is an independent archaeologist based in the city of Cusco. She is a cofounder of Aráoz Delgado Consultores Supervisores and has directed numerous projects across the Andes.

Brian S. Bauer is a professor of anthropology at the University of Illinois–Chicago and an adjutant curator at the Field Museum. He has conducted archaeological research in the Andes for more than 30 years.

Javier Fonseca Santa Cruz is a member of Peru's Ministerio de Cultura. He is especially well-known for his work on the Inca and Wari in the Vilcabamba region.

Kylie E. Quave is a visiting assistant professor of anthropology at Beloit College and a postdoctoral research fellow at the Logan Museum of Anthropology. She directs archaeological research on the Inca in the Cusco region.

Chronology

Early 1400s	The Inca Empire expands into the Vilcabamba region, located northwest of Cusco. Construction of Choquequirao, Machu Picchu, Vitcos, Vilcabamba, and Yurak Rumi begins.
Early July 1537	After his failed siege of Cusco, Manco Inca retreats into the Vilcabamba region.
Mid-July 1537	Rodrigo Orgóñez and Ruy Diaz lead a raid into the Vilcabamba region.
April 1539	Gonzalo Pizarro and followers invade the Vilcabamba region. They remain there for almost two months but do not capture Manco Inca.
Mid-1544	Manco Inca is killed in Vitcos. Sayri Tupac becomes the ruler of Vilcabamba.
1559	Sayri Túpac leaves the Vilcabamba region and visits Lima.
1560	Sayri Túpac dies while in Spanish-controlled Yucay. Titu Cusi Yupanqui becomes the ruler of Vilcabamba.
1565	With the Treaty of Acobamba, Titu Cusi Yupanqui agrees to end resistance against Spanish rule.
1568	Titu Cusi Yupanqui is baptized by Juan de Vivero. Marcos García enters
Circa 1569	Diego Ortiz is given permission to establish a mission in the Vilcabamba region.
February 6, 1570	While in the city of Vilcabamba Titu Cusi Yupanqui dictates a chronicle of his life. García and Ortiz sign the document as witnesses.
March 1570	García and Ortiz burn the Yurak Rumi shrine near Vitcos. García is banished from Vilcabamba while Ortiz is allowed to remain.
1571	Titu Cusi Yupanqui dies suddenly while visiting Vitcos. Ortiz is killed in the aftermath. Túpac Amaru becomes ruler of Vilcabamba.
March 1572	Atilano de Anaya is killed at the bridge of Chuquichaca while attempting to enter Vilcabamba.
April 14, 1572	Viceroy Francisco de Toledo declares war on Vilcabamba.
May 4, 1572	MartínHurtado de Arbieto leaves Cusco with an army to invade the Vilcabamba region.
June 24, 1572	Spanish forces and their Andean allies enter the city of Vilcabamba.
July 29, 1572	Viceroy Francisco de Toledo appoints Hurtado de Arbieto as the governor, captain general, and royal justice of Vilcabamba. The appointment is to last two lifetimes.

August 8, 1572	Hurtado de Arbieto announces his governorship while in the city of Vilcabamba.
Mid-August 1572	Túpac Amaru is captured by Martín García Óñez de Loyola.
September 1572	Hurtado de Arbieto and his forces leave the city of Vilcabamba. Francisco de Camargo y Aguilar is asked to remain to establish a fort in the area. Hurtado de Arbieto establishes a new town, called San Francisco de la Victoria de Vilcabamba, near Hoyara.
September 24, 1572	Túpac Amaru is executed in Cusco.
November 4, 1575	Toledo and Hurtado de Arbieto file the paperwork necessary for the permanent appointment of Hurtado de Arbieto as governor of Vilcabamba.
January 13, 1580	Toledo reprimands Hurtado de Arbieto for having left the province of Vilcabamba without his permission.
August 1582	Hurtado de Arbieto journeys down the Urubamba River into Manarí territory. The trip goes badly, and the troops return in two months.
1583–1584	Hurtado de Arbieto leads an expedition down the Apurimac River into Pilcosuni territory. He returns to Yucay badly wounded.
1588	Antonio Pereyra begins an investigation into the conduct of Hurtado de Arbieto as governor of Vilcabamba.
May 12, 1589	Pereyra recommends that Hurtado de Arbieto be removed as governor of Vilcabamba for failure to comply with the official duties of the office.
November 12, 1589	Hurtado de Arbieto dies in Lima while defending his right as the governorship.
1595	The Augustinians investigate the death of Ortiz.
Circa 1596	Viceroy Luis de Velasco approves the resettlement of the city of San Francisco de la Victoria de Vilcabamba to its modern-day location.
1599–1600	The Augustinians continue their investigations into the death of Ortiz.
Circa 1603	Slaves revolt in the Vilcabamba region.

Acknowledgments

Brian S. Bauer and Miriam Aráoz Silva

Figure A.1. Field crew at Yurak Rumi, 2008 (photograph by Brian S. Bauer and Miriam Aráoz Silva).

FUNDING FOR OUR WORK AT Vitcos was provided by the National Geographic Society, the Curtiss T. Brennan and Mary G. Brennan Foundation, the Institute for New World Archaeology, and the Accelerator Mass Spectrometry Laboratory at the University of Arizona. Additional support was provided by the Office of the Dean (College of Liberal Arts and Sciences) and the Department of Anthropology at the University of Illinois–Chicago. We thank Vincent Lee and David Drew for providing some of the drawings and photographs used in this work, Steven A. Wernke and Steven Kosiba for their comments on parts of this manuscript, George S. Burr for his aid with the radiocarbon dating, and Kylie Quave for her assistance with the ceramic analysis.

Crew members during our Vitcos work included Wilbert Gamarra, Henry Quispe, and Thibault Saintenoy in 2008; Wilbert Gamarra, Geanette Guzman, Vincent Bauer, and Kylie Quave in 2009. During our work in the region, we were also supported by many members of the surrounding committees (Figure A.1). We would especially like to thank Julia and Vicente Cobos for the hospitality they showed us in the village of Huancacalle and Rosa and Juvenal Cobos, who generously helped with our housing during the second year of work at Vitcos. Our excavations at Vitcos were conducted with permission from the former Instituto Nacional de Cultura Region Cusco[1] in 2008 (Acuerdo N° 180) and 2009 (Acuerdo N° 147 and Resolucion Directoral Nacional N° 529/INC). Supervision was provided by Clara Jimenez in 2008 and Reynaldo Bustinza in 2009.

Our work in 2010 at Espíritu Pampa was supported by the National Science Foundation (BCS 0910432) and the Institute for New World Archaeology. Crew members in 2010 included Wilbert Gamarra, Geanette Guzman, and Gladys Cobos Terrazas. During our time in Espíritu Pampa, we lived with Americo Sacsa Cobos and his wife, Reyna, as well as with Ciriaco Huillca and his wife, Victoria. We could not have run the project without them. We also relied greatly on Julian Valeriano, who was always there with horses when we needed them. During the course of our excavations, we rotated our crews every two weeks to include as many members of the community as possible. Thus we are now indebted to nearly all the families of Espíritu Pampa for their work on the project. Among the many individuals who worked with us were Eduardo Tebes, Vidal Puma, Leonardo Puma, Ismael Puma, Milton Luque, Jose Huillca, Gregorio Alvarez, Rosmel Chiclla, Teofilo Alvarez, Ronald Huaman, Walter Huaman, Valentin Balbino, and Rudy Huillca. The 2010 excavations at Espíritu Pampa were conducted with permission from the former Instituto National de Cultura Region Cusco (proyecto Resolución Directoral Nacional N° 1203/INC del 25.05.2010), and the final report was accepted (Resolución Viceministerial N° 013-2011-VMPCIC-MC del 05.01.2011). Supervision was provided by Rene Pilco Vargas with the help of Arminda Gibaja Oviedo and Wilbert San Roman Luna.

Axel Aráoz Silva drafted many of our field maps, and Gabriel E. Cantarutti aided us in almost all aspect of manuscript preparation. In Cusco we were helped by our close friends Jean-Jacques Decoster, Donato Amado, Jesus Galiano Blanco, Goyo Coronal, and Eva Santa Cruz. Madeleine Halac-Higashimori also spent many hours helping us improve the manuscript. Parts of Chapter 3 were published in *Andean Past* (Bauer et al. 2012:195–211) and are reproduced with permission.

Preface

Brian S. Bauer

WE WORKED IN ESPÍRITU PAMPA at a wonderful moment in its long history. Roads, electricity, and telephone services were slowly moving into the Vilcabamba region but were rare enough that they were unreliable. When they did work as intended, they felt almost wondrous. There was regular transportation from the booming, seedy, natural gas–financed river town of Kiteni to the dreary, nearly empty village of Chuanquiri. And a rough road, usable only during the height of the dry season, had been cut from Chuanquiri to the bridge of Azulmayo, where a small regional market, only 50 yards long, had quickly developed. Once a week, villagers from across the uplands would arrive with their horses carrying coffee beans to be exchanged for supplies with a few entrepreneurs who had arrived in large trucks the night before. The trucks came to Azulmayo laden with goods and left full of coffee beans.[2]

Brought to life for only a few hours a week, Azulmayo would be packed with women and men, buyers and sellers, young and old, all shuttling between a series of small kiosks. Filthy and covered in pieces of discarded paper, metal, and plastic, Azulmayo had that special feeling of a temporary frontier settlement where the influence of the combustion engine ended and horses and

Figure P.1. The last of three suspension bridges built between Azulmayo and Espíritu Pampa, 2010 (photograph by Brian S. Bauer and Miriam Aráoz Silva).

manual labor still carried the day. If we were lucky, or if our request, sent the night before from the only radio station in the region, had been heard, we would use a few of the unburdened horses to carry our gear on the four-hour climb from Azulmayo to Espíritu Pampa.[3] The trail was always slippery, and the heat felt oppressive as we tried to adjust from the higher and drier climate of Cusco (Figure P.1).

The community of Espíritu Pampa is composed of a few dozen scattered homesteads at the confluence of the Chaupi and Concevidayoc rivers. Formally the holdings of Julio Cobos, the land was divided up during the agrarian reform and is now occupied by a small number of families, many of which are linked through marriage. Yucca is the major staple. However corn, sugarcane, coca, and various fruits are produced in limited quantities.[4] In this subtropical region, vegetation begins to reclaim abandoned fields within a few months. Although the *maquisapas* (spider monkeys) and peccaries that inhabited the area as recently as 15 years ago have now retreated deeper into the forests, to the newly initiated, the area is filled with exotic animals and plants.

Thanks to the generosity of several families, we lived in two rented rooms in the community of Espíritu Pampa and made the short walk each day to the archaeological site. Leaving the trail and entering the dense forest that still covered patches of the area was like entering a new world or crossing into a greenish night. There are shades upon shades of green and multiple tones of yellow and brown that shift during the day as the light filters down through the high forest canopy. In many places, the forest humus was so thick that we could not feel the ground but instead walked upon a spongy surface that gave off a deep, rich organic smell. In the deep forest, there is no mud, only rotting wood, leaves, and branches. There is, however, a nearly continuous chorus of chirping insects and birds, occasionally interrupted by the crash of a falling tree limb somewhere in the distance and the grinding of tree limbs against each other in the wind. Speaking for the whole crew, we were entranced with our brief stay in Espíritu Pampa and are profoundly grateful for it.

For many years, the ruins of Espíritu Pampa played only a minor role in the lives of the villagers who lived near it. Now, however, the Ministerio de Cultura supports a series of projects in the valley and hires a few local men to keep the central core of the archaeological site free of vegetation. But change is occurring rapidly in and around the site. Each year new fields are cleared and burned and a few more of the towering matapalo

trees, the final remnants of the ancient forest, are carelessly cut with chainsaws. Two years after our work, road construction destroyed the Azulmayo suspension bridge (Figure P. 2) and the end of the road reached Chuntapampa, about an hour walk from Espíritu Pampa. Regrettably, the entire area remains deeply impoverished, the political problems have worsened, development is uneven, and the community of Espíritu Pampa continues to gain little benefit from the important ruins within its boundaries.

The town that the Inca once called Vilcabamba, and that is now called Espíritu Pampa, was set aflame by its own citizens on the evening of June 23, 1572, in anticipation of the soon-to-arrive Spanish forces. The town was burned in an attempt to deny the invading forces the supplies they would need to occupy the region. However, this dramatic act failed to deter the Spaniards; within a few months, they had captured and executed the last Inca ruler, Túpac Amaru, and begun to settle those areas closest to Cusco. The former settlement of Vilcabamba, the final capital of the Incas, was left in ruins and abandoned. Yet because of the remoteness of the ruins and the vegetation that quickly covered (and in many ways preserved) the remains, the site remained remarkably intact over the next four centuries.

Beginning about 10 years ago, the former Instituto National de Cultura Region Cusco began supporting large-scale research in the Vilcabamba region, especially at the site of Espíritu Pampa. This research has emphasized the clearing of sites and making them accessible for tourism. The establishment of networks of cleared and consolidated Inca ruins permits adventure-minded tourists to see the region and to follow in the footsteps of Bingham, Savoy, and other early explorers. However, from a scientific perspective, the field methods and laboratory analysis used in these projects were not sufficient to collect all possible evidence from the contexts being transformed, and the final products of the fieldwork have generally been internal technical reports that have not been widely disseminated. This divide between the aims of academic archaeologists and the development goals of national heritage-management programs can be observed in other parts of Peru and in other countries where tourism constitutes an important part of national economies.

Archaeologists today are deeply engaged in debates over the ethics of professional practice and the multiple voices and constituencies that should take part in discourses on the past (e.g., Scarre and Scarre 2006). While we recognize the claims of national govern-

Figure P.2. The Azulmayo Bridge, 2010 (photograph by Brian S. Bauer and Miriam Aráoz Silva).

ments, descendant communities, and avocational visitors, it is nevertheless regrettable when an emphasis on the speedy removal of archaeological deposits takes precedence over painstaking description of contexts that are inevitably destroyed in the process of studying them. Regrettably, over the past 20 years, the monumental zones of many of the most important archaeological sites in the Cusco region have been irrevocably altered by the Instituto National de Cultura Region Cusco, and the data collected are too often limited, inaccessible, or lost altogether. The task for current archaeologists—one that is becoming all too familiar in many parts of the world—is to conduct new work where possible and to synthesize all available knowledge that can be gleaned from previous fieldwork, remaining mindful of what is not known and can never be recovered.

Endnotes

1   The Institutio National de Cultura Region Cusco was reorganized to become the Ministerio de Cultura Dirección Desconcentrada de Cultura Cusco in October 2010.
2   Alternatively, one could make the three-day hike from Huancacalle to Espíritu Pampa.
3   While many coffee farmers of Espíritu Pampa owned one or two horses, coffee harvests required the use of dozens. These were frequently contracted from relatives or friends in Pampaconas, which, being much higher, was able to support larger herds.
4   Some farmers also have access to potato fields high up the mountain slopes or trade with farmers of Pampaconas and other mountain villages.

Chapter 1

An Introduction to Vilcabamba

Brian S. Bauer

I N LATE JUNE OF 1572, Spanish forces, accompanied by their Andean allies, stormed the remote town of Vilcabamba, the last Inca stronghold.[1] Among the first soldiers to enter the town was Pedro Sarmiento de Gamboa, the standard bearer for the army. He rushed to the central plaza and declared, "I, Captain Pedro Sarmiento de Gamboa, *Alférez General* of this army, at the request of its General, the illustrious Lord Martín Hurtado de Arbieto, claim this town of Vilcabamba, its vicinities, provinces, and jurisdictions." Sarmiento de Gamboa then shouted "Vilcabamba! For Don Felipe, King of Castile and León" three times and planted the flag in the plaza.[2]

The fall of Vilcabamba was a significant victory for the Spaniards in their colonization efforts in the Americas. They had successfully invaded the Andes more than 40 years before, but the Vilcabamba region remained the final bastion of organized indigenous resistance against European hegemony. Forty years earlier, Manco Inca, who at first aided the Spaniards and then rebelled against them, had established a rumpstate in this mountainous region while he attempted to regain control of the realm.[3] After Manco Inca's death, three of his sons (Sayri Túpac, Titu Cusi Yupanqui, and Túpac Amaru) negotiated with the Spaniards while also leading indigenous resistance against them. For their part, the Spaniards sent diplomats, priests, and at times military expeditions into the Vilcabamba region during this period in an effort to bring an end to the conflict and establish uncontested hegemony in the Andes. The Spanish campaign against Vilcabamba ended with the capture and subsequent execution of Túpac Amaru, events that most scholars equate with the end of the Inca Empire (Figure 1.1).

A Short History of the Vilcabamba Region

After his failed revolt in 1536, Manco Inca retreated down the Urubamba River to a vast mountainous region known as Vilcabamba.[4] The Incas had occupied the Vilcabamba area for at least four generations and had constructed three major towns (Choquequirao, Vitcos, and Vilcabamba), established dozens of smaller settlements, and developed an extensive road network in the region. For Manco Inca, Vilcabamba must have been seen as an almost impenetrable refuge, where he could live while attempting to reorganize his loyalists against the Spaniards, who were already taking control of broad areas of the highlands. To enter the Vilcabamba region, Manco Inca and his forces crossed the Chuquichaca Bridge (at the modern settlement of Chaullay) and continued on the central road that leads directly to Vitcos. After crossing the bridge, Manco Inca

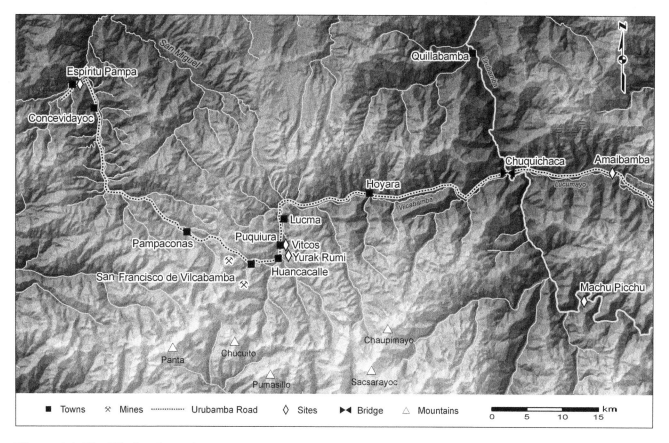

Figure 1.1. The Vilcabamba region
(map by Gabriel E. Cantarutti).

ordered it to be destroyed in the hope that this would prevent the Spaniards from entering the region (Figure 1.2). The Spanish forces, led by Rodrigo Orgóñez and Ruy Diaz and supported by Manco Inca's half brother, Paullu Inca, were forced to stop for a few days as they rebuilt the bridge (Pizarro 1921:365 [1571], 1986:169 [1571]). However on its reconstruction, the Spanish forces quickly traveled on horseback as far as Vitcos. No Spaniard had entered this region before, and what they found amazed them.

The city of Vitcos was built on a high hill at the intersection of three different valleys. It was a natural location for the Inca occupation of the region, and they had built a sprawling town with an impressive central plaza, various elite dwellings, dozens of domestic clusters, and a large shrine complex. The settlement was also surrounded by several large, well-watered terrace systems. However, by the time the Spanish arrived in Vitcos, Manco Inca had fled into the dense forests of the surrounding mountains. Unable to capture Manco Inca, the Spanish troops returned to Cusco with a large hoard of gold and silver taken from the city.[5]

A second raid into the Vilcabamba region, led by Gonzalo Pizarro, occurred three years later, in 1539. As with the first raid, by the time the Spaniards reached the city of Vitcos, Manco Inca had already fled into the

Figure 1.2. Foundations of the Inca bridge of Chuquichaca. These were destroyed in 1998 in a massive flood (photograph by Vincent Lee, circa 1984).

mountains. This time, however, the Spaniards followed the Inca to the village of Pampaconas and then farther into the lowlands. A major battle took place at a small ridgetop settlement called Huayna Pucará[6], about two days from the Inca town of Vilcabamba, but the Inca again escaped. The Spanish stayed in the Vilcabamba region for more than two months; however, they were unable to learn the whereabouts of Manco Inca.[7]

The relationship between Vilcabamba and Cusco was complex. Manco Inca continued to conduct raids on travelers along the mountains routes between Lima and Cusco. In response, the Spaniards founded the town of Huamanga (modern Ayacucho) to help protect highland travel. At the same time, diplomatic connections between Vilcabamba and Inca nobles in Cusco were sustained, as each side eyed the other with concern. Meanwhile, Spanish leadership in Peru entered a period of crisis as a series of conflicts pitted different factions against one other.

In 1544 Manco Inca was assassinated in Vitcos by a band of Spanish rebels who had sought asylum in the Vilcabamba region. His death did not bring peace to the region, however, as resistance against the Spaniards continued under the successive leadership of his sons Sayri Túpac (1544–1560), Titu Cusi Yupanqui (1560–1571), and Túpac Amaru (1571–1572). During this period, the Inca nobility continued to live in both Vitcos and in the more remote town of Vilcabamba.

Sayri Túpac, the eldest of Manco Inca's sons, was far more open to negotiations with the Spaniards than his father had been. In time, the viceroy of Peru was able to negotiate a treaty between Sayri Túpac and the Spanish Crown. The critical feature of the treaty was that Sayri Túpac would be granted the wealthy landholding (*repartimiento*) of Yucay, which included the former country estate of Huayna Capac, the final Inca to rule a united empire and Sayri Túpac's grandfather.[8] In exchange for this land grant, Sayri Túpac agreed to convert to Christianity and leave the Vilcabamba region. In 1559 he left his mountain refuge. He first traveled to Lima to meet the viceroy and then settled in Cusco. Sayri Túpac's arrangements with the Spaniards did not bring peace to the Andes for long, however, since he died within two years of leaving Vilcabamba.

With Sayri Túpac's death, leadership in the Vilcabamba region passed to Titu Cusi Yupanqui. Like his brother, Titu Cusi Yupanqui was interested in gaining access to the Yucay estate, and he held prolonged negotiations with Spanish officials over many years. In 1568, as part of what has become known as the Acobamba Treaty, Titu Cusi Yupanqui allowed two Augustinian priests, Marcos García and Diego Ortiz, to live and proselytize in the area. In 1570 these two priests and a small group of villagers burned the Yurak Rumi complex (a large carved rock and a set of adjacent buildings), the most important shrine in the Vilcabamba region (see Chapter 3).

During the following year, Titu Cusi Yupanqui suddenly died while in Vitcos; Diego Ortiz was subsequently killed under the assumption that he was involved in some way with the Inca's death (Bauer et al.

2014). With Titu Cusi Yupanqui's death, Túpac Amaru, Manco Inca's youngest son, was crowned as Inca.

In 1572, after the death of Atilano de Anaya, a Spanish diplomat who had been sent into the Vilcabamba region, Viceroy Francisco de Toledo organized a massive raid against the Inca. Spanish troops quickly took the town of Vitcos and then moved on to Vilcabamba. When the Spaniards entered the final capital of the Inca, they found it in ruins, still smoldering from fires lit the night before. The royal court and the townspeople had abandoned the settlement and fled into the surrounding mountains in an attempt to escape the invaders. The Spaniards occupied the town for about two months while they sent search parties in different directions looking for leaders of the resistance. In time, the Spaniards hunted down and captured all the members of the royal court.[9]

When the Spanish forces returned to Cusco, they brought with them Túpac Amaru, the last of Manco Inca's sons, who had only recently become ruler of Vilcabamba. After a hastily arranged trial, Túpac Amaru was beheaded in the central plaza of Cusco on the orders of Viceroy Toledo. Scholars widely agree that the fall of Vilcabamba and the death of Túpac Amaru marked the end of the Spanish invasion and the beginning of European control of the Andes.

The town of Vitcos was most likely abandoned soon after the third and final Spanish raid into the region. At that time, Martín Hurtado de Arbieto, the leader of the Spanish forces, established a Spanish *reducción* called San Francisco de la Victoria de Vilcabamba near the modern town of Hoyara, and we presume that the residents of Vitcos were forced to leave their city and were resettled into this township. In time, even the name of Vitcos was forgotten; the ruins came to be called Rosaspata. When the famed geographer Antonio Raimondi (1872) traveled to the region in 1865, the former Inca city was not even worthy of mention.

Built in a more remote and thinly populated region, the Inca town of Vilcabamba was largely abandoned after 1572; the subtropical forest soon began to encroach on this former settlement.[10] During the first decades after the Spaniards annexed the Vilcabamba region, the former Inca town of Vilcabamba was referred to as Vilcabamba the Old, to distinguish it from a newly established settlement in the Vitcos Valley, which the Spaniards named San Francisco de la Victoria de Vilcabamba. With the passing of generations, remembrances of Vilcabamba the Old wore thin, and by the end of the nineteenth century, few in the area could recall the town's earlier importance. Gradually the area became

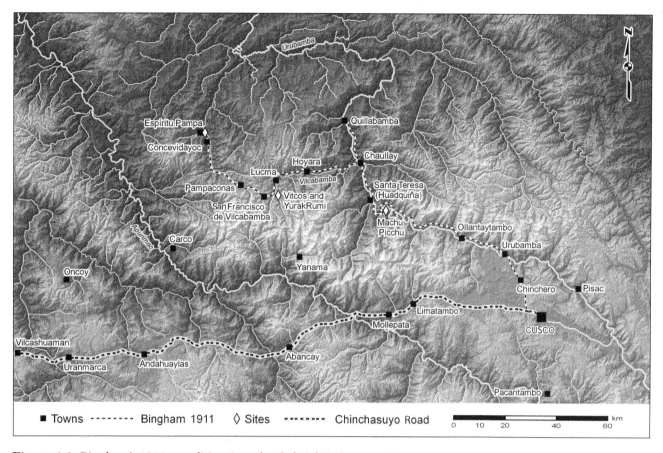

Figure 1.3. Bingham's 1911 expedition (map by Gabriel E. Cantarutti).

overgrown and the largely forgotten ruin of Vilcabamba came to be known as Espíritu Pampa (the Plain of Spirits).

Hiram Bingham and Explorations of the Vilcabamba Region

In 1908 Hiram Bingham conducted a cross-continental journey from Buenos Aires, Argentina, to Lima, Peru.[11] Near the end of the trek, while in the town of Abancay, Peru, Bingham was told of an immense Inca site called Choquequirao by a local official who had recently led a large work party to the ruins looking for treasure. Choquequirao had been known for more than a century and was generally believed to be the city of Vilcabamba, the last capital of the Incas. Bingham spent several days photographing and studying Choquequirao before continuing on his journey to Lima. That visit provided the basis for his first scholarly article (Bingham 1910). A book describing the entire trip from Buenos Aries to Lima soon followed (Bingham 1911).

Up to this point, Bingham was more interested in the colonial history of Latin America and in producing travel accounts than in conducting concentrated research on the Inca, but this was soon to change. On his return to the United States, Bingham learned that recent scholarship questioned the long-standing assumption that the site of Choquequirao was the lost city of Vilcabamba and about the discovery of several archival documents providing additional information on the final years of Inca resistance in the Andes. While researching the topic, Bingham came upon a footnote in Bandelier's (1910) monumental work *Islands of Titicaca and Koati*, suggesting that the mountain of Coropuna near Arequipa might be the highest in South America. As a result, Bingham organized another expedition to Peru with two very different goals. The first goal was to look for the Inca cities of Vitcos and Vilcabamba. The second goal was to climb the mountain of Coropuna.[12] A third goal, walking the seventy-third meridian, was later added and was undertaken largely under the direction of Isaiah Bowman.[13]

Bingham was an unusual person to have organized this expedition. He was not an archaeologist or a mountaineer but a professor of Latin American history. Furthermore, his studies prior to this time had focused on the period of South American independence, the early 1800s. Nevertheless, Bingham was an experienced explorer, and he managed to receive funds from Yale University to support his trip. To his credit, Bingham brought a group of other professionals with him to help collect information. Most important for this study, he recruited topographer Kai Hendriksen and geologist-geographer Bowman; the latter would produce an especially large number of important publications on the Andes and become an internationally known scholar.[14] In this way, Bingham's 1911 trip marked an important break between what had been a series of travel accounts and the formation of a scientific expedition dedicated to collecting a wide range of information (Burger and Salazar 2004).[15]

Bingham arrived in Cusco in early July 1911. Informed by several recently discovered Spanish documents describing the last decades of the Incas, published by Carlos Romero (1909), Bingham suspected that the Inca cities of Vitcos and Vilcabamba would be found in the Vilcabamba region near the town of Puquiura to the northwest of Cusco. Yet he was not certain, since the well-known geographer Raimondi (1872) had visited the region many years earlier and not reported any ruins. Working from several tips concerning the existence of Inca remains in the lower Urubamba Valley, Bingham left Cusco on July 19 and reached Ollantaytambo the following day (Figure 1.3). There he encountered exceptionally good luck. Below Ollantaytambo, the Urubamba Valley begins to narrow, and its steep cliffs, wild rapids, and dense vegetation make travel along its course extremely difficult. For centuries, most trade between Cusco and the region to its northwest had avoided this difficult stretch of the valley by taking a longer but easier route toward the lowlands via the Amaibamba Valley. Bingham found, however, that the Peruvian government had completed a relatively new mule trail along the Urubamba River between Ollantaytambo and Quillabamba. Following advice from acquaintances in Cusco, especially Albert Giesecke, rector of the National University of Cusco, Bingham decided to travel the new route. Two evenings later, while camping near a sharp bend in the river, Bingham learned from a local farmer that there were ruins located on a narrow ridge high above that section of the Urubamba River. Bingham's two U.S. companions selected to remain in camp the next day, so Bingham set out with his military escort and the farmer to visit the site. After stopping briefly for food and water at a hut just before reaching the top of the ridge, he found himself on the edge of a wonderfully preserved, although greatly overgrown, Inca ruin.[16] Less than a week after

leaving Cusco, Bingham had come upon Machu Picchu, one of the greatest ruins of Peru.[17]

Contrary to popular belief, Bingham specifically noted in his early writings that he was not the first to hear of or visit the site of Machu Picchu. In 1875 Charles Wiener (1880), an Austrian-born explorer, was commissioned by the French government to travel through and report on Peru and Bolivia. Wiener arrived in Cusco and spent considerable time in and around the city. He also traveled to the town of Ollantaytambo. While there, he heard of a set of large ruins farther down the Urubamba River called Huayna Picchu and Machu Picchu. Wiener left Ollantaytambo and traveled into the interior following the traditional trade route, via Amaibamba, that linked Ollantaytambo with the low regions of coca and fruit production. By so doing he bypassed the narrowest section of the Urubamba Valley and missed the ruins of Machu Picchu. Nevertheless, the approximate locations of the ruins are marked on a map that was published with his travel account.

Many other travelers before Bingham had made the trip along the new road between the subtropical region of Quillabamba and Cusco. There is no doubt that many had heard stories of the ruins located high above the steep canyon walls, and some may have visited them.[18] For example, Albert Giesecke was told of the ruins of Machu Picchu the year before Bingham visited Cusco, but he was not able to make the climb to the site because of heavy rains. Giesecke passed his information on to Bingham in Cusco before he set out down the Urubamba River; Giesecke encouraged him to visit the site.[19] Furthermore, Bingham notes that he interviewed a prospector in Cusco who had possibly been to the site. More importantly, several farmers were living beside the ruins when Bingham visited, and he found the name of a nearby resident and the date 1902 written on one of the walls of the site.[20]

Eager to continue on and visit the region broadly known as Vilcabamba, Bingham spent only a few days at Machu Picchu before moving downstream to the hacienda of Huadquiña. The haciendas of Huadquiña (now called Santa Teresa)[21] and Santa Ana (located farther downstream near modern-day Quillabamba) were huge estates established by the Jesuits (Cruz Ccorimanya 2009:82). After the Jesuits were expelled from Peru in 1767, it appears that the haciendas were awarded to other religious organizations and then, over the years, entered into private hands. The powerful owners of these haciendas and their descendants dominated the political and social agendas of the region until agricultural reforms of the late 1960s. In Bingham's time, the hacienda of Huadquiña still covered an immense area—more than 200 square miles—and was controlled by Carmen Vargas (Bingham 1948:121).

In his search for the final cities of the Inca, Bingham was especially reliant on Antonio de la Calancha's detailed 1638 description of Diego Ortiz's missionary work in the Vilcabamba region. Bingham showed copies of the relevant passages to all those he met. For example, he writes that in the hacienda of Huadquiña,

> Our hosts, Señora Carmen Vargas and her family, read with interest my copy of those paragraphs of Calancha's chronicle which referred to the location of the last Inca capital. Learning that we were anxious to discover Vitcos, a place of which they had never heard, they ordered the most intelligent tenants on the estates to come in and be questioned [Bingham 1948:121].

Bingham was particularly interested in finding the rock shrine that Calancha called Yurak Rumi (White Rock). In his description of the shrine, Calancha (1981 [1638]) noted that this sacred rock was near the Inca town of Vitcos in an area called Chuquepalta.[22] Bingham was certain that if he could find the shrine of Yurak Rumi, he could then determine which of the many scattered ruins in the area was the former town of Vitcos.

Bingham left the *hacienda* of Huadquiña and traveled down the Urubamba to the next large landholding, the hacienda of Santa Ana (now Quillabamba), which was owned by Pedro Dugue. Bingham had already met Dugue's son while in Cusco, and he had encouraged Bingham to visit his father, who knew a wide range of people who were familiar with the interior regions of the province. When Bingham arrived in Santa Ana, Dugue told him that in 1902, a recently deceased local prospector, Manuel López Torres, had visited a large set of ruins deep within the region of Vilcabamba near a small landholding called Concevidayoc (Bingham 1914b:185).[23]

On August 6, after exploring some minor ruins near Huadquiña and visiting the hacienda of Santa Ana, Bingham left the Urubamba River valley by way of the well-known Chuquichaca Bridge beside the town of Chaullay and then headed up the small Vilcabam-

ba River in the direction of Puquiura (Figure 1.4).[24] As he traveled, Bingham began encountering place-names that matched those provided in the historical texts (Bingham 1912d:175–192, 1912c; Hemming 1970:482–485).

At the end of the first long day up the Vilcabamba River, Bingham arrived at the hamlet of Paltaybamba. The next day he passed the area of Hoyara, which he recognized as the site of the first Spanish town established in the Vilcabamba region following the capture

Figure 1.4. Bingham's team traveling toward the town of Puquiura in 1911 (National Geographic Image Collection: negative 785981, photograph by Hiram Bingham).

of Túpac Amaru (Ocampo Conejeros 2013 [1611]). In conversations, Bingham was specifically told that there were Spanish ruins within the nearby cane fields (Bingham 1912d:176). That evening his group rested in the small town of Lucma. The next day, Bingham visited and mapped the ruins of Inca Huaracana, situated on a ridge directly behind the small community. Bingham was eager to continue his explorations, as he was told by several local residents that there was a large carved rock called Ñusta España near the village of Puquiura, just

Figure 1.5. Millstone photographed by Bingham in 1911 (National Geographic Image Collection: negative 785895, photograph by Hiram Bingham).

Figure 1.6. Millstone photographed by Bingham in 1911 (photograph by Brian S. Bauer and Miriam Aráoz Silva).

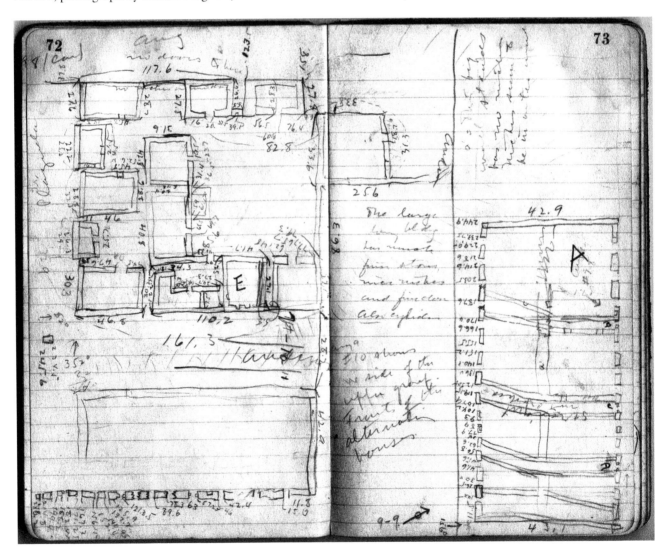

Figure 1.7. Bingham's 1911 field notes on the ruins of Vitcos (Rosaspata) (Yale Peruvian Expedition Papers, Manuscript 664. Manuscripts and Archives, Yale University Library).

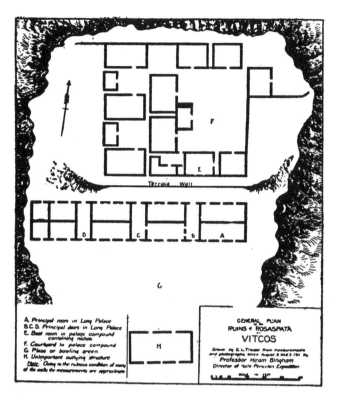

Figure 1.8. Bingham's (1912d:181) plan of the monumental core of Vitcos (Rosaspata).

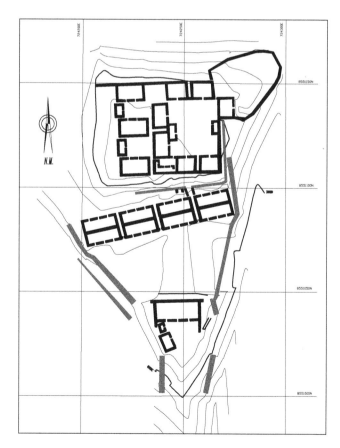

Figure 1.9. Plan of the monumental core of Vitcos (Rosaspata) (map by Axel Aráoz Silva).

Figure 1.10. Two doorways at Vitcos (Rosaspata), circa 1983 (photograph by David Drew).

Figure 1.11. Doorway at Vitcos (Rosaspata) after reconstruction (photograph by Brian S. Bauer and Miriam Aráoz Silva).

an hour or so farther upstream.

On August 8 Bingham made the short trip from Lucma to Puquiura and crossed the Vilcabamba River at the village of Huancacalle. Near the river crossing he noted the remains of a colonial era ore-crushing mill (Figures 1.5 and 1.6). Bingham was intrigued by the mill, since Baltasar de Ocampo Conejeros (2013:29, 36, 50 [1611]) had written that Cristóbal de Albornoz, a longtime resident of Vilcabamba, owned a mill near the town of Puquiura. Bingham continued, passing the ruins of a single large building at Uncapampa, and arrived at the impressive ruins of Rosaspata. Although the site was overgrown, Bingham could tell that it contained a large central plaza as well as a number of impressive structures (Figures 1.7–1.11).[25]

Bingham spent the night near the former mill. He returned to the Rosaspata area the next day, wanting to search for the large rock that he had been told about. Bingham found the rock late in the afternoon, in an

Figure 1.12. The north and west sides of Yurak Rumi being cleared of vegetation in 1911 (National Geographic Image Collection: negative 785910, photograph by Hiram Bingham).

area that is still called Chuquepalta (Figure 1.12).[26] Years later, Bingham could still clearly remember his arrival at the shrine:

> It was late on the afternoon of August 9, 1911, when I first saw this remarkable shrine. Densely wooded hills rose on every side. There was not a bird to be seen; scarcely a sound to be heard. It was an ideal place for practicing the mystic ceremonies of an ancient cult. The remarkable aspect of this great boulder and the dark pool beneath its shadow had caused this to become a place of worship [Bingham 1922:247].

Bingham correctly inferred that the large carved rock of Yurak Rumi (also called Ñusta España) was a major Inca shrine. In so doing, he also had a strong argument that the nearby site of Rosaspata was the town of Vitcos, which Calancha had specifically noted was located close to a large rock shrine. Yurak Rumi and its connection with the former Inca town of Vitcos became the focus of a series of preliminary reports published the following year (Bingham 1912a, 1912b, 1912c, 1912d).

Bingham spent the next day, August 10, clearing the shrine site, taking photographs, and sketching maps of

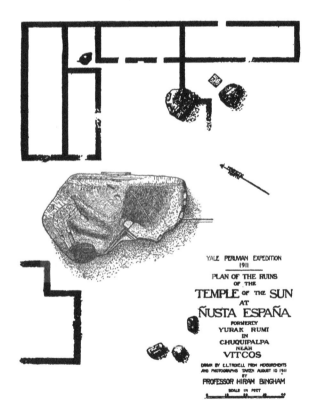

Figure 1.13. Bingham's (1912d:185) first plan of Yurak Rumi.

Yurak Rumi and Vitcos (Bingham 1912d:185). He then traveled to the Spanish town of Vilcabamba (formally known as San Francisco de la Victoria de Vilcabamba), about three hours away. This town was widely known as a former mining center and is marked on a host of seventeenth- and eighteenth-century maps (Figure 1.14). It was constructed at its current location around 1596, when Spanish settlers wanted their center near the largest mines of the region. Baltasar de Ocampo Conejeros (2013 [1611]) describes the founding of the town and construction of its church in his lengthy *Description of the Province of San Francisco de la Victoria de Vilcabamba* (circa 1611), a document that Bingham had read and perhaps even carried with him into the field.

However, Bingham had arrived at the town of San Francisco de la Victoria de Vilcabamba with the specific goal of locating places named by early Spanish writers. For example, he asked about the location of a village called Pampaconas, which is mentioned in documents related to the Vilcabamba region. Most importantly, Bingham had read Rodriquez de Figueroa's 1565 report that describes his meeting with Titu Cusi Yupanqui at Pampaconas. The report notes that the Inca had traveled to Pampaconas for the meeting from a town located farther down in the lowlands. Bingham correctly assumed that this unnamed town was the Inca town of Vilcabamba.

While in the Spanish town of Vilcabamba, Bingham was told that the village of Pampaconas was only half a day's walk away. He also heard rumors of more ruins beyond Pampaconas, deep in a subtropical region called Concevidayoc (Figure 1.15).[27]

On August 12, Bingham made the easy walk to the village of Pampaconas. After spending the night, he made the more difficult trip to the hacienda of Concevidayoc, dropping down into the subtropical area of Vilcabamba. On his arrival, the owner of Concevidayoc, Juan Cancio Saavedra, showed Bingham various Inca vessels and other objects recovered from a number of nearby structures. He confirmed that there were numerous additional ruins a few hours farther downriver in a small valley called Espíritu

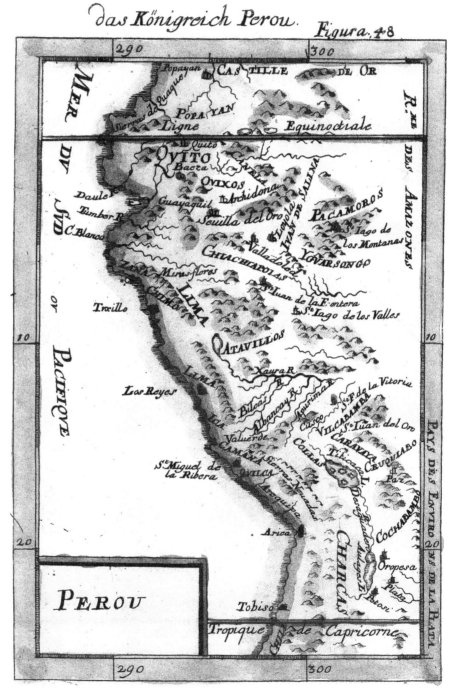

Figure 1.14. A 1683 map showing the Vilcabamba region and the town of Sa(n) F(rancisco) de la Victoria (de Vilcabamba) (Mallet 1683).

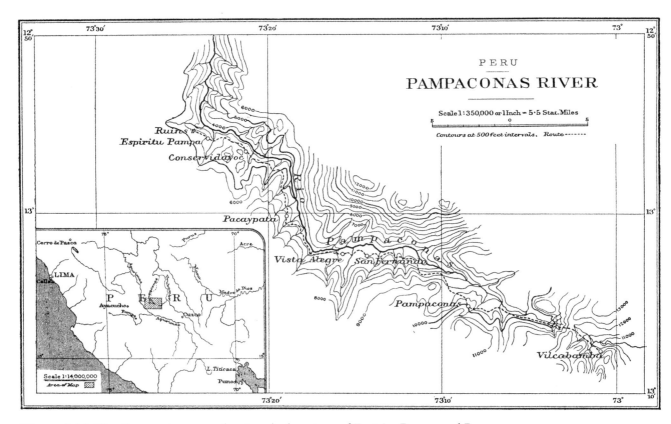

Figure 1.15. The first modern map showing the locations of Espíritu Pampa and Pampaconas was made by topographer Kai Hendriksen, a member of Bingham's 1911 team (Bingham 1914a).

Pampa (Figure 1.16).[28] The following day, Cancio Saavedra took Bingham to the site.

In an article, the first of numerous accounts of his explorations in the Vilcabamba region, Bingham (1912d:190) describes his initial impressions of the site of Espíritu Pampa:

> We followed a foot trail which leads from the present Vilcabamba basin down the Pampaconas valley to a place called Concevidayoc, or Espíritu Pampa, or Vilcabamba, near which we found ruins of a number of well-built houses of characteristic Inca architecture. The presence of the customary types of Inca pottery and the characteristics of the architecture which resembles in many respects the buildings of Choquequirao, led me to believe that the Incas had a settlement here, and that there must have been a well traveled foot path from the Vilcabamba valley certainly down as far as Espíritu Pampa.

When Bingham arrived at Espíritu Pampa, he found it occupied by a small group of swidden agriculturists. Members of the Campas tribe, these individuals were most certainly Machiguenga speakers who had fled up from the Amazonian piedmont to escape the growing oppression of rubber collectors (Figure 1.17). There appears to have been a large settlement of Campas in Concevidayoc and a smaller group living in Espíritu Pampa. Bingham (1914b:213) writes:

> At Concevidayoc, we found a small settlement of Campas Indians who were locally referred to as Pichanguerras. The married men wore a single long tunic, composed of a square of roughly woven cloth, with a hole cut in the centre for the head, and the sides partly stitched up to make armholes. The unmarried men wore a few rags around the waist. These people were timid, and we learned that they had run away from rubber gatherers in the valleys below. They did some hunting, using bows and arrows but appeared to rely chiefly on their little plantations of yucca and camotes. The huts were small, oval in shape with steeply pitched roofs, the sides made of small logs driven into the ground and fastened together with vines.

Beside modern huts, Bingham also noted a large number of low circular ruins within the clearing. Numerous others could be found within the forest.

Led by local members of the Campas (Machiguenga), Bingham was then shown more substantial ter-

Figure 1.16. The homestead of Juan Cancio Saavedra in Concevidayoc, September 1911 (National Geographic Image Collection: negative 785757, photograph by Hiram Bingham).

races and the remains of a large rectangular building. He writes, "Half an hour's walk from the ruined village of circular houses is a place called Eromboni Pampa, where there are several terraces and a long rectangular building, 192 feet in length and 24 feet in width, with twelve doors in front and twelve doors behind. . . . Near there was a fountain with three short spouts" (Bingham 1914a:186). We now know that these features are located in the center of the former Inca town, but at that time the jungle growth was extremely thick; Bingham had difficulty understanding the scale, layout, and importance of the ruin.

It took local workers several days to clear the trail from Concevidayoc to Espíritu Pampa. A few more days were spent clearing selected areas of the ruins. Although the dense vegetation allowed only glimpses of the former settlement, after days of cutting, it became clear that Espíritu Pampa held the remains of an Inca town that contained buildings, canals, plazas, terraces, and roads. During his brief visit, Bingham (1914b:188) made a detailed map of a small complex of exceptionally well-made buildings that the Campas called Tendi Pampa. Although this complex was located several hundred meters away from the other ruins he found, Bingham noted that the buildings held the finest Inca pottery seen at the site. It was also clear that these buildings had been occupied after Spanish contact, since fragments of Spanish-style clay roof tiles were found among them.

Figure 1.17. Members of the Campas tribe were living among the ruins of Espíritu Pampa when Bingham visited the site in 1911 (Yale Peruvian Expedition Papers, Manuscript 664. Manuscripts and Archives, Yale University Library).

After visiting the ruins of Espíritu Pampa, Bingham began the long hike back to Cusco. He was extremely pleased with the results of the expedition. In less than a month, Bingham had found an incredible series of Inca sites. These included Machu Picchu, Rosaspata (Vitcos), Ñusta España (Yurak Rumi), Espíritu Pampa (now known to be the Inca town of Vilcabamba), and a host of smaller Inca sites. As Hemming (1970:488) notes, although Bingham directed a series of other expeditions into the region in 1912 and 1914–1915, both to clean the ruins he had found and to gather additional scientific information, "nothing discovered by these two great expeditions could compare in brilliance or importance with the places found during Bingham's first extraordinary month in the area."

In his earliest reports, Bingham seems ambivalent about the idea that Espíritu Pampa could be the Inca town of Vilcabamba.[29] On the one hand, he had care-

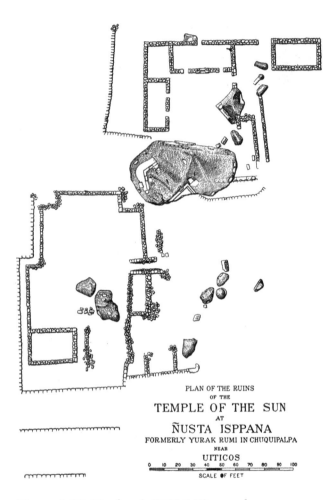

PLAN OF THE RUINS
OF THE
TEMPLE OF THE SUN
AT
ÑUSTA ISPPANA
FORMERLY YURAK RUMI IN CHUQUIPALPA
NEAR
UITICOS
0 10 20 30 40 50 60 70 80 90 100
SCALE OF FEET

Figure 1.18. Bingham's (1922:248) second map of Yurak Rumi.

fully followed the places mentioned in several Vilcabamba documents, and they had led him directly to the overgrown town of Espíritu Pampa. A host of known landmarks including Chuquichaca, Hoyara, Lucma, Puquiura, Vitcos (Rosaspata), the Spanish town of Vilcabamba, and Pampaconas were all found within the historical narratives of the Vilcabamba region, and they were all positively identified by Bingham as he journeyed across the area. On the other hand, the site of Espíritu Pampa appeared to be smaller than what Bingham imagined the last capital would be, and it did not contain the impressive stone workmanship that he had

seen at other state installations. Bingham's ambivalence toward the site is reflected in his early writings, where he admits that Espíritu Pampa is located where he expected to find the final town of the Incas and that it had been occupied during the early colonial period, but he stops short of calling the site Vilcabamba. Instead Bingham (1914a:198–199) assigns the site a vague classification as an unnamed "residence of the Inca Titu Cusi Yupanqui."

The reoccurring problem for Bingham was that the ruins of Espíritu Pampa seemed to lack both the size and the monumentality needed to mark the last Inca capital. In contrast, the architecture of Machu Picchu was unsurpassed and it covered a large area. When Bingham returned to the United States, the roles that Espíritu Pampa and Machu Picchu held in the final years of the conquest remained unresolved.

The 1912 Yale University – National Geographic Society Expedition

Bingham turned to Yale University and the National Geographic Society to support a second expedition to Peru. The 1912 Yale University–National Geographic expedition focused on the greater Cusco region and included various topographic surveys, archaeological reconnaissance work at many of the most important sites, ethnographic research on highland peoples, and the mapping and excavation of selected ruins. Of course, it also included months of work clearing, photographing, and mapping the site of Machu Picchu.[30]

Bingham's 1912 fieldwork in the Vilcabamba region beyond Machu Picchu was complicated by widespread epidemics of smallpox and typhoid. Nevertheless, his team conducted several treks across the region, recording a series of Inca roads and various small archaeological sites (Bingham 1913). Bingham also excavated at Yurak Rumi on August 25 with some eleven local laborers, concentrating on the area near the rock where the spring emerged. Bingham (1913:520) notes, "I drained the marshes that partly surround the rock at Ñusta España and excavated as far as was practicable. To our surprise and mortification we were unable to find any artifacts whatever and only a handful of rough potsherds." He did, however, uncover an exceptionally well-made wall with nine niches at the base of the rock (Figures 1.18–1.20).

That year Bingham and other members of his research team made numerous treks across the Vilcabamba region, but they did not return to Espíritu Pampa. As

Figure 1.19. Bingham excavated near the base of Yurak Rumi in 1912 (National Geographic Image Collection: negative 786000, photograph by Hiram Bingham).

Figure 1.20. The base of Yurak Rumi (photograph by Brian S. Bauer and Miriam Aráoz Silva).

the extent and architectural grandeur of Machu Picchu became clear, Bingham turned away from the straight-forward interpretation of the historical documents that had guided his 1911 research and his conservative interpretations of the archaeological ruins that he found. Enchanted by Machu Picchu, Bingham developed a poorly supported theory that Machu Picchu was the mythical origin place of the Inca (called Pacariqtambo) as well as the final capital of the empire. It was an odd and distorted reading of the colonial documents and the archaeological record, yet it served to add mystique to Machu Picchu. Unfortunately, Bingham's search for the last capital of the Incas ended at Machu Picchu and his illogical theory remained unchallenged for decades.

The 1914–1915 Yale University – National Geographic Society Expedition

Building on the success of the 1912 expedition, both Yale University and the National Geographic Society agreed to support a final expedition to Peru (Bingham 1915, 1916, 1930). The topographical team left the United States in 1914 and spent almost a year and half in the highlands; other members left in the spring of 1915 and spent less time in the field. In 1914 the Inca road that leads from Machu Picchu to Cusco was found. It was soon cleared to help support research at the site.[31] During previous expeditions, Bingham had worked out of Cusco, but for this field period he established his headquarters in Ollantaytambo. From this base, the crew conducted several more treks across the Vilcabamba region and penetrated deep into the Amazonian piedmont.[32] In 1915 Bingham and team members also traveled to Bolivia to visit the Island of the Sun and the Island of the Moon in Lake Titicaca (Bauer and Stanish 2001).[33] Although not well documented, it is also clear that Ellwood C. Erdis, the chief engineer of the expedition, conducted excavations at Rosaspata (Vitcos) from mid-June through mid-July 1912.[34] Bingham (1922:244) writes, "Our excavations in 1915 yielded a mass of rough potsherds, a few Inca whirl-bobs and bronze shawl pins, and also a number of iron articles of European origin, heavily rusted—horseshoe nails, a buckle, a pair of scissors, several bridle or saddle ornaments and three Jew's harps."

While the public readily accepted Bingham's outlandish assertion that Machu Picchu was the final capital of the Incas, academics did little to dissuade them, selecting instead to remain mum on the topic. In this regard, it is worth noting that Philip A. Means, who as an undergraduate at Harvard University was a member of Bingham's 1914–1915 expedition, became a leading scholar of Andean prehistory. While Means did not agree with Bingham's suggestion that Machu Picchu was the final capital of the Incas (Bingham 1989), he chose not to publicly voice his concerns. The site of Machu Picchu, one of the most important archaeological findings of the early twentieth century, is scarcely mentioned in Means's monumental two-volume overview of the prehistoric Andes (*Ancient Civilizations of the Andes* [1931] and *Fall of the Inca Empire and the Spanish Rule in Peru* [1932]). The next generation of academics also elected to ignore the misidentification of Machu Picchu. For example, the site is not mentioned in George Kubler's (1944, 1946, 1947) extensive articles on the Inca occupation of the Vilcabamba region and the early colonial period of Peru. Nor is it discussed by John H. Rowe in his monumental overview of the Inca (Rowe 1946). Perhaps the first person to publicly question Bingham's association of Machu Picchu with the Inca town of Vilcabamba was Victor von Hagen (1955:111), an amateur historian who led a well-publicized expedition along several parts of the former Inca road system. A direct challenge to Machu Picchu's role in the final days of the Inca Empire did not come until half a century after Bingham's work in Vilcabamba. It was voiced by the self-aggrandizing adventurer Gene Savoy.

Christían Bües and the Mapping of Vilcabamba

Although the site of Vitcos (Rosaspata) and the shrine of Yurak Rumi were both described in Bingham's work, and they were even mentioned in a small travel guide for the Cusco region by José Gabriel Cosio (1924:111–112),[35] few outsiders traveled into the Vilcabamba region to see these remarkable sites during the decades following their discovery. The most notable exception was Christían Bües, a German-born Cornell-educated agronomist who eventually settled in Quillabamba in 1915 (Cruz Ccorimanya 2009; Lee 2000:121–122; Savoy 1970:80). Bües traveled across the Vilcabamba region many times and wrote a series of articles on a wide range of topics, including petroglyphs in the Urubamba River valley. He is widely mentioned in early- to mid-twentieth-century literature concerning the Quillabamba region. However, Bües is best known among Cusco archaeologists for drawing a series of maps of the Vilcabamba region.[36] His only published map fo-

Figure 1.21. Clearing the ruins of Espíritu Pampa. Benjamin and Flavio Cobos stand above a newly cleared building (photograph included in dispatch by the Central Press Association, August 14, 1964, sent by Alberto J. Schazin).

cused on the San Miguel Valley, one valley to the east of Concevidayoc Valley (Cruz Ccorimanya 2009), which he visited in 1935. Unfortunately, he did not publish his other, larger maps, but copies of them have survived. One of his maps, drafted in 1921, was copied in 1937 and subsequently copied in 1952 for use on von Hagen's expedition (1955).[37] This version was also used by Lee (2000) and Thomson (2003:236–237) during their studies of the region. The von Hagen copy shows only a small area west of Vitcos and does not reach Vilcabamba (Lee, personal communication 2010). A 1931 map, marked with the initials CAB and believed to be made Bües, was used by John Beauclerk in his late-1970s work and more recently by Thibault Saintenoy (2011). A third map, signed by Bües in Quillabamba in December 1935, was redrawn by Emilio Araujo in 1958. This map was published by Pardo in 1972, but the reproduction is so blurred that it is difficult to read. The 1931, 1935/1958, and 1939 maps show the area of Pampaconas as well as Espíritu Pampa, while the 1921

map does not. The 1935/1958 map is the most detailed, but all of the maps have important toponymic information not preserved elsewhere. Bües maps were used in the development of the 1959 Instituto Geográfico Militar map of the area north of Cusco and by most researchers working in the Vilcabamba region between the 1960s and the 1980s.

Gene Savoy and the Search for Vilcabamba

Bingham ended his 1911 explorations at the intriguing but heavily overgrown ruins of Espíritu Pampa. Although Bingham spent several days at the site, he was unimpressed with its size, and he returned to Cusco unsure of the historic role that the ruins once played. Unfortunately, over the following year, Bingham abandoned the clean logic that had led him to Espíritu Pampa and proclaimed that Machu Picchu was the town of Vilcabamba. Bingham's illogical association of Machu Picchu with the Inca settlement of Vilcabamba remained largely unchallenged for over half a century, until traveler Gene Savoy (1964a, 1964b, 1970) visited Espíritu Pampa in 1964.[38]

Inspired by the findings of Bingham and driven by his own quest to find "lost cities," in the 1960s Savoy returned to the question of the "lost city of Vilcabamba." Unlike many academics of the time, who appear to have passively accepted that Machu Picchu was Vilcabamba or who simply chose not to enter into the debate without a substantial ruin to serve as an alternative, Savoy was intrigued by the jungle-covered remains that had been briefly described by Bingham and then largely forgotten. Using essentially the same historical sources to guide his journey as Bingham had used a half century before, Savoy headed into the Vilcabamba region.

Savoy's travels took him to the Chuquichaca Bridge, the ruins of Vitcos (Rosaspata), the Spanish town of Vilcabamba, and the plain of Pampaconas and then down into the subtropical area of Concevidayoc and Espíritu Pampa. By that time much of Espíritu Pampa had been purchased by Julio Cobos and was being worked by him and his two eldest sons, Benjamín and Flavio.[39] The Machiguengas had left the plain and resettled a few kilometers farther downriver some years before, but they occasionally returned and had shown the Coboses several of the largest ruins deep in the forest. The Cobos family gave the ruins little thought, however, as they were primarily concerned with clearing the area for coffee. When Savoy arrived on July 12, 1964, Benjamin Cobos first took him to the ruins of Tendi Pampa. Savoy (1970:98) writes, "[T]he two-story platform group was found to consist of twelve rooms graced with niches and doorways, including a semicircular room, inner and outer courtyards, a fountain, hallway and stairways, the whole surrounded by high walls decorated with roof pegs." Like Bingham, Savoy (1970:97–98) also saw roof tiles at this site. He noted that several tiles were painted and that one contained serpentine lines (also see Pardo 1970:116–117). He was then led to what we now know is the center of the site and reports seeing the remains of a stone bridge, several fountains, and an extremely large building with many doorways (the Kallanka).

Over the next several days, Savoy paid local workers to clear parts of the central ruins, and slowly the large scale of the ruins became apparent (Figure 1.21). Savoy made three different trips that year (1964–1965) to Espíritu Pampa, clearing the ruins, revisiting sites, and investigating new areas. Although he immediately and unabashedly announced his findings in the *Lima*

Times, the newspaper that had helped financed his trip, a more formal description would not be published until six years later and a preliminary map of the site itself, drawn by Peruvian architect Emilio Harth-Terre from Savoy's field notes, would not appear for an additional eight years (Savoy 1964a, 1964b, 1970, 1978a, 1978b). Savoy's published descriptions of the site are taken mostly from his diary entries and are difficult to follow if one has not been to the site. Nevertheless, the breathless narrative lends the overwhelming impression of both the massiveness of the site and the density of the vegetation that covered it.

Savoy, a relentless self-promoter, immediately announced his belief that Espíritu Pampa was the Inca town of Vilcabamba in a series of newspaper articles and five years later in a memoir of his time in the field.[40] At the same time Savoy was in the Vilcabamba region, historian John Hemming (1970) was using newly found archival records and a more complete understanding of the region's history and geography to help establish that the site of Espíritu Pampa was in fact the Inca town of Vilcabamba. Nevertheless, due to its remote location, the site of Espíritu Pampa remained uninvestigated for most of the twentieth century.

Recent Work in the Vilcabamba Region (1960–1990)

Following Savoy's well-announced visit to Espíritu Pampa, numerous individuals journeyed into the area. These expeditions provided little information on the ruins, since the travels were largely motivated by self-promotion. For example, shortly after Savoy first publicized his findings at Espíritu Pampa, two British adventurers, Mark Howell and Tony Morrison, briefly visited the site. After spending just a few days there, they left and asserted in a book the following year that they believed that Espíritu Pampa was not Vilcabamba (Howell and Morrison 1967). This conclusion was based largely on two observations. The first was that they, like others before, saw roof tiles at the site; the second was that they saw evidence that some of the buildings had been burned at the time of site abandonment. Incorrectly believing that the town of Vilcabamba had remained free of European influence and that it was never destroyed by fire, Howell and Morrison felt sure that the last capital of the Incas remained to be found. Ironically, these two observations would later be used by scholars, such as Hemming (1970), to suggest that the ruins of Espíritu Pampa were indeed those of Vilcabamba. Still, the tone for Vilcabamba research—one that was light on facts and fieldwork but heavy on public relations—had been set.[41]

Until the 1960s, the Peruvian archaeological community had not been especially engaged in exploring the Vilcabamba region, beyond studying the ruins of Choquequirao.[42] However, following Savoy's 1965 announcement, expeditions began to visit the region. One of the first Cusco archaeologists to conduct research in the area was Florencio Fidel Ramos Cóndori (2007). He visited Choquequirao in 1964, Vitcos in 1968, and many other locations during the decades that followed. Remarkably, his 1968 photographs of Vitcos are among the earliest for the region, after those taken by Bingham some fifty years earlier.[43]

The 1970s saw increased interest in the Vilcabamba region. Thanks to the nearly simultaneous printing of Savoy's (1970) book *Antisuyu*, in which he describes his work at Espíritu Pampa, and Hemming's (1970) landmark *Conquest of the Incas*, the story of Vilcabamba became better known. Hemming, a master historian, identified several critical documents that described the final days of the Inca that had not been brought to bear on the question of Vilcabamba by earlier researchers. These included Martín de Murúa's *Historia General del Peru* (1987 [1611–1616], 2008 [1616]), a massive work that contains several chapters on the final decades of the Vilcabamba resistance movement. They also included important field dispatches send to Viceroy Toledo by Martín Hurtado de Arbieto, the general in charge of the 1572 expeditionary force to occupy the Vilcabamba area. Furthermore, his research exposed the fact that an extremely large volume of documents related to the Vilcabamba region had been published in 1906; these had been largely ignored by researchers interested in the last city of the Incas (Maúrtua 1906). Although Hemming (1970:475–500) had yet to visit the site of Espíritu Pampa himself, he identified numerous passages in these documents that supported the view that

Figure 1.22. A polished black-ware vessel recovered by Amelia Perez Trujillo in 2003 at Vitcos (Rosaspata) (Museo Amazónico Andino Qhapaq Ñan de Quillabamba. Photograph by Brian S. Bauer).

Espíritu Pampa was the town of Vilcabamba. Most importantly, Hemming was able to trace the exact movements of various Spaniards (missionaries, ambassadors, and military forces) in and out of the region through the use of modern and old place-names. Like the few documents used by Bingham to originally find Espíritu Pampa, these new sources suggested that the town of Vilcabamba was a one- or two-day walk downstream from Pampaconas.[44] Hemming's studies also provided details on the layout, altitude, architecture, and destruction of Vilcabamba, which had not been highlighted before. Most specifically, Hemming's research indicated that the Inca town of Vilcabamba was located in a broad valley in a subtropical region, that some of the buildings were covered with roof tiles, and that the town had been burned in 1572. All these observations supported Hemming's assertion that Espíritu Pampa was the final capital of the Inca. The field identification of the town of Vilcabamba had finally been resolved.

In the mid- to late 1970s, research momentum began to build in the Vilcabamba region as numerous individuals visited it and wrote about its many archaeological remains. In 1972 Luis A. Pardo, a leading Cusco historian, wrote an extensive overview of the Incas' activities in the Vilcabamba region. Although Pardo did not visit the region, his lengthy article included photographs of Vitcos by Ramos Cóndori and a detailed description of Espíritu Pampa provided by Antonio Santander Caselli,[45] who had been with Savoy in 1964. It was also at this time that Stuart White visited and described in detail (1984) the remote and wonderfully preserved Inca site of Puncuyoc.[46] The Cusichaca Project, based between Machu Picchu and Ollantaytambo, also helped sponsor a series of treks across the Vilcabamba region (Beauclerk 1980; Drew 1984). Moreover, new archival research provided additional information on the final decades of the Incas. For example, Edmundo Guillén Guillén (1977a, 1977b, 1978, 1979, 1980, 1981, 1994, 2005) published a vast array of books and articles on the topic, which included many newly found archival documents. Guillén Guillén visited the Vilcabamba region in the 1980s and added greatly to our understanding of the sequence of events that took place in the region.

By the early 1980s the Vilcabamba region was beginning to be seen as a destination for hikers and travelers, especially those interested in the history of the Inca.[47] This interest was encouraged by a popular review of sites in the region by Angles Vargas (1988). Vincent Lee first entered the Vilcabamba region in 1982 as a hiker, but he soon began a systematic exploration of the region. Unlike most researchers who visited the region once or a few times, Lee returned again and again to slowly build up a massive database. Trained as an architect, Lee was especially interested in the standing structures of the Inca; he provided the first comprehensive maps of Vitcos and Espíritu Pampa as well as a wealth of detailed studies of individual buildings and other smaller sites (Lee 2000). Resisting the temptation to call press conferences to announce his finds, which in the wake of Savoy had become common for privately supported research in the region, Lee wrote a series of publications documenting his finds and resolved a number of issues concerning the location of different places mentioned in the Spanish accounts of the Vilcabamba campaigns. Lee's work ended all serious debate concerning the relationship between Espíritu Pampa and the Inca town of Vilcabamba, confirming that they were one and the same.

Unfortunately, the 1980s also witnessed the rise of the Maoist revolutionary group the Shining Path (Sendero Luminoso). This brutal organization was first centered in Ayacucho, but its violence soon spilled over into much of the central Andes and the large urban centers of Peru. The province of La Convención, a longtime hotbed for public unrest and a traditional area for coca production, was quickly pulled into the conflict. With a vengeful military, fanatical revolutionaries, and a skittish peasantry, travel through the Vilcabamba region became increasingly hazardous. Even after the capture of Abimael Guzmán, the leader of the Shining Path, in 1992, parts of the region remained dangerous, as radical cells, individuals with connections to the drug trade, and nervous police continued to cross the area. With the stabilization of the Peruvian economy in the mid-1990s and a demobilization of armed forces from the area, various researchers began fieldwork. For example, Samanez and Zapata (1996) published an article on Yurak Rumi, including a set of detailed drawings of the compound. In 2002 the former Institutio National de Cultura Region Cusco took interest in the monumental sector of Vitcos and sponsored a number of excavations. These included those conducted by Amelia Pérez Trujillo (2002), who uncovered a fine Inca burial with a host of ceramic and metal objects.[48] Pérez also recovered a finely polished black-ware vessel that appears to have been imported from the Chimú area on the north coast of Peru (Figure 1.22).[49] Additional excavations took place at Vitcos in 2004 and 2005 under the direction of Luz Marina Merma Gómez and Ana María Díaz Yampi. These excavations were followed by a massive reconstruction effort in 2007 by Ricardo Huayllani (Figures 1.23 and 1.24). Unfortunately, information on these excavations and reconstruction projects is limited and is not available to the public.

Political tensions have remained high in the region. For example, between 2008 and 2013, there were many reports of armed members of the drug trade passing through the region. In 2009 two farmers in the village of Pampaconas were mistakenly killed by police at night during confused circumstances. In 2010 much of La Convención was brought to a standstill in May and August by regional strikes over the proceeds of gas exploration. In 2011 several members of the army, en route to help with upcoming elections, were killed near Choquetira. Furthermore, in April 2012 there was a massive kidnapping of gas workers, all of whom were later released unharmed. In response, the government increased the number of soldiers in the region. According to local farmers, the military strafed ridgetops near

Figure 1.23. Buildings of Vitcos (Rosaspata) before reconstruction, circa 1983 (photograph by David Drew).

Espíritu Pampa with indiscriminate machine gun fire from several helicopters. Then, in October 2012, three helicopters were destroyed in the small airport of Kiteni. Soon afterward two policemen were killed in the region. Additional attacks on gas companies continued throughout 2012 and 2013 and are widely believed to be linked to extortion threats.

This was the general state of research and conflict as we began our research in the region. In 2008 Bauer and Aráoz Silva began work in the Vitcos region. The first year of their project, they conducted a survey of the area immediately surrounding Vitcos and conducted excavations at the site of Yurak Rumi. The following year they directed excavations at two additional building in Vitcos and returned to complete their research at Yurak Rumi. In 2008 Fonseca Santa Cruz began his excavations at the site of Espíritu Pampa, sampling two buildings in Tendi Pampa as well as various other buildings across the site. The following year, 2009, he focused his excavation on Tendi Pampa. It was during that field season that Bauer and Aráoz Silva were able to visit Fonseca Santa Cruz in Espíritu Pampa. The following year, 2010, Fonseca

Santa Cruz gracefully welcomed Bauer and Aráoz Silva as they dug a set of Inca buildings within Espíritu Pampa while he began excavations at a newly found Wari site, about 1 km away (Fonseca Santa Cruz 2011; Fonseca Santa Cruz and Bauer 2013). The three authors agreed that it would be best to merge their data sets into a single volume, and we are pleased to present this summary of our various field seasons working in the Vilcabamba region.

This chapter has provided a general overview of the state of Vilcabamba research. Chapter 2 draws upon intensive survey data to explore the Late Intermediate period (circa AD 1000–1400) and Inca period–colonial period (AD 1400–1572) settlement patterns in the Vitcos region. Within this chapter we also present the results of our excavations at the largest single building of Vitcos, commonly called the Kallanka, and our work within two nearby buildings, which we call the Double Structures. The third chapter focuses on our excavations in the shrine complex of Yurak Rumi. This massive carved stone, and the suite of buildings that the Inca built adjacent to it, was burned by the Augustinian priests in late February or early March

Figure 1.24. Vitcos (Rosaspata) after INC reconstruction, 2007 (photograph by Brian S. Bauer and Miriam Aráoz Silva).

1570. Chapter 4 moves the focus of investigation from Vitcos to the town of Vilcabamba (now called Espíritu Pampa). In the fifth chapter we present the results of Fonseca Santa Cruz's excavations at the Tendi Pampa compound. His work has revealed a remarkable set of intact objects and suggests that the compound was one of the most important locations within the settlement. The recovery of glass beads, various iron objects, and an astonishing vessel that portrays Spaniards fighting indigenous people of the region adds to the importance of his research. In the sixth chapter we discuss the results of Fonseca Santa Cruz's excavations at various other locations at the site of Espíritu Pampa. These include excavations within what we believe to be the last complex to be built at the site, as well as the recovery of outstanding Andean and European artifacts. The seventh and final chapter presents the results of Bauer and Aráoz Silva's excavations concentrated on two different sets of buildings near the monumental core of the site.

Endnotes

1   Parts of this introduction can also be found in Bauer et al (2015).

2   For a comprehensive review of the final decades of the Inca Empire, see Hemming (1970).

3   In contrast to a government in exile, the leaders of a rump-state control only a small portion of the territory and political power that they once held. In other words, theirs is but a remnant of what had formally been a much larger polity.

4   There are several insightful books describing the collapse of the Inca Empire from the arrival of the first Europeans to the invasion of Vilcabamba. The highest level of scholarship has been set by John Hemming in his book *Conquest of the Incas*. Other important books and articles have been produced by Edmundo Guillén Guillén, Catherine J. Julien, and Kerstin Nowack, to name only a few authors. More popular works have been written by Vincent R. Lee and Kim MacQuarrie.

Because the narrative of the Vilcabamba experience is well developed and is accessible in other writings, in this work we focus on the archaeological results of our research. Readers interested in a series of newly translated documents concerning Vilcabamba can see Bauer et al. (2015).

5   At first Inca resistance against the Spaniards was centered in the town of Vitcos. However, as this settlement proved too vulnerable to Spanish raids (1537, 1539), the royal court soon pulled back even farther into the mountains to the town of Vilcabamba.

6   Another battle took place at Huayna Pucará when the Spaniards entered the Vilcabamba region in 1572.

7   It is possible that the Spaniards visited the Inca town of Vilcabamba during this period.

8   The Yucay *encomienda* was taken by Francisco Pizarro after the conquest and was later passed to his two sons. It was later claimed by Francisco Hernández Girón; on his death, it returned to Crown control. The Crown then gave it to Sayri Túpac in return for his abdication. Beatriz Clara Coya became the owner of the estate after the death of her father, Sayri Túpac. Since she was still in her early teens, Clara Coya's inheritance rights became the focus of the Acobamba Treaty negotiations between Titu Cusi Yupanqui and the Spaniards (Guillén Guillén 1977a, 1977b; Nowack 2004). Control of the Yucay *repartimento* continued to be the center of a complex legal dispute over the next century (see Covey and Amado González 2008).

9   Túpac Amaru was captured by Martín García Oñez de Loyola. Numerous accounts of this event are recorded by García Oñez de Loyola; the most recently published account can be found in Covey and Amado González (2008).

10   A Spanish outpost was established in the ruins of Vilcabamba in 1572; it appears to have been abandoned only a few years later.

11   Hiram Bingham was born in 1875 to longtime missionaries in Honolulu, Hawaii. After receiving his primary and secondary education in Hawaii, he attended Phillips Academy for two years, preparing for university. When Bingham graduated from Yale University in 1898, little did he know that he would soon be returning to this institution and that through his affiliations with it, he would become a world-famous explorer. After earning a master's degree from the University of California at Berkeley and a doctorate in Latin American history at Harvard University, Bingham decided to retrace the route of the South American liberator Simón Bolívar, from Caracas, Venezuela to Bogota, Colombia. On his return to the United States, he briefly taught Latin

American history at Harvard and Princeton before returning to Yale as a part-time lecturer. During this period, he also wrote his first book, a travelogue on his recent journey to northern South America.

12   Coropuna proved not to be as high as suggested, so Bingham's trip to the mountain was a bitter disappointment (Bingham 1912a). In contrast, Bingham's work northwest of Cusco was a spectacular success.

13   Bowman's classic book *The Andes of Southern Peru* (1916) is a direct product of his research on the Yale expedition of 1911.

14   A partial project bibliography is provided by Bingham (1922:347–351).

15   The 1911 expedition took approximately five months.

16   Bingham's discovery of Machu Picchu is extensively described in his own publications as well as by various other authors (Bingham 1989; Burger and Salazar 2004; Hemming 1970; MacQuarrie 2007). As a result, we provide only a summary, highlighting those aspects of his research that are most relevant to our work in the Vilcabamba region.

17   Several weeks later, members of Bingham's team spent 10 days mapping parts of Machu Picchu.

18   José B. Samanez y Ocampo (1980) traveled down the Apurímac and Urubamba Rivers in 1883 and 1884. His notes do not provide any information on the areas of Vilcabamba or Machu Picchu, however.

19   In their later guide to Cusco, García and Giesecke (1925) note that Bingham was the first researcher to visit the site.

20   For additional information on pre-Bingham explorations in the Urubamba River valley near Machu Picchu, see Buck (1993).

21   The hacienda of Huadquiña was a major stopping point for many early travelers along the Urubamba River, including Charles Wiener and Leonce Angrand. It also served as the starting point in Conde Eugène de de Sartiges de Sournia trip to Choquequirao, which was included within its immense landholdings.

22   Calancha's information on the sacred rock was itself taken from the 1595 testimony of Angelina Llacsa Chuqui. Centuries later this information was published by Urteaga (1916). Although Bingham continued to retell the story of his work at Yurak Rumi until the late 1940s, he never cites this work or an even more important collection of documents on the Vilcabamba region published in 1906 (Maúrtua 1906).

23   The site was of course known by those living in the area and perhaps by various miners, muleteers and rubber explores who had crossed the region.

24   Bingham (1912d) reports that while he was at Santa

Ana, he was told that a rubber explorer named Manuel López Torres had visited the area of Concevidayoc in 1902 and had reported seeing a large set of ruins there.

25 One of the earliest references to the site of Rosaspata is in Cisneros's (1904:41) list of important archaeological sites in the Cusco region. This list also includes a reference to Huayna Picchu (Daniel Buck, personal communication 2010) and dates to some eight years before Bingham's first expedition to the site.

26 Although Bingham did not know it at the time, the location of Chuquepalta was also marked on a map made by Pablo José Oricain (2004 [1790]).

27 Other team members who visited the site in early September made a topographical map of the area from San Francisco de la Victoria de Vilcabamba to Espíritu Pampa (Bingham 1914a; Bowman 1916).

28 Following 1572 sugarcane was immediately planted in the Vilcabamba region; it quickly became the region's most important cash crop. When Bingham visited Espíritu Pampa in 1911, he noted that sugarcane was one of the few cash crops in the valley but that the difficulty of transporting sugar out of the region reduced its value (Bingham 1922:290). While sugar continues to be an important crop elsewhere in the province, today coffee is the most important cash crop of Espíritu Pampa. Nevertheless, the rotting remains of the old sugar mills can still be found scattered across the coffee fields.

29 Also see Bingham (1912b:24; 1914a:213).

30 The National Geographic Society dedicated an entire volume to Bingham's 1912 expedition and published more than 240 of his photographs.

31 Additional research on this road was later conducted by Paul Fejos (1944). It is now known as the Inca Trail and is a greatly popular trek for visitors to the region.

32 It appears that members of his team attempted to retrace the journey of Martín García Óñez de Loyola, traveling far down the Urubamba River, but little is known about this expedition.

33 A smaller group of team members had already visited the Lake Titicaca region in 1912.

34 A note within the National Geographic photographic collection suggests that Erdis collected 19 boxes of sherds and Spanish artifacts at Vitcos (Rosaspata).

35 Cosio (1912, 1961) was sent by the Peruvian government as well as the National Geography Society of Lima to work with Bingham during his second expedition. Cosio (1951) later published an article on Vitcos based on Bingham's early work. A member of Bingham's final expedition, Osgood Hardy (1918), also published a few pictures of Rosaspata (Vitcos) in a popular article.

36 While on a short trip from Lucma to San Fernando in September 1934, Bües provided an early description of the site now called Puncuyoc, writing "La ruina incaica de Idma Huasi de dos pisos, bien conservado, sin techo que cierra al abra de Idma Huaicco" (Cruz Ccorimanya 2009:189).

37 Victor von Hagen headed a well-publicized group that traveled along several of the major Inca roads. Members of his team visited the remote site of Puncuyoc, although they provide few details of it (von Hagen 1955:112). Von Hagen also visited the site of Vitcos (Rosaspata) and was told of Espíritu Pampa, but he did not travel there. As noted by Lee (2000:122), von Hagen (1955:111) was one of the first writers to publically question Bingham's association of Machu Picchu with the city of Vilcabamba.

38 In the late 1950s, two different groups of mountain climbers trekked across parts of the Vilcabamba region (see Clark 1959; Imhof 1966; Spiess 1966). Clark (1959:84–85) specifically mentions Vitcos but adds little to our understanding of the site.

39 The Cobos family has played a critical role in supporting scientific research at Vitcos and Espíritu Pampa. They have worked as collaborators and support personnel in numerous projects, large and small, in the region since the 1960s.

40 Savoy went on to found his own religious cult and died in 2007 in Reno, Nevada.

41 Fieldwork in the province of La Convención, which includes the Vilcabamba area, was made even more difficult in the 1950s and 1960s as it became the center for a series of antigovernment, agrarian reform movements lead by Hugo Blanco and others.

42 As our work is centered on Vitcos and Vilcabamba, we do not to review the large and growing literature on Choquequirao.

43 Larco (1934:123) also provides a single photograph of Yurak Rumi.

44 It is disconcerting to see how Bingham, who spent at least two nights in the village of Pampaconas as he traveled to and from the site of Espíritu Pampa and who even wrote an article on his work in the Pampaconas region (Bingham 1914a), was able to convince himself that Machu Picchu was the final capital of the Incas.

45 Antonio Santander Caselli was a seasoned explorer of La Convención who joined up with Savoy when he first arrived in Cusco. In Pardo's 1972 article, Santander Caselli claims that he arrived at Espíritu Pampa on July 11, 1964, the day before Savoy, and that he believed as a result that he should be considered the discoverer of the city of Vilcabamba (Lee 2000:140; Pardo 1972:115).

46 This site is also called Inca Huasi. We prefer the name

Puncuyoc since it helps to distinguish this site from the many other locations also called Inca Huasi.

47 For additional information on the history of exploration of the Vilcabamba region, see Ridgway (1987), Savoy (1970:210–211), Lee (2000), Thomson (2003), and Ramos Cóndori (2007:60–61).

48 The impressive collection of objects recovered by Amelia Pérez Trujillo is currently held in the Museo Amazónico Andino Qhapaq Ñan de Quillabamba.

49 This vessel is especially interesting to us, since we also recovered various fragments of polished black-ware in our excavations at Vitcos and Espíritu Pampa.

Chapter 2

Settlement Patterns and Excavations in the Vitcos Region

Brian S. Bauer and **Miriam Aráoz Silva**

LTHOUGH THE VILCABAMBA region is best known for the events that occurred within it during the post-contact period, it is important to place those events within a broader chronological context. We begin this chapter with the results of our archaeological survey of the Vitcos region. In doing so, we focus on settlements patterns of the region during the Late Intermediate period and the Inca period. We then present the results of excavations we conducted in two different buildings at the site of Vitcos.

Since the 1980s, there has been increased interest in the organization and archaeology of settlements dating to the Late Intermediate period (circa A.D. 1000–1400).[1] The Late Intermediate period is now seen as a critical era of regional development across the highlands, and a growing number of research projects seek to understand the history of different ethnic groups during this period. For example, the Upper Mantaro Archaeological Research Project focused on the Wanka ethnicity and found that most of the scattered villages on the valley bottoms were abandoned early in this period in favor of a smaller number of much larger hilltop settlements encircled by large stone walls. This shift from valley-bottom to higher-elevation settlements corresponded with a parallel shift from maize to high-altitude grains and tubers (D'Altroy and Hastorf 2001). Following the Inca conquest of the Wan-

ka region, the settlement shifted from the hilltops back down to the valley floor. Building on this work, Arkush (2011) has examined the Colla of the Lake Titicaca basin, and Bauer et al. (2010) have researched the Chanka of the Andahuaylas region (see also Kellett 2010). While the details of these studies differ, the general settlement pattern of their Late Intermediate period sites is the same: the occupations are clustered on hilltops, many of which are fortified. There also appears to have been a shift from valley to highland resources in each of these areas. Furthermore, after each of these different regions fell under Inca control, settlements were reestablished on the valley bottoms.

Settlement patterns of the Late Intermediate period are of special interest to archaeologists working in the Cusco region, as this era includes the period of early Inca state growth (see Bauer 2004; Bauer and Covey 2002; Covey 2006; Kosiba 2011, 2012). The presence of ridgetop sites in the Vilcabamba region—although not always recorded as specifically Late Intermediate period sites—has been long noted. For example, Drew (1984:361) describes the site of Unnuyoc, located in the upper branches of the Santa Teresa River valley: "Here, at Unnuyoc, above the level of the montana, are 35 structures of broadly circular ground-plan spread out along the ridge in small clusters for about half a kilometer. Their dimensions vary from two and a half to six

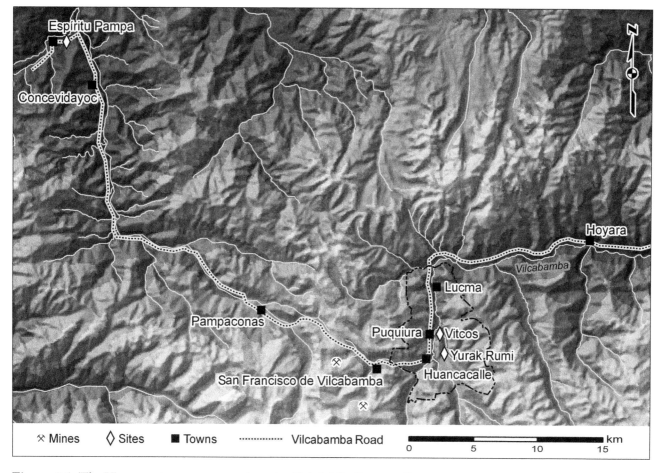

Figure 2.1. The Vitcos region survey area (map by Gabriel E. Cantarutti).

meters in diameter. . . Their condition is not good and little more than the outlines of walls remain." We now know that this site most certainly dates to the Late Intermediate period. Other descriptions of ridgetop sites are provided in a number of different reports, including Beauclerk (1980), Kendall (1984), White (1987), Lee (2000), Ramos (2007), and von Kaupp and Fernandez Carrasco (2010). Most importantly, Thibault Saintenoy (2008, 2009, 2011) conducted a large survey project along the Apurímac River within the Vilcabamba region and recorded dozens of Late Intermediate period ridgetop sites.

The Vitcos Survey

At the time of our research, the locations of most Inca-period sites in the Vitcos region had already been documented by Lee (2000). However, we believed that more systematic coverage that focused on sites of all time periods would enrich our understanding of the region's prehistory. Accordingly, we conducted an archaeological survey in the Vitcos region from August to November 2008 (Figure 2.1). We began this phase of research hoping to conduct a tightly controlled systematic survey of the area, but we soon realized that this

would not be possible. The steep mountain slopes and the dense vegetation prevented us from walking in organized lines separated by a fixed number of meters. In addition, we found that our surface collections at most sites were limited because of thick ground cover. In the end, we relied on an intensive coverage of the region in which team members covered almost all possible occupation areas and surveyed through the vegetation wherever possible.

Because we were interested in establishing the settlement pattern for the prehistoric occupations of the area, we tended to end the survey at around 3,900 m, above the maximum altitude for agriculture. The areas above this altitude (3,900–4,400 m) are extremely steep and generally covered with rock outcrops. In other words, although there may be a few scattered platforms on the summits of the surrounding mountains, we did not cover the mountaintops. We felt that our time was best spent in the lower altitudes working with the occupation sites. By the end of the fieldwork, we had covered approximately 52 km² and recorded the remains of some 90 possible archaeological sites.

During the survey, one possible Archaic-period site was found, and several other sites that appeared to have pre–Late Intermediate period materials were recorded.

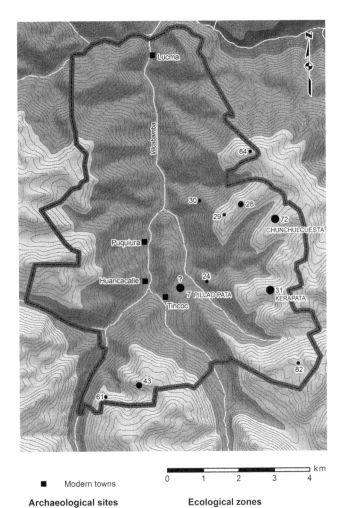

Figure 2.2. The Late Intermediate period settlement pattern of the Vitcos region (map by Gabriel E. Cantarutti).

However, the ceramics were of unknown local styles. Furthermore, in reviewing our collections, we believe that the pre–Late Intermediate period sites of the region are underrepresented. Many of these sites may be located near the valley bottom and are now covered with meters of deposits. It is also worth noting that although we did not find any clear evidence of Wari remains, there is intriguing evidence that the Wari colonized parts of the eastern Andean slope. For example, Savoy (1970:81, 99) reports seeing what were certainly Wari vessels in Puquiura and Espíritu Pampa.[2] Savoy's observations seemed unlikely until 2010, when excavations in the Espíritu Pampa area revealed the remains of a surprisingly large Wari occupation and a set of elaborate tombs (Fonseca Santa Cruz 2011;

Fonseca Santa Cruz and Bauer 2013). Furthermore, in 2011 several additional Wari vessels, now on display at the Museo Amazónico Andino Qhapaq Ñan de Quillabamba, were unearthed during construction work in the town of Quillabamba (personal communication Wilbert Gamarra, 2012). With these remains it is becoming clear that the Wari established and maintained colonies in the eastern lowlands. In many ways this is not surprising since this region contained important resources, such as coca, and it lies relatively close to the Wari heartland.

The Late Intermediate Period Settlement Pattern for the Vitcos Region

Across the Andean highlands, the Late Intermediate period is characterized by a very distinct settlement pattern (Covey 2008). This may also be true of the Vitcos area, where we identified 10 sites that we believe were established and occupied during this period. Because of the thick grass cover, no surface ceramics were found at these sites. They are believed to date to the

Figure 2.3. Site 43 (Ch'ectaqaqa) is at the end of a narrow ridge (photograph by Brian S. Bauer and Miriam Aráoz Silva).

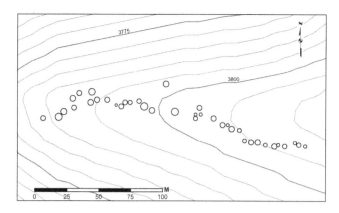

Figure 2.4. Site 43 (Ch'ectaqaqa) forms a continuous line of structures along the ridge (map by Rebecca A. Friedel).

Late Intermediate period based on their non-Inca architecture (that is, circular buildings) and their high-elevation locations (Figure 2.2). We offer the following descriptions of the four most important Late Intermediate period sites within the survey area.

SITE 43: CH'ECTAQAQA

The site of Ch'ectaqaqa (also called Pacopata) is located at approximately 3,850 m on a narrow, undulating ridge on the eastern side of Pacopata Mountain, immediately south of the town of Huancacalle (Figures 2.3 and 2.4). It contains more than 40 circular to oval structures spread across a narrow rolling ridgetop. The ridge is so narrow that the structures form a continuous line from one end of the site to the other, running approximately 250 m. The western end of the site is delineated by two trenches cut perpendicular to the ridge. These trenches, measuring approximately 3 m wide, 20 m long, and 2 m deep, provide protection along the most accessible route to the site. Extremely steep, rocky slopes mark the eastern, northern, and southern sides of the ridge.

While the ridge is relatively free of trees and bushes, it is covered with thick mountain grass as well as patches of lichens and moss. A few foundation stones are visible on the surface, but there are no discernible doorways or other internal features to the buildings. The location of most of the buildings is revealed by roughly circular depressions on the surface of the

ridge. The largest of the buildings measures some 5.5 m in diameter, while most are within the 3 to 4 m in diameter range. A small pond is located a short distance to the west of the site.

SITE 31: KERAPATA

The site of Kerapata (also called Cochapata) is spread across a high (3,700–3,800 m), broad, gently rolling ridge east of Huancacalle (Figures 2.5 and 2.6). The site contains more than 28 circular structures, but it is in poor condition, with the locations of many buildings marked by only circular depressions. There are a few better-preserved structures that still display circular foundations and discernable doorways, and one struc-

Figure 2.5. An example of a circular building at Site 31 (Kerapata) (photograph by Brian S. Bauer and Miriam Aráoz Silva).

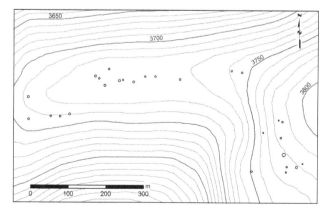

Figure 2.6. The site of Kerapata (map by Rebecca A. Friedel).

ture contains a large grinding stone in its interior. The largest building recorded at the site measures approximately 8.5 m in diameter, while the majority measure between 4 and 6 m in diameter. There are several ponds within a short distance of the site.

SITE 28: VIRACOCHAN

The site of Viracochan is situated near the upper end of a large ridge that rises to the east of Vitcos. The ridge looms above the site of Yurak Rumi and is one of the better-known ridges of the Vitcos region. The site is located between 3,700 and 3,750 m and is covered in mountain grass, lichen, and moss. Bushes and small trees have also grown within the foundation stones. Viracochan is the largest Late Intermediate period site in the region, with more than 50 circular to oval structures visible on the surface (Figure 2.7). There is a wide range of structure sizes, varying between 2 and 6.5 m in diameter, and the foundations are widely spaced across the site. Some of the foundations are clearly marked by rows of standing slabs. However, most are poorly preserved and barely discernible. Only a few structures were complete enough for us to determine where the doors were.

In recent times, the site has been used for potato cultivation. Hand plowing, the clearance of rocks from fields, and the use of foundation stones for modern field

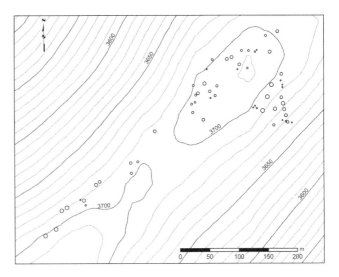

Figure 2.7. Viracochan is the largest LIP site in the Vitcos region (map by Rebecca A. Friedel).

boundaries have destroyed numerous structures at the site. Nevertheless, there are the faint remains of low terraces and possible internal boundary walls. Both ends of the site are delimited by low walls (not shown on the plan) that may date to ancient times, and several small ponds are located near the site.

SITE 72: CHUNCHULCUESTA

The site of Chunchulcuesta is located on an extensive

Figure 2.8. Site 72 (Chunchulcuesta). Note the scattered circular buildings and the pond (photograph by Brian S. Bauer and Miriam Aráoz Silva).

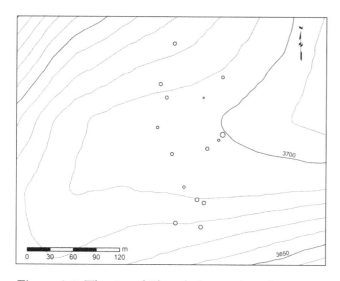

Figure 2.9. The site of Chunchulcuesta (map by Rebecca A. Friedel).

idence of large-scale public works (for example, temple mounds, platforms, or sunken courts) at any site.

The larger Late Intermediate period sites of the Vitcos area contain a pattern of dispersed circular buildings or a concentration of buildings clustered along a single ridge. In both of these cases, the internal organization of the sites appears to be informal and organic. Most of the sites are unremarkable and match the descriptions provided by Saintenoy (2011) across the greater Vilcabamba region. There is no single, disproportionately large Late Intermediate period site in the Vitcos region indicative of a paramount village. All the large Late Intermediate period sites in the Vitcos area also have small ponds within a short distance; some appear to have defensive works (walls or ditches) across their most accessible entrances. Finally, we note that the majority of the Late Intermediate period sites are

plain near the upper altitude of the Chunchulcuesta ridge (3,800 m). This ridge is located to the north of the Viracochan ridge and to the south the Qerapata ridge. Currently there are some 14 large circular foundations (< 4 m in diameter) and various small circular foundations visible on the surface (Figures 2.8 and 2.9). Most of the foundations are in poor condition, and the former location of some buildings can be identified only by depressions in the ground surface. There is a small pond immediately adjacent to the occupation.

In sum, the largest Late Intermediate period sites of the Vitcos region share many common features. They are generally located on prominent ridges, between 3,700 and 3,800 m, at the upper limits for cultivation in the region. The preservation at these sites is extremely poor, with the locations of many buildings marked only by circular depressions in the ground. However, at most sites a few structures still display circular foundations and doorways. The buildings present a continuum of sizes: from small (2–3 m) to large (6–8 m). We presume that the smallest buildings represent storage structures while the large structures were houses. There is no evidence of large elite structures or central plazas at any of the sites, and beyond the construction of fortification ditches and a few possible defensive walls, there is no ev-

Figure 2.10. Like several sites in the Vitcos area, Pincollunca (Site 78) displays impressive Inca stonework (photograph by Brian S. Bauer and Miriam Aráoz Silva).

located on the east side of the Vitcos Valley, a fact that we cannot fully explain.

The Inca Settlement Pattern in the Vitcos Region (circa A.D. 1400–1572)

The settlement pattern of the Vitcos region underwent substantial changes as it was incorporated into the early expanding Inca state. The largest settlements on the ridge summits were abandoned, and a host of new sites with various functions (quarries; religious, residential, and agricultural sites) were developed near the valley floor. The buildings of this period are clearly distinguished by their rectangular forms and the inclusion of various canons of Inca architecture, including well-made stone blocks, slightly inclining walls, trapezoidal doors, and rectangular-trapezoidal internal niches (Figures 2.10 and 2.11). Radiocarbon samples from our excavations indicate that the Inca constructed the Yurak Rumi shrine complex in the early fifteenth century, a date that is consistent with the expansion of the Inca beyond the Cusco region (Chapter 3). We presume that this is when construction of other Inca installations of the region also began.

The strong hand of the Inca state can be clearly seen in the construction of several large terrace complexes near Vitcos. The easy access to water, the moderate climate, and the development of irrigating systems within the terrace complexes assured nearly constant agricultural production (Figure 2.12). It is presumed that the produce from these newly created lands was used to help support the Inca occupation of the region, which included the establishment of elite households as well as ritual complexes such as Yurak Rumi.

There are also several stone quarries located within the Vitcos Valley. Like the terrace systems, the quarries present strong evidence of the Inca state organizing the local population and most likely demanding tribute labor to construct the monumental buildings of the region. Inca construction activities at the site of Vitcos most likely started in the early fifteenth century and lasted for more than 150 years, but they were suddenly terminated with the 1572 Spanish raid into the Vilcabamba region.[3] Lee (2000:471) has documented the location of many large building stones that appear to have been left en situ on trails within Vitcos; their transportation appears to have been stopped at a specific moment. These blocks indicate that construction was still an ongoing activity at Vitcos when the site was abandoned (Figures 2.13 and 2.14).

Finally, we also note a concentration of carved outcrops on the valley floor. While clusters of carved outcrops are common in the Cusco Valley, they grow increasingly rare in the Inca hinterlands. Although the exact meaning of these carved rocks is not understood, they certainly mark the Vitcos Valley as a special place within the expanding state (Figure 2.15). Several of these carved outcrops appear to be stopped in midproduction, which is another indication that site planning was still occurring when the Spanish took over the region in 1572.

Excavations at the Kallanka (Vitcos)

In 2009 we conducted excavations within the building in Vitcos that is currently called the Kallanka (Site 20 in

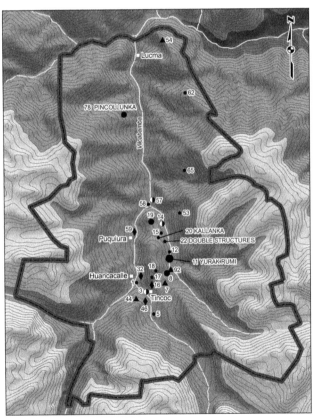

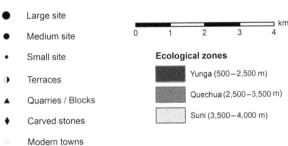

Figure 2.11. Inca settlement patterns in the Vitcos region, A.D. 1400–1572 (map by Gabriel E. Cantarutti).

Figure 2.12. Large Inca terrace works at Vitcos (photograph by Brian S. Bauer and Miriam Aráoz Silva).

Figure 2.13. A large Inca stone block left in mid-production near Vitcos. Note the pecked areas on its surface (photograph by Brian S. Bauer and Miriam Aráoz Silva).

Figure 2.14. A large stone lintel in mid-production near Vitcos (photograph by Brian S. Bauer and Miriam Aráoz Silva).

Figure 2.15. A large carved rock and an adjacent niched wall near Vitcos (photograph by Brian S. Bauer and Miriam Aráoz Silva).

Figure 2.11). Bingham documented this building on his first visit to Vitcos in 1911. In his very first publication concerning the results of his Vilcabamba fieldwork, Bingham (1912d:180) notes that his local guide called this building and its immediate terrace Uncapampa. He describes this site as containing "the ruins [of] a single house, 166 feet long by 33 feet wide. . . . There were six doorways in front, none on the ends or in the rear walls." Bingham also provides a plan of the structure, which shows a series of interior niches that are still visible in the southeastern corner of the building. Elsewhere he provides a photograph of the interior of the building (Bingham 1912d:89). Although Bingham returned to the Vitcos region in 1912 and 1914–1915, there are no indications that he, or any member of his team, conducted excavations at the Kallanka (Figure 2.16).

The only other researcher to describe this building in detail is Lee (2000:179–180, 468). In his book *Forgotten Vilcabamba: Final Stronghold of the Incas* (2000), Lee provides a detailed map of the Vitcos region and a plan of the Uncapampa structure, which he called the Kallanka (Figure 2.17). Lee's name for the building is derived from the observation, first noted by Gasparini and

Figure 2.16. Uncapampa at the time of its first clearing in 1911 (Bingham 1912c:689).

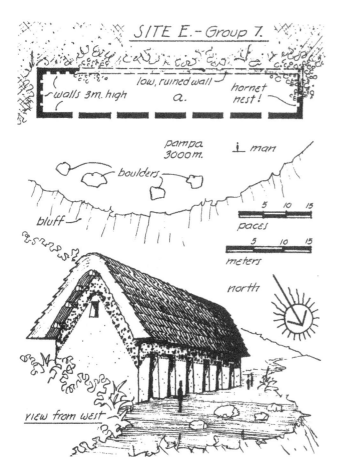

Margolies (1980), that most Inca administrative centers contain large structures with multiple doorways called *kallankas* (also see Barraza Lescano 2010). Following the writings of Garcilaso de la Vega (1960 [1609]), these buildings are generally thought to have been used for public rituals during the rainy season.

The Kallanka of Vitcos is located on the steep northeastern slope of Cerro Hatun Moqo within the Rosaspata National Archaeological Park, somewhat isolated from other buildings in the site of Vitcos (Figure 2.18). It is situated approximately .5 km from the monumental sector of Vitcos to the northwest and more than 1 km from the shrine complex of Yurak Rumi to the southeast. To make room for the building, the Inca excavated into the natural subsoil of the mountain slope. There is a small, flat area extending 8 to 10 m directly in front of the building, which was most likely made with the earth removed from the mountain slope as the building was being constructed.

The building measures approximately 50 m in length and 8.5 m in width. Its back wall is cut some 2 m

Figure 2.17. Map and reconstruction of the Kallanka (Uncapampa) of Vitcos (drawing by Vincent Lee, 2000:468).

Figure 2.18. The Kallanka is located on a mountain slope within the site of Victos (photograph by Brian S. Bauer and Miriam Aráoz Silva).

Figure 2.19. The Kallanka after being cleared of vegetation, 2009 (photograph by Brian S. Bauer and Miriam Aráoz Silva).

into the slope of the mountain. The building is in a poor state of conservation, with eroded earth covering most of its back wall and interior. Its front wall, which contains six slightly trapezoidal doorways, is also poorly preserved, with sections in various stages of collapse (Figures 2.19 and 2.20). The building had 5 internal niches on each end wall and perhaps as many 20 niches along its back wall. The remaining interior niches indicate that they were rectangular rather than the traditional trapezoidal shape. It is possible that the building also contained niches between the various doors in its front wall, but no evidence of them has survived.

The walls of the Kallanka are constructed with granite stones and earth mortar. The corners of the building, as well as those of the doorways and niches, were built with slightly larger and more carefully squared granite blocks. Some of the walls still stand over 1.6 m high, but these are currently being supported by informal wooden supports and are on the verge of collapse.

In 2008, when the former Institutio National de Cultura first cleared the Kallanka, it was covered in dense underbrush and large eucalyptus trees. At the beginning of our work (June 2009), the building was covered in secondary growth, thick grass, and bushes. Several looter's pits were also visible; the largest of these were located in the northeastern and southwestern corners of the building.

INTERIOR EXCAVATIONS AT THE KALLANKA

During the course of our research, three approximately 2-x-8-m excavation units (U1–U3) running wall to wall were placed within the structure (Figure 2.21).[4] These three interior excavation units contained nearly identical depositional sequences.[5] Beneath the modern humus was a level of semicompact, redeposited material that had eroded into the building from the mountain slope above. This strata contained small amounts of extremely eroded ceramics from farther up the mountain. Next was a thick level of wall fall composed of large rocks and yellow mortar. In some units, it was clear that sections of the wall had fallen in

Figure 2.20. The southeastern corner of the Kallanka at Vitcos. The building still displays several features noted by Bingham in 1911 (photograph by Brian S. Bauer and Miriam Aráoz Silva).

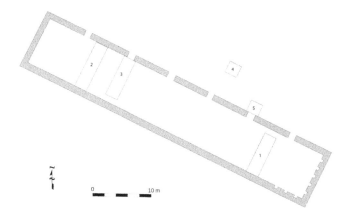

Figure 2.21. Excavation plan of the Kallanka (map by Axel Aráoz Silva).

Figure 2.22. Profile of an excavation unit in the Kallanka (photograph by Brian S. Bauer and Miriam Aráoz Silva).

a single event, while in others it appeared that the wall had collapsed more gradually. Beneath the wall fall was an occupation level, approximately 10 cm thick, containing scattered ceramic fragments, flecks of carbon, and minute fragments of burnt bone. One miniature, copper/bronze *tupu* (pin) was also recovered. While patches of hard, packed earth were found, there was no

evidence of a well-prepared floor. The occupation level rested directly on the natural subsoil of the mountain that was exposed when the Incas dug into the hill slope to build the building (Figure 2.22).

All three of the excavation units within the Kallanka revealed similar features. There were many slight depressions in the floor, perhaps made to help support the base of large storage vessels. Two of the units exposed numerous postholes scattered across the floor. The postholes averaged 20 cm in width and 20 to 30 cm in depth. Many had pieces of ceramics or small stone slabs wedged around their edges, placed in an effort to better support the posts (Figure 2.23). Our excavation also revealed the remains of narrow drainage canals cut into the subsoil, running perpendicular to the building, in two of the units. These trenches were cut at the time of construction, relieved water pressure on the back (upslope) wall of the building, and allowed groundwater to drain under the building. The drainage channel in Unit 3 was the best defined (Figure 2.24). It crossed the width of the building. A hole at the far end allowed water to pass under the foundation of the building.

EXTERIOR EXCAVATIONS AT THE KALLANKA

Two 2-x-2-m units were also placed in the small terrace to the east of the Kallanka. Unit 4, located near the middle of the terrace, was only 30 to 40 cm deep and provided a few unremarkable ceramics. Unit 5 was positioned in front of one of the doorways. A hard, gravel floor was found across the unit at a depth of ap-

Figure 2.23. Example of a posthole in the Kallanka. Note the different materials, both in and around the hole, that were used to help support the post (photograph by Brian S. Bauer and Miriam Aráoz Silva).

Figure 2.24. Excavations revealed a series of drainage canals under the floor of the Kallanka. Note the many postholes scattered across the floor (Unit 3) (photograph by Brian S. Bauer and Miriam Aráoz Silva).

were found. Instead there was a dispersed scatter of small sherds across the floor. The identification of the vessel types used in the building was especially difficult because of the eroded nature of the artifacts.[6] Approximately 38 percent (n = 61) of the rim sherds were from cooking pots, and 25 percent (n = 40) were from large storage vessels. These were followed by bowls and plates (35 percent; n = 56), lids (18 percent; n = 29), and drinking cups (2 percent; n = 3), with .6 percent of the rim sherds being from unidentifiable vessels. Overall, the distribution of vessel types shows a variety of functional classes. The most common forms also include miniatures, or vessels with diminutive dimensions.

About 13 percent of the total sherds were decorated (n = 267). Over 25 percent were composed of pastes that were similar to Cusco-Inca pastes (Bauer 1999, 2002) found in the Cusco region (n = 528). Nearly all the rest appear to be made from local clays (Quave 2010). However, a small percentage (> 1 percent) of the vessels were made of a fine blackware. This ware may be associated with the black Chimú pottery encountered in Sacsayhuaman (Valcárcel 1946:181), in Machu Picchu

proximately 25 cm. A thin level of cultural material, including small eroded pieces of ceramics and three iron nails, was recovered immediately above the floor (Figure 2.25). The location of these nails suggests that they were used in a wooden door, which has long since rotted away. These nails were the only materials of Western manufacture recovered in the building.

Summary of Excavations at the Kallanka

The excavations conducted within and outside the Kallanka yielded 2,057 ceramic fragments (Quave 2010). No complete or reconstructable vessels of ceramics

Figure 2.25. Three iron nails were recovered in Unit 5, directly in front of one of the doors of the Kallanka (photograph by Brian S. Bauer and Miriam Aráoz Silva).

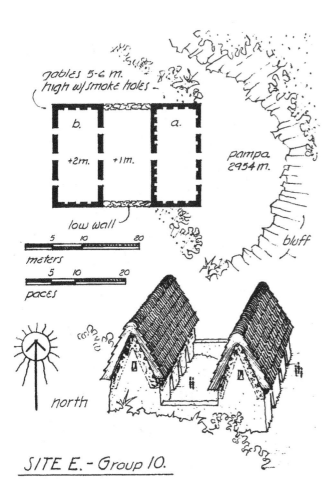

Figure 2.26. The Double Structures (drawing by Vincent Lee, 2000:469).

(Bingham 1922), and by Amelia Pérez Trujillo (2002) at Vitcos. In the Kallanka, the fine black-ware fragments were identified as coming from a miniature bowl, two miniature plates, and a drinking vessel. Special finds in the Kallanka also include a fragmented duck head plate and a broken llama head plate, both made of a Cusco-Inca paste. A worked disk associated with fiber spinning was also recovered. Thus it appears that the Kallanka hosted a variety of activities, from the quotidian to perhaps the ceremonial, with a mixture of locally and Cusco-produced vessels and a very small number of exotic pots.

Excavations at the Double Structures (Vitcos)

In 2009 we also conducted excavations in two buildings that we call the Double Structures (Figure 2.26). These buildings are located on the east side of Hatun Urco, about halfway down the slope, approximately 300 m to the southeast of the Kallanka (Site 22 in Figure 2.11).

They are perched near the edge of a mountain shelf and overlook the small, heavily terraced river valley to the east. The two structures are relatively isolated from other buildings at the site and remain in fair condition. José Cobos and Vincent Lee first documented the buildings in 1983 (Lee 2000:178, 469). At that time, the buildings had never been cleared and were covered in thick brush and trees.

The buildings were cleared of trees several years before our 2009 work. However, they were heavily overgrown with underbrush. While the structures were still standing and various interior niches could be seen, most of the walls were supported by informal wooden poles and were near the point of collapse (Figures 2.27 and 2.28)

The site consists of two parallel structures measuring 18.5 x 9 m each (Figure 2.29). There is a small rectangular flat area, 4 m wide, between the buildings. Each of the buildings has three downhill-(east-)facing trapezoidal doorways, with five interspersed interior niches. Each of the short sides of the buildings contained three slightly trapezoidal niches, while the longer back walls contained nine niches.[7] The interior corners of the buildings contained large looter's pits.

Figure 2.27. One of the doors in the lower structure (photograph by Brian S. Bauer and Miriam Aráoz Silva).

Figure 2.28. The lower structure after clearing but before excavations began (photograph by Brian S. Bauer and Miriam Aráoz Silva).

During our work at the site, we placed one approximately 2 x 7 m unit in the interior of the upper building and a similar unit in the lower building (Units 1 and 2). The exact length and placement of the units were influenced by the conditions of the remaining walls and the location of looter's pits. Although the details of each unit differed slightly, their stratigraphic profiles were essentially the same. The profiles included a level of topsoil several centimeters deep, followed by a stratum of eroded sediments that in turn covered large areas of wall fall. This was followed by an occupation level, of approximately 10 to 15 cm in depth, that contained small, scattered ceramic sherds, a few minute burnt bone fragments, and, in the case of Unit 2, iron nails. There was no evidence of a formally prepared floor. The occupation level rested directly on the rocky, sterile subsoil of the hill slope, which had been cut into and leveled in certain spots when the buildings were originally constructed. Unlike the excavations in the Kallanka, no interior post-molds were identified.

Units 3 and 4 were both 2 x 2 m units in the area between the two buildings. Unit 5 was a 2 x 2 m excavation in front of a door of the lower building. All three of these units yielded a small number of ceramics and various iron nails (Figure 2.30).

Discussion of the Artifacts Recovered at the Double Structures

Excavations in the interior and exterior of the Double Structures recovered only 235 pottery fragments. No intact or reconstructable ceramic vessels were found. The identification of the vessel types was especially difficult in the Double Structures because of the eroded nature of the artifacts. The most common, identifiable, rim sherds were from plates and bowls (81 percent; n = 22), followed by large storage containers (11 percent; n = 3), cooking pots (4 percent; n =1), and lids (4 percent; n = 1).[8] Half of the rim sherds from bowls and plates were from miniatures; two of these were made of the fine black-ware paste discussed in our description of the Kallanka (Quave 2010).

Approximately 4 percent of the sherds recovered were decorated (n = 10). About 18 percent of the sherds

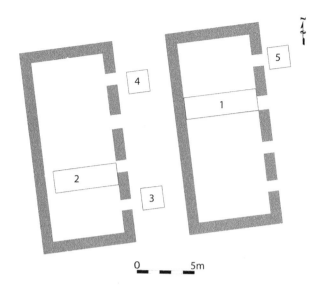

Figure 2.29. Plan of the Double Structures at Vitcos (map by Axel Aráoz Silva).

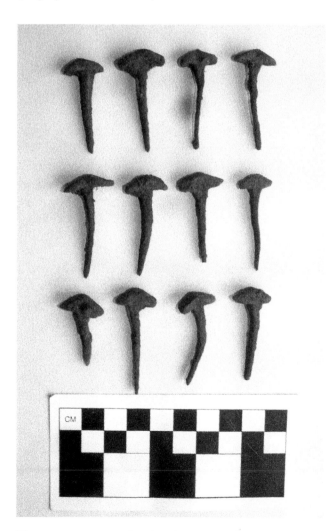

Figure 2.30. A sample of nails recovered from the Double Structures (photograph by Brian S. Bauer and Miriam Aráoz Silva).

were made with a Cusco-Inca paste (n = 42); 72 percent (n = 169) were made from local pastes, and 10 percent (n = 24) were made with a fine black-ware paste (Quave 2010). The low quantity of finds in the Double Structures makes a comparison with other excavated sites difficult.

While our excavations in the Double Structures provided very limited ceramics, they did yield various metal objects. Twenty iron nails were recovered in Unit 2. Most of these nails were found near the doorway of the upper building. Unit 3 contained three nails, Unit 4 provided four nails, and Unit 5 yielded a single nail, for a total of 28 iron nails. No other objects of European origin were recovered in the excavations.

Endnotes

1   See Covey (2008) for a comprehensive overview.
2   Savoy reports being shown "Tiwanaku-style" vessels in these areas, an understandable mistake for the 1970s.
3   As in many other regions of the Andes, several of the colonial churches in the Vitcos region contain stones taken from Inca buildings of the region.
4   All excavations described in this report followed the same excavation methodology. The excavations proceeded in 10-cm levels or until a natural soil change was detected. All soil removed during the excavations was screened through 1/4-inch wire mesh. Ten-liter flotation samples were collected from all features and floors as well as from each excavation level. After the excavations were finished, profiles were drawn, final photographs were taken, and the units were backfilled. During our research, we elected to leave 50 percent or more of the interiors of selected buildings unexcavated for future research.
5   The poor stability of the walls of this building limited the size and location of our excavations units.
6   Approximately 91 percent of the sherds from the Kallanka were non-rim sherds from unidentifiable vessels.
7   The full set of interior niches is visible only in the lower building.
8   Approximately 89 percent of the sherds from the Double Structures were non-rim sherds from unidentified vessels.

Chapter 3

The Yurak Rumi Shrine Complex

Brian S. Bauer, Miriam Aráoz Silva and **Kylie Quave**

THE YURAK RUMI SHRINE IS located in a small but steep-sided river valley at an altitude of approximately 3,080 m.[1] Now, as in Inca times, the valley slopes are covered in dense vegetation while the valley floor is cleared and carefully terraced. The complex is relatively small, less than 50 x 50 m in total area, and is situated some 20 minutes by foot from the monumental plaza of Vitcos. The relative seclusion of the shrine, the natural beauty of the carved rock, and the richness of the surrounding vegetation lend an idyllic quality to the shrine complex (Figure 3.1).

A Brief History of Yurak Rumi

During the period of organized indigenous resistance to Spanish rule (1536–1572), many of the major rituals organized by the Inca were held at the shrine of Yurak Rumi (also known as Chuquepalta). In 1568, while the Inca were still in control of the Vilcabamba region, the ruling Inca, Titu Cusi Yupanqui, invited an Augustinian priest named Marcos García to enter the area and establish a mission. About a year later, a second Augustinian, Diego Ortiz, was also given permission to live in the area.[2] As Titu Cusi Yupanqui contemplated a full conversion to Christianity,[3] the relationship between the Incas and the Christians was stable, and the missions run by Ortiz and García lived in an uneasy state

of truce with the Yurak Rumi shrine and its attendants. But in 1570, perhaps angered by their recent poor treatment by Titu Cusi Yupanqui in the Inca town of Vilcabamba and emboldened by a growing number of converts to Christianity, the two priests organized the burning of the Yurak Rumi shrine complex. The burning of the shrine by García and Ortiz is best described in the 1595 testimony of Juana Guerrero:[4]

> A month or so after the fathers returned to the town of Puquiura, this witness saw that some natives came looking for them and told them [that] near Vitcos, in a place called Chuquepalta, there was a white rock above a spring, from which many dreadful death curses were cast upon them, because the devil was there and because when they passed it they no [longer] prayed to it or gave it offerings as they had in the past. And they asked the fathers who were there to exorcise it and deliver them from that evil. And so those religious went there with a number of Indians and young men carrying firewood, and they exorcised and burned it. And since that was done, no harm has come to any Indian [Aparicio López 1989:164–165; translation by the authors].[5]

In the wake of this provocative act, Titu Cusi Yupanqui quickly returned to Vitcos to restore order and

Figure 3.1. The shrine complex of Yurak Rumi (photograph by Brian S. Bauer and Miriam Aráoz Silva).

to save the priests from an angry mob (Figure 3.2). The next year, however, the Inca suddenly died while in Vitcos.[6] Soon afterward (April 1572) the Spaniards entered the Vilcabamba region; a general depopulation of the area soon followed. The city of Vitcos was abandoned, and the important rituals that had been performed at the shrine of Yurak Rumi slowly faded from local memory, until it was visited by Bingham in 1911.

Description of Yurak Rumi

For the purposes of our investigations at the site, we divided the Yurak Rumi shrine complex into a series of distinct areas, including the rock, the plaza, the southwestern courtyard, the northeastern courtyard, and the second fountain area (Figures 3.3 and 3.4).

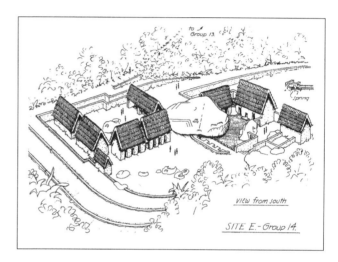

Figure 3.2. Reconstruction of Yurak Rumi (drawing by Vincent Lee, 2000:473).

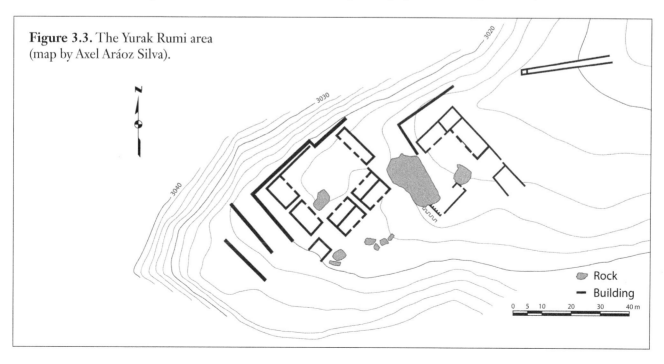

Figure 3.3. The Yurak Rumi area (map by Axel Aráoz Silva).

Rock

— Building

0 5 10   20   30   40 m

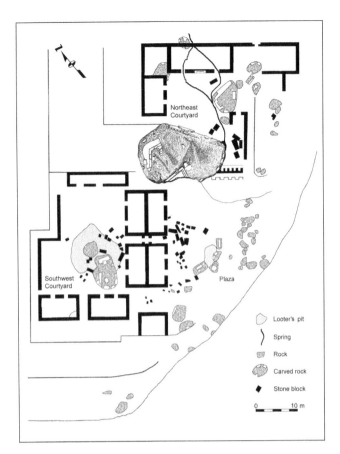

Figure 3.4. The Yurak Rumi complex (map by Brian S. Bauer and Miriam Aráoz Silva).

Figure 3.5. Detail of the north side of Yurak Rumi in 1911 (National Geographic Image Collection: negative 785908, photograph by Hiram Bingham).

THE WHITE ROCK

The immense and complexly sculpted rock of Yurak Rumi (in Quechua, *yurak* means "white" and *rumi* means "rock") is located at the center of the shrine compound. The rock is roughly oval in outline and somewhat pyramidal in form. Composed of a single block of white granite, it is now darkened by black lichen. Yurak Rumi measures approximately 21 x 10 m. Each side of the sculpted rock offers a radically different but impressive facade.

The north side of Yurak Rumi contains a sheer face, which stands 8 m above the current ground level. This remarkable rock face contains a series of 10 square protuberances, 7 of which run in a single line, as well as some more subtle, steplike carvings near its base (Figures 3.5–3.8).

The south side of the rock contains a series of carved, triangular, horizontal plains. The angularities of these carvings stand in sharp contrast to the smoothness of the rock surface, so the south side of Yurak Rumi is especially impressive. This side of the rock also contains a thin, slightly incised line that runs 9 m from the

Figure 3.6. The north side of Yurak Rumi (photograph by Brian S. Bauer and Miriam Aráoz Silva).

summit of the rock to its edge (Figure 3.9).

The east side of the rock contains a few minor carved "seats" and "steps," and it overhangs the spring that emerges from below it (Figures 3.10–3.12). Finally, the western side is covered in a complex series of "seats" and "steps."

Figure 3.7. The north side of Yurak Rumi in 1911 (National Geographic Image Collection: negative 602413, photograph by Hiram Bingham).

Figure 3.8. The north side of Yurak Rumi contains a steep face and various square protuberances (photograph by Brian S. Bauer and Miriam Aráoz Silva).

Figure 3.9. The east side of Yurak Rumi in 1911 (National Geographic Image Collection: negative 785902, photograph by Hiram Bingham).

Figure 3.10. The east side of Yurak Rumi contains a few small "seats." It also overhangs the spring that gives fame to the complex (photograph by Brian S. Bauer and Miriam Aráoz Silva).

Figure 3.11. The south side of Yurak Rumi contains a series of carved, triangular, horizontal plains. It is a stunning combination of carved and natural surfaces (photograph by Brian S. Bauer and Miriam Aráoz Silva).

Figure 3.12. The west side of Yurak Rumi is covered in a complex series of carvings (photograph by Brian S. Bauer and Miriam Aráoz Silva).

THE PLAZA

The area immediately to the south of the sacred rock contains a large open plaza (approximately 25 x 20 m). Near the center of the plaza is a cluster of four carved boulders and an adjacent looter's pit (Figures 3.13 and 3.14).

The plaza is flat, and our test excavations indicate that the Inca leveled parts of it with fill during construction of the shrine complex. The east side of the plaza is marked by the edge of the valley and a series of natural boulders. The west side of the plaza is defined by a pair of twin buildings that face the plaza.

One of the most notable features of the shrine complex is an east–west passageway that leads between the twin buildings and connects the plaza with an interior courtyard (*cancha*). Although now poorly preserved, the entrances to this passageway contain exceptionally large and well-worked granite blocks. Other large blocks, including lintels, are found scattered in disarray on either side of the passageway. The shapes of some of the fallen stones indicate that both of the entrances once contained double niches. The twin buildings on either side of the passageway also display the remains of four large rectangular stones set in the gables.[7] At the time of occupation, these stones served as entrances to second-story rooms (Figure 3.15).

Although the entrances of the passageway are built with well-carved blocks, the twin buildings are constructed with smaller stones and earth masonry. The nearby site of Vitcos (Rosaspata) also displays similar architectural traits in its large plaza. In Vitcos the entrances to the three major passageways that lead off the plaza are built in a

Figure 3.13. One of four small carved rocks in the plaza area of Yurak Rumi (photograph by Brian S. Bauer and Miriam Aráoz Silva).

Figure 3.14. One of four small carved rocks in the plaza area of Yurak Rumi (photograph by Brian S. Bauer and Miriam Aráoz Silva).

Figure 3.15. An east–west passageway was a major feature of Yurak Rumi at the time of the Inca occupation (photograph by Brian S. Bauer and Miriam Aráoz Silva).

Figure 3.16. (left) Door support hole at Yurak Rumi (photograph by Brian S. Bauer and Miriam Aráoz Silva).

monumental style, with oversize double-niched doorways constructed of large granite blocks. The adjacent building walls are constructed of far less noble material.

Two small rectangular holes are on either side of the west entrance of the passageway that leads between the plaza area and the southwestern courtyard (Figure 3.16). Similar holes have been noted at many other imperial Inca sites, and they may have supported some kind of door. Identical holes can be found in the three major passageways that lead off the central plaza of Vitcos (Rosaspata).

THE SOUTHWESTERN COURTYARD

The area to the southwest of the rock contains a small courtyard about the same size as the plaza (25 x 20 m). There are two buildings on the south side of the courtyard, both of which contain two doorways, and there are the poorly preserved remains of a single large building on the north side. The two twin build-

Figure 3.17. Near the center of the southwestern courtyard is a large carved rock. The area surrounding it was looted before Bingham's 1911 visit (photograph by Brian S. Bauer and Miriam Aráoz Silva).

timate that the second rock would have been 1 or 2 m below the surface of the *cancha* while the shrine was in use. The fact that Bingham's drawing of the site shows this flat rock suggests that the large looter's pit was dug before his visit to Yurak Rumi in 1911.

THE NORTHEASTERN COURTYARD

The area to the north of the rock is more than 3 meters lower than the south sector of the shrine complex. Its most important feature, which is marked by a wondrously carved stone bench, is the small spring that emerges from beneath the rock (Figures 3.18 and 3.19). The ground surface at the base of the rock is about at water level, and even a light rain can create areas of standing water and swampy conditions. An informal, shallow ditch now takes surface water from this area and drains it to the north of

ings, which separate the plaza and the courtyard, define the east side of the courtyard. The west side is clearly marked by a long wall that runs parallel to a large terrace built into the valley slope. This wall and its adjacent terrace form a narrow passageway that runs for some 30 m. This narrow passageway appears to have been constructed to enclose and restrict access to the west side of the courtyard.

A large (8 x 4 m) rock, which holds several carved "seats" and "steps," dominates the center of the southwestern courtyard. An immense looter's pit and its resulting back dirt surrounds this carved rock (Figure 3.17). The looting event has also exposed a second, slightly smaller rock. Although this second rock is flat, it does not appear to have been worked. We es-

Figure 3.18. A finely carved bench at the base of Yurak Rumi marks the emergence of a sacred spring (photograph by Brian S. Bauer and Miriam Aráoz Silva).

Figure 3.19. (above) The finely carved bench at the base of Yurak Rumi after Bingham's 1912 excavations (National Geographic Image Collection: negative 786176, photograph by Hiram Bingham).

Figure 3.20. A page from Bingham's field notes. It is labeled "August 26 cont." and contains a drawing of what Bingham called the "rock seats [at] Yurak Rumi" (Yale Peruvian Expedition Papers, manuscript 664. Manuscripts and Archives, Yale University Library).

the site.[8] The spring beneath the rock is specifically mentioned by Juana Guerrero in 1595 (Aparicio López 1989:164; Bauer et al 2014). Not surprisingly, this is also the area in which Bingham concentrated his excavations when he dug at the site in 1912.[9]

The spot at which the spring emerges beneath the rock is marked by an exceptionally well-crafted stone bench with a series of nine niches. The bench is approximately 9 m long and has been crafted from four large granite blocks. Bingham was especially impressed with this feature of the site. He took several photographs showing its excavation (Bingham 1913:553–554, 1922:250) and included a drawing of it in his field notes (Figure 3.20).

The area north of the rock also contains three buildings, a passageway, and various carved rocks. The three buildings combine with the sacred rock to form a courtyard. The building closest to the rock forms

Figure 3.21. The northeastern courtyard during Bingham's 1912 excavations. The trench that he dug to drain the courtyard can clearly be seen in this photograph, as can the large single-block external niche that faces the Yurak Rumi (National Geographic Image Collection: negative 786180, photograph by Hiram Bingham).

Figure 3.22. The building directly facing the rock contains a large niche made from a single block of granite (photograph by Brian S. Bauer and Miriam Aráoz Silva).

Figure 3.23. There are several carved rocks in the area north of Yurak Rumi. The stream that winds around this carved rock comes from beneath Yurak Rumi. In Inca times, the water would have flowed along a different course within a stone-lined canal (photograph by Brian S. Bauer and Miriam Aráoz Silva).

the west side of the courtyard. This building had two doorways and is now badly looted. The northernmost building is the only structure at the site that directly faces the rock. This building has two doorways, but it is most notable for a large central exterior niche, built from an impressive single block of granite, that faces the rock (Figures 3.21 and 3.22). No other building at the site contains a similar feature. The third building, now poorly preserved, forms the northeastern corner of the courtyard.

There are also the remains of a walled passageway that may have once linked the plaza area of the site with the northeastern courtyard, as well as a double-niched doorway that served as the formal north entrance to the shrine complex. Near the center of the northeastern courtyard is a large, ornately carved rock (Figure 3.23); a series of smaller carved rocks are scattered across the

area. As with the southern courtyard, access into this area of the site appears to have been limited.

THE SECOND SPRING

A second, much larger spring is located about 45 m north of the rock. The water emerges at the base of a large terrace and flows through a stone-lined canal to an elegant two-spouted fountain and bath (Figures 3.24 and 3.25). The water then continues within a wide canal for some 30 m down the course of the valley.

Building Construction at the Site

The craftsmanship of the carved bench beside the sacred spring cannot be overlooked. The bench, composed of four large stone blocks that were carved in

Figure 3.24. The Inca fountain at Yurak Rumi (photograph by Brian S. Bauer and Miriam Aráoz Silva).

Our excavations recovered various stone pegs, used to secure the roofs of buildings to the walls. Similar roof pegs can be seen in place in many different Inca sites in the Vilcabamba region and across the imperial heartland. As the pegs were generally recovered well above the 1570 destruction level, it seems that they were pulled from the gables during a later looting or general desecration event; in some cases, they may have simply fallen as the upper walls of the buildings became unstable over the centuries (Figure 3.29).

It is worth noting that one of the larger blocks found in the plaza area has a T-shaped joint carved into its surface (Figure 3.30). While rare, T-shaped joints have been noted at important Inca compounds, including within the Coricancha in Cusco and in Ollantaytambo.[10]

exactly the same way and then placed together, rivals any stonework found in the Inca Empire.

The shrine complex also contains more than a dozen smaller carved stones (Figure 3.26). Most of these appear to be boulders that were deposited in the valley during its glacial past and then worked by the Inca. While most of the carved rocks seem to be in their final desired forms, one of the largest carved rocks at the site contains an incomplete "shelf," suggesting that the carving may have been ongoing until the site was abandoned (Figure 3.27).

The buildings at the site are mostly made of moderately sized worked and natural stones held together with small spacer stones and earth mortar. The doorways, corners, and niches of the buildings are built with slightly larger, well-shaped, closely fitting granite blocks (Figure 3.28). The stones that define the entrances to the southwestern courtyard represent exceptions. Like the blocks used in the doorways in the plaza of Vitcos (Rosaspata), the courtyard passageways at Yurak Rumi were outlined with large stone blocks, many measuring more than 1 m in length and height. The entrances also contained massive lintel stones, which can still be seen lying nearby.

Figure 3.25. The large canal leading down from the dual fountain and bath (photograph by Brian S. Bauer and Miriam Aráoz Silva).

Figure 3.26. The plaza of Yurak Rumi, showing many stone blocks (foreground) used in construction of the buildings and several carved rocks. In this picture, a suite of four carved stones can be seen in the background (photograph by Brian S. Bauer and Miriam Aráoz Silva).

Figure 3.27. This large outcrop, located in the northeastern courtyard, has an unfinished "shelf." Craftsmen were working from the left side toward the center of the stone but stopped midway through the process. This suggests that rock carving was a continuous process occurring at the site until its final abandonment (circa 1572) (photograph by Brian S. Bauer and Miriam Aráoz Silva).

Figure 3.28. (left) The large passageway stone blocks at Yurak Rumi (photograph by Brian S. Bauer and Miriam Aráoz Silva).

Figure 3.29. (above) Unit 3 contained various roof pegs at the same level. They appear to have been pulled from the gables after the building was abandoned (photograph by Brian S. Bauer and Miriam Aráoz Silva).

Figure 3.30. (below) Stone with a T-shaped joint in Yurak Rumi (photograph by Brian S. Bauer and Miriam Aráoz Silva).

The Terraces of the Shrine Complex

The Yurak Rumi compound is located in the middle of a narrow valley. The ground level drops approximately 15 m across the length of the site. This declination is divided between four sets of terraces that run perpendicular to the valley. The southernmost terrace stands about 1.3 m high and is composed of natural stones of varying sizes supported with small filler stones and earth mortar. The second terrace is of slightly better construction and stands between 1.5 and 2 m in height. At the edge of the valley slope, this terrace makes a 90-degree turn and runs for approximately 40 m, forming a retention wall for the western side of the site. The third terrace is substantial, standing more than 2.5 m high. It separates the northern and southern halves of the site. This terrace is composed of moderately sized, roughly shaped stones. The final terrace begins adjacent to the sacred rock and runs west for approximately

11 m before it makes a 90-degree turn, forming a western retaining wall for this area of the site. This terrace is composed of much larger worked stones, many of which are over 1 m long (Figure 3.31).

Test Excavations at Yurak Rumi (2008)

During 2008 we dug a series of small (generally 1 x 1 m) test excavations across the site to gain information on its stratigraphy and occupational history (Figure 3.32). These test excavations are labeled P1 through P11. The test units dug outside the buildings ended at bedrock or at a mixture of small stones and gravel, while units placed within buildings were terminated at the Inca floor level.

Test Excavations P1–P3 were dug as a line of test units, set approximately 10 m apart, along the southeastern edge of the plaza. Each of the units varied in depth be-

Figure 3.31. The third and lowest terrace of Yurak Rumi is made with large, well-worked stones (photograph by Brian S. Bauer and Miriam Aráoz Silva).

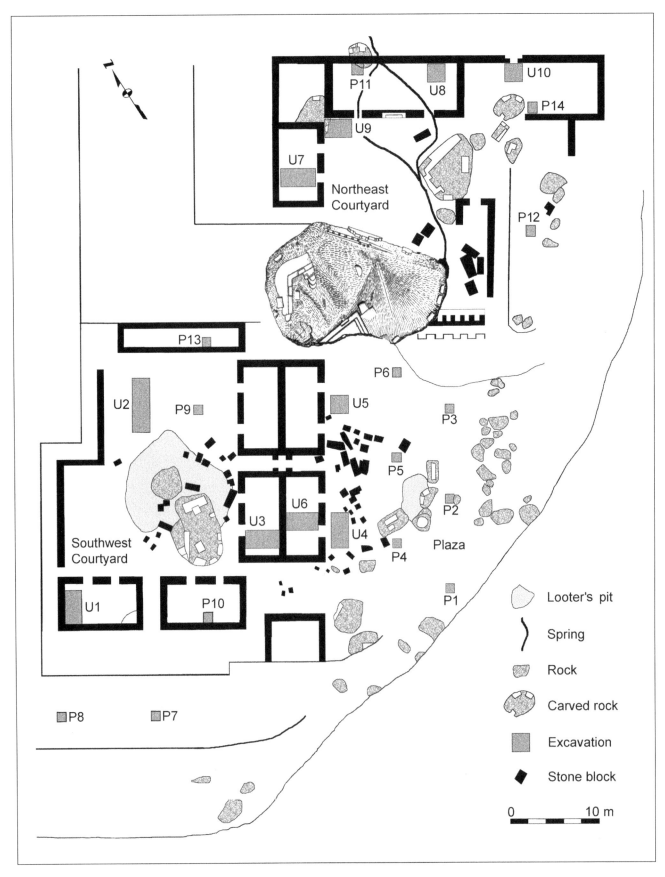

Figure 3.32. Map of Yurak Rumi showing locations of test excavations (P1–P13) and larger excavation units (U1–U10) (map by Brian S. Bauer and Miriam Aráoz Silva).

tween 70 and 113 cm. Each unit was dug to bedrock, and they all yielded a minimal number of eroded ceramics in their upper levels. Unit P1 marked the limits of detected cultural activities at the site. Excavation P2 revealed what appeared to be a thick (about 60 cm) stone-and-earth fill, which was used to level this area of the plaza. No clear floor was identified. Excavation P3 contained patches of a prepared gravel floor above similar fill materials.

Test Excavations P4–P6 were dug as a line of test units through the center of the plaza. These pits were spaced approximately 10 m apart and were offset from Units P1–P3 to provide better coverage of the plaza. Each unit was excavated to the natural bedrock and yielded a few small eroded ceramic sherds. Excavation P4 was placed near one of the carved rocks near the center of the plaza. The northwestern corner of the unit intersected a narrow pit (30 cm in diameter, 70 cm deep) sealed with small capstones. The pit was dug long after the site had been abandoned. It may have once held an offering, which has not endured. The excavation also revealed a compact, well-preserved gravel floor constructed on more than 1 m of multilayered fill deposits (Figure 3.33). A single flat slab of green schist was found resting on the gravel floor. Similar green schist slabs were also noted in excavations U4, U5, and U6 and are believed to have been used during the brief reoccupation of the site after its destruction in 1570. Excavation P5 was located near the center of the plaza on the edge of a looter's pit. This excavation revealed a concentration of redeposited burnt plaster, similar to

Figure 3.34. The northeastern profile of P8 (photograph by Brian S. Bauer and Miriam Aráoz Silva).

what we found in the interior of all the buildings we excavated, and the possible remains of a gravel floor. Test excavation P6 was placed near Yurak Rumi. It was relatively shallow, with a maximum depth of 60 cm, and provided no noteworthy results.

Test Excavations P7 and P8 were placed approximately 10 m apart on an artificially constructed agricultural terrace in the southwestern corner of the complex. The terrace stands some 1.5 m high. Although the profiles of the two pits differed slightly, they both revealed a similar construction sequence for the terrace. The modern plow zone was followed by an organically rich terrace fill, approximately 80 cm deep, of soil and small rocks (Figures 3.34 and 3.35). Next came a prepared level of red clay and gravel (3 to 6 cm thick), which appears to have been laid down to seal the bottom of the terrace fill. The base of the terrace was established with cobble-sized rocks resting on bedrock.

Test Excavation P9 was placed relatively near to, and north of, the large looter's pit that dominates the southwestern courtyard (Figure 3.36). The excavation revealed a humus-and-topsoil level followed by a thick stratum of disturbed soil, representing the back dirt

Figure 3.33. The southwestern profile of P4. Note the gravel floor, about 40 cm below the current ground level, which was built on many levels of fill (photograph by Brian S. Bauer and Miriam Aráoz Silva).

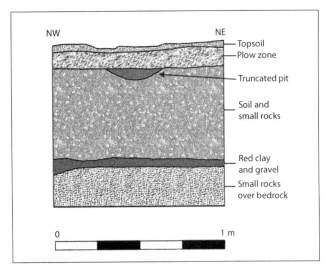

Figure 3.35. A simplified profile of P8. Note the lines of red clay and gravel resting above the lowest fill level (drawing by Brian S. Bauer and Miriam Aráoz Silva).

Figure 3.36. The northeastern profile of P9. Note the crushed-white-granite floor level just below the 50 cm mark on the photographic scale (photograph by Brian S. Bauer and Miriam Aráoz Silva).

of the looter's pit. The third stratum was composed of redeposited materials (slope wash) laid down after the site was abandoned. Next came a series of closely spaced, relatively thin (2 to 3 cm) levels. The first was a floor of small pebbles and gravel that extends across much of the courtyard area. This rested directly above a floor of crushed white granite. Next came a lens of dark earth followed by another floor of crushed white granite. Under the second granite floor was a thin level of earthen fill and a then thick stratum (30-plus cm) of very dark brown soil mixed with rocks, which is believed to be the natural sediment of the valley before the Inca occupation.

Test Excavation P10 was located against the interior back wall of one of the buildings that define the southwestern courtyard (Figure 3.37). In this unit we first removed the current topsoil and a level of wall fall. We then encountered a thin level of redeposited materials and melted adobe, within which we found a small piece of blue-on-white majolica ceramic. The next level consisted of a 30 cm thick stratum of destroyed building materials, including burnt wall plaster and carbonized roof remains, which rested on a prepared floor made of green clay.[11] Fragments of a crushed storage vessel were recovered on the floor.

Test Excavation P11 was a 1.2 x 1 m unit placed in the northeastern sector of the site against the back wall of the building that faces the sacred rock (Figure 3.38). The excavations soon revealed a hard-packed but very irregular earth-and-pebble floor with large fragments of classic Inca pottery, carbon, and some minute burnt bone fragments (Figures 3.39 and 3.40). Beneath the earthen floor was a fill level, approximately 20 cm thick, which rested on a second thin (2 to 4 cm) fill level, followed by a second floor of crushed white granite. This second floor was flat and well made. It rested above a thin (less than 1 cm) level of red

Figure 3.37. (left) Detail of Inca floor covered by destroyed building materials in P10 (photograph by Brian S. Bauer and Miriam Aráoz Silva).

Figure 3.38. (above) Northwestern profile of P11. The crushed-white-granite floor is marked with a slash (photograph by Brian S. Bauer and Miriam Aráoz Silva).

Figure 3.39. (below) Large Inca plate fragment found in P11 (photograph by Brian S. Bauer and Miriam Aráoz Silva).

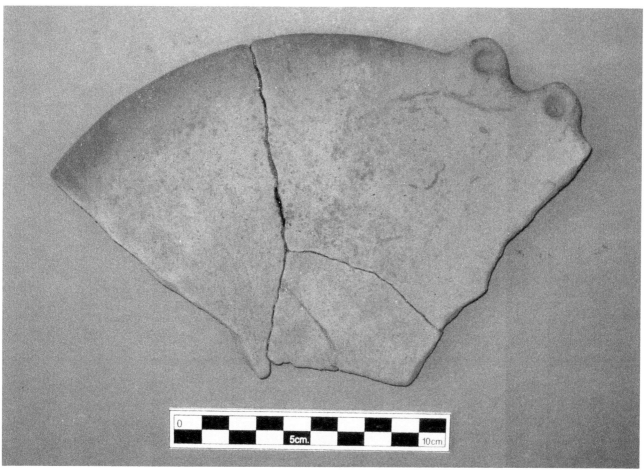

Figure 3.40. Flat-bottom Inca dish found in P11 (photograph by Brian S. Bauer and Miriam Aráoz Silva).

Figure 3.41. This test excavation exposed a patio-facing wall and a vessel resting upside down on the floor of the building (photograph by Brian S. Bauer and Miriam Aráoz Silva).

clay, which may have been used as a sealant to protect the granite floor in this waterlogged area of the site.[12] Beneath the red clay level was a thick stratum (50 to 60 cm) of multiple fill levels, which appear to have been used to raise the interior area of the structure.

Test Excavations P12 and P14 were placed on the edge of the site to the east and northeast of the rock. While the excavations in P12 did recover a small number of ceramic remains, the area appears to have been disturbed, perhaps during Bingham's 1912 excavations. P14 was placed within a structure. Unfortunately, this test unit soon reached the water table, and it was not completed.

Test Excavation P13 was a 1 x 1.5 m unit placed within the structure that marks the northern edge of the southwestern courtyard (Figure 3.41). The excavation helped define the courtyard-facing wall of the building that was no longer visible on the surface and that had not been well documented in early studies. The excavation also identified a thick (30 cm) stratum of burnt building materials within the structure. Below this destruction level was a green-clay floor, on top of which rested a complete, although upside down, pedestal vessel (Figure 3.42).[13]

Larger Excavations at Yurak Rumi (2008 and 2009)

During the 2008 field season, we dug six larger excavation units (U1–U6) in the southern parts of the shrine complex to collect more data on the open areas of the site and the preservation of its buildings. The areas sampled included the plaza and the southwestern courtyard, as well as the interiors of three buildings. We returned to the site in 2009 to conduct excavations of four additional units on the north side of the sacred rock (U7–U10). The larger excavations of our project varied between 2 x 2 m and 2 x 6 m. When these excavation units were placed inside structures, we generally

Figure 3.42. The pedestal vessel recovered in P13 (photograph by Brian S. Bauer and Miriam Aráoz Silva).

positioned them widthwise, to run from the back wall to the front wall on the building. Most of the excavations did not go below the Inca floor levels, although in a few cases, we dug much smaller test squares through the floor to document the underlying strata.

Excavation U1 was a 2 x 4 m excavation located within the easternmost building in the southwestern courtyard. Beneath the wall fall of the structure, the excavation revealed a thick stratum of burnt building materials, including wall plaster and carbonized roof remains, resting on a preserved green-clay floor (Figure 3.43). The interior of the building was cleared of objects at the time of the fire, except for a bronze *yauri* recovered during the excavation (Figures 3.44 and 3.45). The position of this halberd-like weapon, just slightly above the floor and within a matrix of burnt clay and roof materials, suggests that it was originally stored within the rafters of the building and that it fell to the ground when the roof burned and the building collapsed. Two 1 x 1 m units were dug through the green-clay floor and revealed that this area of the shrine complex had been leveled with fill material before construction of the buildings began.

Excavation U2 was a 2 x 6 m unit placed in the southwestern courtyard of the shrine complex on the edge of a large looter's pit. Beneath the current topsoil and the spoil from the looter's pit, the excavation revealed a lev-

Figure 3.43. Exposed green-clay Inca floor in Unit 1 (photograph by Brian S. Bauer and Miriam Aráoz Silva).

Figure 3.44. A bronze *yauri* found within the burnt and collapsed remains of Unit 1 (photograph by Brian S. Bauer and Miriam Aráoz Silva).

el of redeposited materials (slope wash), laid down after the site was abandoned, resting above a 10-cm-thick gravel floor. No artifacts were recovered on the gravel floor. Continued excavations in part of the unit reached bedrock, revealing that the gravel floor had been constructed on fill that was used to level this area of the site

(Figure 3.46). It is worth noting that the same gravel floor was also identified in test excavation P9, 5 m away.

Excavation U3 was a 2 x 4 m unit placed within one of the twin buildings that separate the plaza area from the southwestern courtyard. Our work revealed that the roof pegs had been pulled from the gables sometime after the structure burned but before the collapse of its major walls (see Figure 3.30). This may represent a looting event that occurred early in its post-abandonment phase. As in the interior of all other buildings at the site, this unit exposed a well-made green-clay floor directly beneath a thick (about 30 cm) level of burnt wall plaster and charred roof materials. No items were recovered on the floor of the structure.

Sometime after the building was abandoned, a small offering containing unidentified organic and inorganic

Figure 3.45. The Inca *yauri* recovered in Unit 1 (photograph by Brian S. Bauer and Miriam Aráoz Silva).

remains, as well as a few small pieces of silver lamina, was burned and buried within it. The offering documents that the site continued to be seen as a special location well after its major structures had been destroyed.[14]

Excavation U4 was a 2 x 4 m excavation positioned in the plaza directly in front of one of the twin structures. After the removal of the topsoil, we identified a stratum of wall collapse that originated from the nearby building. The next level contained redeposited materials, including burnt plaster, melted adobe, and carbon, most of which also appeared to come from the adjacent building. Under this level, we found an irregular arrangement of flat slabs of blue-green schist, which had been used to resurface a gravel floor that once covered much of the plaza area (Figure 3.47). Several small fragments of white majolica ceramics were found within the resurfaced floor level. No artifacts were recovered on the lower gravel floor.

Excavation U5 was a 2 x 2 m unit situated in the plaza in front of the twin structure nearest to the sacred rock. The first two strata included topsoil followed by wall fall and other redeposited materials. As with U4, we then found a well-preserved gravel floor that had been partially resurfaced with flat slabs of green schist (Figure 3.48).

Excavation U6 was a 2 x 4 m unit placed within one of the twin structures that separate the plaza from the

Figure 3.46. Unit 2 facing east. Note the remains of the gravel floor on the right and left sides of the excavation. The modern ground level is uneven because of a large looter's pit located to the right of this excavation (photograph by Brian S. Bauer and Miriam Aráoz Silva).

southwestern courtyard. Excavations began with removal of the topsoil and recent wall fall from the structure. Beneath the wall fall was a flat living surface with much carbon, which we believe represents a brief reoccupation of the building following the burning of the site by the Augustinian priests. At this level we recovered the remains of two iron nail fragments and several sherds of white majolica pottery. The next stratum consisted of nearly 30 cm of burnt plaster and other building materials resting on a green-clay floor. The burnt materials were especially well preserved within this building, and we were able to identify pieces of the collapsed roof, including rafters, battens, thatch (burnt and unburnt),[15] and rope. These materials are discussed in more detail below (Figures 3.49–3.52). We also re-

Figure 3.47. (left) Unit 4 exposed the gravel floor that once covered much of the shrine area. This floor was later resurfaced with a patchwork of blue-green schist slabs (photograph by Brian S. Bauer and Miriam Aráoz Silva).

Figure 3.49. Excavations in U6 revealed various burnt but well-preserved parts of the roof of the building as well as a crushed storage vessel on a green-clay floor (photograph by Brian S. Bauer and Miriam Aráoz Silva).

Figure 3.48. Unit 5 showing the gravel floor and Yurak Rumi in the background (photograph by Brian S. Bauer and Miriam Aráoz Silva).

Figure 3.50. (above) Carbonized roof battens held together with rope resting on the green-clay floor in U6 (photograph by Brian S. Bauer and Miriam Aráoz Silva).

Figure 3.51. Parts of a carved wooden staff were recovered on the floor of U6 (photograph by Brian S. Bauer and Miriam Aráoz Silva).

Figure 3.52. Fragments of an iron nail found in U6 (photograph by Brian S. Bauer and Miriam Aráoz Silva).

covered a complete but shattered storage jar and the remains of a carved carbonized staff on the floor of the building.

Excavation U7 was a 2 x 3.4 m unit placed in one of the buildings that form the northwestern courtyard. The northern end of the building had been badly looted, so our excavation was placed in the southern half. The excavation revealed a level of topsoil followed by a level of stony, redeposited slope wash marking a prolonged time of abandonment. Beneath this was the wall fall of the building. In some areas, the wall had fallen in a single block and the stones were still in their original positions relative to each other. The wall fall covered a relatively thin (1 to 2 cm) level of carbonized materials, including roof batten remains resting on a green-clay floor (Figure 3.53). No other artifacts were recovered from the interior of the building.

Excavation U8 was a 2 x 2 m unit placed in the building that faces the rock in the northeastern courtyard. The building, which was also sampled in 2008 by excavation P11, is especially noteworthy for its large exterior niche. The interior of the building has been badly disturbed by two ditches dug to drain the northeastern courtyard of water from the spring and general seepage from the rock area. Beneath the topsoil and wall collapse we found an irregular earthen and pebble floor, on top of which were various fragments of Inca ceramics. The floor appears to have been resurfaced in parts with slabs of blue-green schist, similar to those found in the units excavated in the plaza. Unlike the interiors of other buildings of the site, this building did not yield evidence of a massive burning event, although some burnt pieces of plaster and adobe were recovered.

Excavation U9 was a 3 x 2 m unit placed in one corner of the northeastern *cancha*. The excavation revealed that the *cancha* was once covered with a hard-packed gravel floor and that this floor had been resurfaced at least once with additional gravel and scattered slabs of blue-green schist (Figure 3.54). The excavation also re-

Figure 3.53. Northeastern profile of U7 showing a collapsed wall (photograph by Brian S. Bauer and Miriam Aráoz Silva).

Figure 3.54. As seen in U9, the northeastern *cancha* was originally covered with a hard-packed gravel floor. This floor was later resurfaced with additional gravel and large slabs of blue-green schist (photograph by Brian S. Bauer and Miriam Aráoz Silva).

vealed carved portions of a natural rock outcropping that were not formerly visible and revealed that the gravel floor rested on the natural subsoil of the area.

Excavation U10 was a 2 x 2 m unit placed on the interior side of the double-jamb doorway that leads from the shrine complex to the north. The excavation revealed several additional Inca blocks that had made up the doorway and the remains of a stone canal (25 cm wide, 35 cm high) that once drained water away from the compound.

Artifact Analysis of Materials Recovered from Yurak Rumi

At least 944 ceramic sherds were recovered in the Yurak Rumi shrine complex (Quave 2010). The wet conditions at the site seem to have eroded the surface of many pottery fragments, likely erasing painted designs, slipped finishes, and polishing. Approximately 68 percent (n = 81) of the identified rim sherds were from cooking pots, 20 percent (n = 24) were from large storage vessels, 6 percent (n = 7) were from plates and bowls, 5 percent (n = 6) were from lids, and 2 percent (n = 2) were from drinking vessels.[16] One intact pedestal pot was also recovered.

About 10 percent (n = 97) of all the sherds recovered were decorated. Approximately 15 percent (n = 144) of the sherds were made with a Cusco-Inca paste, about 81 percent (n = 769) were made of local pastes, and .4 percent (n = 4) were made with a fine black-ware (Quave 2010).

Flotation soil samples (10 kg) were collected from each level and feature of the complex. The flotation was conducted in the field, and the resulting collections were sent to Lima for analysis by Gabriela Bertone at the Laboratorio de Arqueobotánica in the Museo de Historia. While her analysis confirmed our identification of the burnt roof remains, no cultigens were identified.

Comparison of Ceramics from the Kallanka, the Double Structures, and Yurak Rumi

European materials recovered during our excavations in the Vitcos region included 25 iron nails. The majority of nails came from the Double Structures. However, both the Kallanka and Yurak Rumi also provided examples. All the iron nails were of the same style, with

a relatively large head and a short (2 to 4 cm) shaft. Many of these nails were recovered near the doorways of buildings, suggesting that they were used in the construction of wooden doors. Similar nails have been recovered in other contact-period and early-colonial context—for example at Huánuco Pampa (Morris et al. 2011).

An intersite comparison of the ceramic assemblages recovered from the Kallanka, the Double Structures, and the Yurak Rumi excavations revealed a variability in paste types.[17] When the frequencies of Cusco-Inca pastes, local pastes, and fine black-wares were compared between and within loci, there were statistically significant differences (using an χ^2 test and Freeman-Tukey deviates). The Kallanka had significantly more sherds made with Cusco-Inca pastes than the other two sites, while the Yurak Rumi excavations yielded significantly more fragments made with local pastes. These findings support the view that state-sponsored festivals occurred in the Kallanka while Yurak Rumi was a regionally important shrine. Finally, the unique fine black-ware, which is thought to have been imported into the highlands from the coast, was significantly present at the Double Structures, supporting the belief that this building may have been used as a residence for an elite individual.

Another way of evaluating site function is through vessel morphology. The results should complement the differences in paste types. However, no matter how vessel morphology is assessed, there are no statistically significant differences between the three sites. This may be because of the relatively small number of ceramic fragments recovered from each site. The frequencies of large storage vessels, cooking pots, drinking vessels, lids, and bowls/plates indicate that all three sites have equal evidence of activities associated with the storage, preparation, and serving of food.

It is worth noting, however, that the only majolica ceramics recovered were found at Yurak Rumi. Majolica, or glazed pottery, was brought to the Vilcabamba region in the colonial period. A total of 27 majolica sherds were found in four excavation units (P10, U3, U4, and U6); many of them appear to have been deposited during a brief reoccupation of the site following the initial destruction of the shrine. The units containing majolica ceramics are clustered together on the south side of the white rock. Although the most common majolica form in Spanish America is a bowl, associated with table service and wealth display (Jamieson 2003:256), the identified majolica forms at Yurak Rumi are a narrow-mouth jar, a plate, and a lid. The glaze colors include primarily green but also white, yellow, red/brown, and blue (Figures 3.55–3.57).

Most majolica arriving in Peru was traditionally assumed to have originated in Panama Vieja, which produced majolica until 1671. However, at Yurak Rumi, all majolica sherds have an orange paste, while Panama Vieja produced a characteristic dark brick-red paste (Lister and Lister 1974). The origin of the majolica vessels is unresolved, as neither historians nor archaeologists have yet unveiled all the centers of majolica production in the Andes. The glazed ware was also used and produced in Lima and other major centers of Spanish occupation in Peru, but there are no published descriptions of the different paste types (Flores Espinoza et al. 1981:52).[18]

Another rare ware type recovered from the excavations is a finely polished black-ware. This ware, which

Figure 3.55. (above) A majolica sherd (green and red-brown over yellowish white) from a narrow-mouth jar found at Yurak Rumi (photograph by Brian S. Bauer and Miriam Aráoz Silva).

Figure 3.56. (left) White-glazed majolica fragments found in U6 (photograph by Brian S. Bauer and Miriam Aráoz Silva).

Figure 3.57. (below) Additional fragments of glazed majolica recovered at Yurak Rumi (photograph by Brian S. Bauer and Miriam Aráoz Silva).

was recovered at all three excavated sites, is highly fired in an oxygen-deficient environment, rendering it black with some areas of partial oxidation within a vessel. Nonplastic inclusions include very fine (about .5 mm) fragments of mica, quartz, feldspars, and an unknown red mineral. The vessels are highly polished inside and out and have thin (about .5 cm) walls.

In total, 59 polished black-ware sherds were found, representing a minimum of nine different vessels. The Double Structures had at least three separate vessels including bowls and plates; at least two of them were miniatures. Excavations at the Kallanka yielded the greatest

number of polished black-ware sherds, including several bowls and plates and a cup. Two of the plates and two of the bowls appear to be of miniature proportions. Yurak Rumi yielded only one black-ware fragment. It is from an unknown vessel type. As noted above, the highly polished black-ware vessels appear to be related to ceramics being produced by the Chimú culture on the north coast of Peru. Small numbers of such vessels are being increasingly noted in excavations conducted in the greater Cusco region.

Dating the Construction and Destruction of the Yurak Rumi Shrine

Our research suggests that the Yurak Rumi shrine was established early on during the expansion of the Inca Empire. Furthermore, we find overwhelming evidence that the shrine was destroyed by fire and that the ritual complex was then briefly reoccupied before being completely abandoned. These archaeological data support Cobo's (1979 [1653]) and Cabello de Balboa's (1951:300 [1586]) description of the expansion of the empire into the Vilcabamba region as well as the 1595 narrative account by Juana Guerrero (Aparicio López 1989:164–165; Bauer et al. 2014) that describes the burning of the shrine by two Augustinians. Nevertheless, we felt it was important to obtain radiocarbon dates to provide greater clarity regarding the timing of these two events. Accordingly, at the conclusion of the fieldwork, six charcoal samples were submitted for dating at the Accelerator Mass Spectrometry Laboratory at the University of Arizona.

DATING THE CONSTRUCTION OF THE SHRINE

Excavations in the plaza and the southwestern courtyard of the shrine complex documented that they were covered with hard-packed gravel and pebble floors during their final years of use. Furthermore, excavations in the buildings that surround the sacred rock revealed that they all contained well-prepared green-clay floors. Nevertheless, we also found evidence of earlier floors, made with crushed white granite, in two units in the shrine complex.

Evidence of two deeply buried floors made with crushed white granite was first identified in Unit P9 in the southwestern courtyard (Figure 3.58). A similar floor was then found in Unit P11 beneath a structure north of the rock (Figure 3.59). There is little doubt that the crushed white granite contained in these floors

is the direct by-product of the Incas carving the many granite boulders that lie within the shrine complex. A carbon sample (AA 83415) collected from the upper crushed-granite floor in Unit P9 yielded an AMS radiocarbon date of 601 ± 34 B.P. A carbon sample (AA

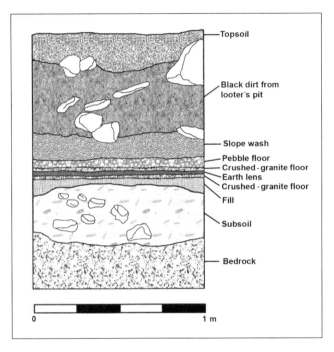

Figure 3.58. A simplified profile of P9. Note two crushed-white-granite floor levels approximately midway through the profile. Carbon collected from the upper floor provided a radiocarbon date of 601 ± 34 B.P.

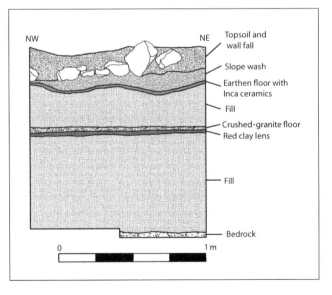

Figure 3.59. Simplified drawing of the northwestern profile of P11. A charcoal sample from the crushed-white-granite floor provided a radiocarbon date of 496 ± 51 B.P.

83416) collected from the crushed-granite floor in Unit P11 provided an AMS date radiocarbon age of 496 ± 51 B.P.

These dates suggest that the shrine was built around A.D. 1400 and support the writings of Bernabé Cobo, who states that the region was incorporated relatively early into the growing Inca Empire. Cobo writes, "[Pachacuti Inca Yupanqui] began his conquests with the provinces of Vitcos and Vilcabamba, a very difficult land to subjugate because it is so rough and covered with dense jungle and many *arcabucos* [dense forests] (Cobo 1979:136 [1653:Book 12, Chapter 12])."[19] Since Machu Picchu is thought to have also been established by Pachacuti Inca Yupanqui (Rowe 1990), it has been proposed that the Vilcabamba region was incorporated into the Inca Empire during the same military campaign (Hemming 1970; Lee 2000).

DATING THE DESTRUCTION OF THE SHRINE

With the help of Juana Guerrero's 1595 testimony, the destruction of the Yurak Rumi shrine can be narrowed down to a relatively short time period. The two Augustinian priests, Ortiz and García, witnessed and signed a document dictated by Titu Cusi Yupanqui (2005:139 [1570]) in the Inca city of Vilcabamba on February 6, 1570, after which they returned to the town of Puquiura near Vitcos.[20] According to eyewitness Juana Guerrero, when García and Ortiz arrived in Puquiura, a group of recent converts was waiting for them (Aparicio López 1989:164–165 [1595]; Bauer et al. 2014). Some of these individuals trembled in fear over the havoc and destruction caused by the "demon" of Yurak Rumi, because they had been baptized and no long paid respect to the shrine. Angry, and perhaps humiliated by certain events that had taken place in the city of Vilcabamba, García and Ortiz, announced that converts should gather the next day and bring firewood, since they were going to burn the shrine. The following day the priests and their followers gathered in Puquiura and then marched to Yurak Rumi. After conducting an exorcism, they burned the temple and the rock. According to Juana Guerrero's timeline, the burning of the shrine appears to have taken place sometime between mid-February and mid-March 1570.

Our 2008 and 2009 excavations at Yurak Rumi confirm that the shrine was destroyed in a massive fire. Each of the buildings that we sampled on the south side contained thick levels of burnt building materials, including large amounts of burnt plaster and adobe as well as carbonized roof remains. The buildings on the north side of the complex were also destroyed by fire. However, the destruction does not appear to have been as complete as on the south side.

Our excavations also revealed that each of the buildings in the shrine complex had well-maintained floors at the time of the destruction. A few complete ceramic vessels (including those for storage, cooking, and serving) were found on the floors, and one structure yielded a bronze *yauri* (halberd) head, which may have been left in the rafters of one of the buildings when it burned. Furthermore, some organic artifacts in use at the time of the burning were preserved in carbonized form. For example, we recovered a carved wooden staff on one of the floors. It should be noted, however, that overall our excavations found very few artifacts within the structures, suggesting that the priests and attendants had time to remove items and flee before the complex was burned.

The most intriguing information on the massive burning of the shrine comes from the U6 excavation, where the roof of the structure collapsed while it was still burning (Figure 3.60). During the course of the excavation, we exposed samples of burnt and unburnt mountain grass (*Stipa ichu*) used as thatch, carbonized mountain bamboo (*Chusququea scandens*) used as battens, carbonized rafters made from alder (*Alnus acuminata*), and carbonized rope made from local grass (*Calamagrostis heterophylla*), used in lashing the battens and rafters. These charred materials rested directly on the green-clay floor of the building and were covered with a 30 cm thick stratum of burnt plaster and other materials.

A hard-packed earthen floor enhanced by a few slate paving stones, above the burnt stratum but below a large-scale collapse of the structure walls, provided evidence of a brief reoccupation of the shrine after it had been burned by the Augustinians.[21] It appears that this reoccupation also ended in fire, since the hard-packed earthen floor was also covered with a lens of ash and burnt wood.

The recovery of various identifiable organic ceiling and roofing materials within a building with a known destruction date provided a unique investigative opportunity. We wanted to examine how the dates of various plant species incorporated into the different parts of the roof correlated with each other as well as with the known destruction date of the shrine (mid-February to mid-March 1570). As a result, a total of nine AMS measurements were run on a rope (AA 83417 [1], AA 83417 [2]), a batten (AA 83418 [1], AA 83418 [2]), the outer layers of a rafter (AA 83419 [1], AA 83419 [2]), the grass thatch (AA 83422), and carbon associated with the reoccupation of the structure (AA 83420, AA 83421).[22] The results of the radiocarbon assays are presented in Figure 3.62.

Discussion of Radiocarbon Dates

The Inca Empire is well-known for its elaborately carved rocks, many of which were worshiped as shrines. One impressive example of such a rock shrine is Yurak

Rumi in the Vilcabamba region. A series of radiocarbon tests were run on carbon collected at the shrine during excavations in 2008 to help determine: (1) when the shrine was first established; (2) when roof elements were refurbished; (3) when it was destroyed; and (4) when it was reoccupied. Not surprisingly, the two carbon samples (AA 83420 and AA 83421) from the reoccupation level provided the latest dates. However, they were only slightly later than the majority of the ceiling and roofing materials, which burned when the shrine was initially destroyed. Although we may never

know with certainty, it is possible that parts of the shrine were immediately reconsecrated by local inhabitants following the actions of Ortiz and García and that those more limited structures were burned again approximately two years later, in 1572, as Spanish forces swept through the region in their successful campaign to capture Túpac Amaru and to end the Inca resistance centered in the Vilcabamba region.

The burnt ceiling and roofing materials of the shrine also provided intriguing results. The sampled thatch (AA 83422), batten (AA 83418 [1], AA 83418 [2]), and rafter (AA 83419 [1], AA 83419 [2]) all yielded similar calibrated dates, which clustered in the late-1400s to mid-1500s. These age estimations make sense if the shrine was established, as suggested by the dates from the crushed-granite floors, during the early 1400s. However, the rope that was used to tie the thatch together provided surprisingly early dates. Our samples (AA 83416 [1], AA 83416 [2]

Figure 3.60. Reconstruction of Building 6 at Yurak Rumi (drawing by Vincent Lee).

Figure 3.61. Reconstruction of two buildings at Yurak Rumi (drawing by Vincent Lee).

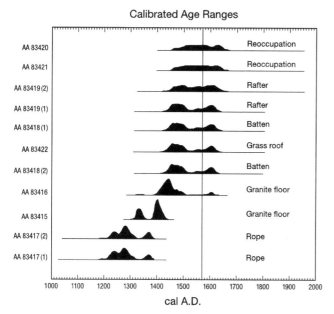

Figure 3.62. Calibrated dates from Yurak Rumi.

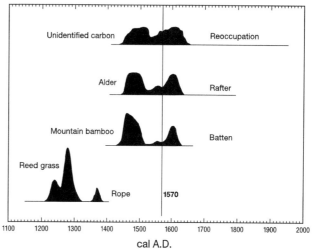

Figure 3.63. The pooling for dates from Yurak Rumi.

yielded calibrated probability dates in the late 1200s, suggesting that the rope was more than 200 years older than the rest of the roof. Indeed, the results suggest that the rope may have even predated the Inca occupation of the Vilcabamba region. Contamination agents could have been introduced as a result of fiber preparation before the weaving of the rope, but the Inca are not known to have used such agents.[23] While it is possible that the Inca used older materials in the construction of the shrine, the dates of the rope seem excessively early, and we currently cannot fully explain the results.

The precision of radiocarbon assays can be increased by using pooled means of different but closely related samples. In this study, the two samples from the reoccupation can be pooled together,[24] as can the samples taken from the batten,[25] the rafter,[26] and the rope.[27] The results of the pooling, presented in Figure 3.63, help illustrate how close the reoccupation dates are to the roof dates and how much earlier the rope dates are.

Two separate test excavations found the remains of crushed-white-granite floors in the Yurak Rumi shrine complex. The pulverized white granite would have been a by-product of the extensive rock carving that occurred when the shrine was first established. The incorporation of the crushed white granite into the floors of the complex would have been architecturally stunning and would have reinforced the ritual nature of the area surrounding the central sacred stone. In other words, the "wastage" from the actual carving of the Yurak Rumi as a paving material for the plaza space is consistent with Inca aesthetics.[28] The pulverized debitage from a major regional shrine would not have been

categorized as raw spoilage but something more akin to a religious relic. Its use as a floor material would have helped bind the site together as a single, sacred complex.

Carbon samples were collected from two of the granite floors.[29] Although the radiocarbon ages of these two samples are separated by some 100 years (601 ± 34 B.P., 496 ± 51 B.P.), their calibrated 1 sigmas do share considerable overlap in the earliest decades of the cal A.D. 1400s. Because these dates are consistent with suggestions that the region was incorporated into the Inca Empire relatively early (Cobo 1979 [1653]), we currently believe that they date the establishment of Yurak Rumi as a shrine and document when the Inca first expanded into the Vilcabamba region. However, as the original floors of the shrine were later buried, and additional floors were established above them, it is also clear that modifications continued at the shrine after its initial dedication.[30]

Endnotes

1   Parts of this chapter and several of the illustrations have appeared in Bauer et al. (2012). We thank the editors of *Andean Past* for their permission to reproduce the information.

2   Marcos García was expelled from the Vilcabamba region soon after the burning of the shrine. Diego Ortiz was killed in Vitcos by Inca loyalists in 1571, after being mistakenly linked to the death of Titu Cusi Yupanqui. His activities in Vilcabamba are documented, since the Augustinians collected information on his death in 1582, 1595, and 1599–1600 (Aparicio López 1989; Bauer et al. 2014; Hemming 1970:476; Levillier

1935:344). There is overlap in the information presented by Murúa (1987 [1611–1616]) and Calancha (1981 [1638]) on the death of Ortiz, since both of these authors had access to the earlier investigations while writing their own accounts.

3 Titu Cusi Yupanqui was baptized in Cusco as a youth and again in the Vilcabamba region as an adult in 1568 as part of the Acobamba treaty. However, his relationship with Christianity remained ambiguous.

4 At the time that the shrine was burned, Juana Guerrero was married to Martín de Pando, the longtime translator and scribe of Titu Cusi Yupanqui. Her testimony was recorded as part of the Augustinians' 1595 attempt to gain sainthood for Diego Ortiz (Bauer et al. 2014). Her testimony was later repeated and slightly altered by other writers (see Calancha 1981:1800–1801 [1638:Book 4, Chapter 2]; Murúa 1987:270 [1611–1616:Book 1, Chapter 75]).

5 "[J]unto a Vitcos, en un puesto que se dice Chuquipalta, donde estaba una piedra blanca encima de un manantial de agua, de la cual les significaron les redundaba muchos daños de asombros y muertes, porque estaba allí el diablo y porque pasando por allí no le mochaban y ofrecían, como lo solían hacer antiguamente; y les pidieron a los dichos padres fuesen allá y la conjurasen y los librasen de aquel peligro; y así los dichos religiosos fueron allá con cantidad de indios y muchachos cargados de leña y la conjuraron y quemaron; y que, desde que hicieron esto, nunca más sintieron daño ninguno los dichos indios" (Aparicio López 1989:164–165; Bauer et al. 2014:81–82).

6 The exact date of Titu Cusi Yupanqui's death is not known, but it most likely occurred in 1571.

7 These gable stones are shown on Bingham's map of the site (1922:248) and remained intact until sometime in the 1990s (see Lee 2000:472). Since that time, one has fallen. It lies within the passageway.

8 This informal ditch currently bifurcates in the open area at the base of the rock. Both branches drain across the Inca building facing the rock.

9 At that time, Bingham did not have direct access to Juana Guerrero's 1595 testimony, which was first published in 1916 by Romero and Urteaga. Instead he was following Calancha's (1981 [1638:Book 4, Chapter 2]) account of the scared rock. However, Calancha had copied his information from Guerrero's statement.

10 T-shaped joints were also used in Tiwanaku times (Lechtman 1996).

11 Excavations did not proceed beyond the green-clay floor.

12 Similar thin levels of red clay were also noted within the profiles of two excavation units on the terrace above the shrine complex.

13 Excavations did not proceed beyond the green-clay floor.

14 Yurak Rumi continues to be viewed as a sacred location by the families living near it. Our excavations at the site proceeded with the permission of local authorities and were accompanied by appropriate dedication ceremonies. For a discussion of similar activities, see Bauer and Stanish (2001:75–78).

15 The thatch of the structure fell in such large amounts and was so quickly covered by other collapsing materials that patches of unburnt ichu grass were identified.

16 About 87 percent of all sherds were from unidentified vessels (n = 824).

17 All diagnostic and nondiagnostic pottery sherds were examined by excavated context, with data on style and technology entered into a spreadsheet for inter- and intraloci comparisons. Within each excavated context, sherds were divided into the smallest possible groups. We grouped fragments with similar characteristics that might belong to the same vessel together (with numbers of fragments recorded) to assess the minimum number of vessels represented. Vessel forms are based on Craig Morris's Huánuco Pampa rim profile system (Morris et al. 2011), with new forms identified from Vilcabamba added into the inventory. We used five major form categories—large storage vessels (distinguished by a greater ratio of vessel height to diameter than for pots), pots, bowls/plates, cups, and lids—and there are subdivisions within each category.

18 However, an analysis of paste geochemistry by instrumental neutron activation on majolica samples from Quito, Cusco, and Panama Vieja has shown that each center had distinct paste characteristics (Olin et al. 1978; also see Jamieson 2003:252).

19 Cobo (1979:135–137 [1653:Book 12, Chapter 12]) suggests that Pachacuti Inca Yupanqui passed through the Vitcos region and arrived at the plane of Pampaconas. It was in Pampaconas that the Inca negotiated with local lords, who agreed to submit to the empire. Also see Cabello de Balboa (1951 [1586]).

20 February 17, 1570, in the Gregorian calendar.

21 The reoccupation of Yurak Rumi may have been limited to only certain areas of the shrine complex. Sometime after this brief reoccupation, many of the buildings of the shrine complex were systematically destroyed, with their major architectural features, such as the stone roof pegs, pulled from the walls.

22 All samples were processed in the National Science Foundation–University of Arizona Accelerator Mass

Spectrometry Laboratory. Calibrated dates were generated by Calib 5.1 beta, courtesy of the University of Washington (Stuiver and Reimer 1993) and were adjusted using southern hemisphere data (ShCal04 calibration curve) (McCormac et al. 2004). See Bauer (2012:203) for additional details on each of these samples.

23 In other cases, conservation agents might make a rope test older than it really is, but in this case, the sample was taken in the field and sent directly to the laboratory for analysis.

24 Samples AA 83420, AA 83421.

25 Samples AA 83418 (1), AA 83418 (2).

26 Samples AA 83419 (1), AA 83419 (2).

27 Samples AA 83417 (1), AA 83417 (2).

28 For example, Polo de Ondegardo (1965:118–119 [1571]) reports that the Inca had covered the central plaza of Cusco with sand, perhaps transported from the coast.

29 Samples AA 83415, AA 83416.

30 Continuous work at the site is also evident in unfinished carved rocks.

Chapter 4

An Introduction to the Site of Espíritu Pampa

Brian S. Bauer

ESPÍRITU PAMPA IS A VAST SITE, the full extent of which is still unknown. It is located at an altitude of 1,500 m, near the confluence of two streams. Built in a hot and humid climate, the site is now covered with towering trees and thick undergrowth. The central core of the ruins includes some 15 ha of buildings, platforms, canals, and terraces. Many other clusters of buildings, some monumental and others residential, are located across the valley and in nearby tributaries (Figure 4.1). The ridgetops that surround the area also contain concentrations of ruins, ranging from small groups of circular buildings to multitiered platforms. Although the dense vegetation prevents an accurate count, it is clear that there are many, perhaps hundreds, of structures within the forest. Because of their remote location and the thick forest cover, the ruins have been spared intensive looting, and as a whole the former Inca settlement remains in a remarkable state of preservation (Figure 4.2).

The Rectangular Buildings

Two structure types dominate the ruins of Espíritu Pampa: rectangular and circular.[1] Most of the rectangular buildings are constructed of moderately sized stones. These include waterworn examples taken from nearby streams and more rectangular, fractured blocks of dark, bluish-gray schist or white granite taken from nearby outcrops. The mortar used in the walls is composed of clay and gravel. No additional materials have been added to strengthen the mortar, although small stones are frequently set in the walls to help level the tiers. The walls of the rectangular buildings are slightly inclined, a hallmark of Inca construction. The doors, niches, and corners of the rectangular buildings are frequently made of slightly worked stone. A few buildings, including one unfinished building in the New Sector and a set of four buildings in the so-called Palace Compound, are constructed with worked, well-fitting granite blocks.

The rectangular buildings across the site vary greatly in size but follow the proportional canons of Inca architecture (Gasparini and Margolies 1980; Protzen 1993). The smaller rectangular buildings contain a single narrow, slightly trapezoidal doorway, while the larger structures have two or three doorways. Despite the ready availability of large trees, slabs of stone—most commonly schist—are used as lintels. Some of the rectangular buildings at the site have slightly off-center doors, and excavations have revealed that these buildings tend to have interior walls that divide buildings into two parts. A limited number of buildings at the site also have corner doors. These features (off-center doors, interior walls, and corner doorways) are un-

Figure 4.1. The monumental core of Espíritu Pampa is located beneath the trees between the two open fields in this photograph. However, the site is much larger, and scattered foundations can be found across the valley (photograph by Brian S. Bauer and Miriam Aráoz Silva).

usual for Inca architecture and may mark a later construction phase at the site.

The combination of weak mortar, heavy rains, and aggressive vegetation has caused many of the buildings to collapse. The exterior walls of many of the rectangular structures stand less than 1 m high. In a few well-preserved cases, the walls reach over 2 m high, and holes for second-floor crossbeams can be seen. Some of the larger structures had stone gables. In a few cases of well-preserved corners, interior corner crossbars were noted near the top of walls. These are relatively common features in Inca architecture and were used to help secure roof lattices. While most of the rectangular buildings were made of stone and mortar, excavations in the New Sector revealed that the upper portions of at least one building at the site were made of adobes.

Excavations have also revealed that most of the rectangular buildings were once covered with a dark red (Munsell 7.5 YR 4/6 strong brown) clay plaster. Many of the rectangular buildings at Espíritu Pampa

may also have had trapezoidal to square interior niches. However, only a few of the buildings are preserved well enough to reveal the former locations of interior niches. The few surviving niches show a range of dimensions.[2]

The Circular Buildings

While the rectangular buildings that dominate the central core of Espíritu Pampa have attracted the attention of archaeologists, various circular buildings are scattered across the site. The circular buildings are less common within the monumental areas of Espíritu Pampa but increase in number with distance from the center. In fact, the circular buildings are so widely spread across the forested valley that it is difficult to estimate how many there are.

The circular buildings vary in size, ranging from 3 to 9 m in diameter. Their locations are marked by low foundation walls that generally stand less than 50 cm high. These foundations are thinner and less substantial than those of the rectangular buildings, having been built with smaller stones. All of the circular buildings have single doorways marked by upright standing slabs. Since there is no wall fall within the circular buildings, we assume that their walls were made of wooden poles lashed together with bark cord. They also most likely had conical roofs.

Bingham noted the presence of circular buildings at Espíritu Pampa even before he reached the center of the site:

> In one of the clearings we located the ruins of a village which had eighteen or twenty primitive circular dwellings. All that remained were walls from two to three feet in height with a single door opening. . . . These houses were arranged in an irregular group. In the woods not far away there seemed to be the remains of other circular houses of about the same size, with walls from three to four feet in height [Bingham 1914b:185–186].

Bingham (1922:293) suggested that the circular buildings were inhabited by the indigenous people of the region at the time of the Inca occupation or by a native group that the Incas brought into the region.

The next visitor to describe the site of Espíritu Pampa, Savoy was also intrigued with the number of circular buildings he found while clearing the ruins.[3] In the end, Savoy suggested that these structures may have been the remains of Machiguenga speakers, such as those who were living at the site when Bingham first visited.[4] It is also possible, however, that some of the circular structures predate the Inca occupation of Espíritu Pampa, as it is known that the Late Intermediate period (A.D. 1000–1400) groups of the region built similar circular dwellings. Furthermore, with the recent discovery of Wari remains in the valley (Fonseca Santa Cruz 2011; Fonseca Santa Cruz and Bauer 2013), it is also possible that some of the buildings date to Middle Horizon times. Clearly, additional research is needed to determine what period or periods the circular buildings date to and what activities occurred within them.[5]

The Monumental Core of Espíritu Pampa

Since 2003 the Ministerio de Cultura has supported several large excavation programs in and around the site of Espíritu Pampa. Many of these projects have been centered on the buildings that form the monumental core of the Inca town.[6] Varying amounts of information are available on these different projects, and some of the reports have already been lost or were never completed. Nevertheless, it is important to review the previous projects because they provide a history of research at the site and an introduction to the organization of the monumental core of Espíritu Pampa (Figure 4.3).

The Palace Compound

At the northeastern end of the central plaza is a group of four structures, separated from the rest of the site by a large, nearly rectangular enclosure wall with a single entrance. The four buildings are laid out in pairs with small patio areas between them. Each pair contains its own entrance. The buildings are constructed of unusually well-worked stone blocks. Scattered fragments of ceramic roof tiles can still be seen on the ground near these buildings. Although there is currently no direct evidence that he occupied the structures, the compound is currently referred to as the Palace of Sayri Túpac, named for the eldest son of Manco Inca, who ruled the Vilcabamba region from about 1544 to 1557. The four buildings are among the best-constructed structures at the site, and there is no doubt that they once served an elite function. While it is certainly possible that the compound was the official residence of a ruling Inca in Espíritu Pampa, it is also possible that the structure served other functions.

The Palace Compound was first described by Savoy (1970:102–103), and it was excavated in 2003 by José Pilares Daza.[7] Pilares Daza dug in all four of the buildings and their two patios. He also excavated two large units within the compound. Combined, the excavations within the Palace Compound yielded a rather small and unremarkable collection of 90 identifiable rim fragments, including large storage vessels (49 percent), cooking vessels (18 percent), plates (16 percent), drinking vessels (8 percent), jugs (7 percent), and lids (3 percent), along with an unknown number of roof tiles. Other than the roof tiles, no European-style items are reported.

The Kallanka

Many Inca centers contain one or more long buildings with multiple doors along one side of their central plaza (Barraza Lescano 2010; Gasparini and Margolies 1980). These structures are now referred to as *kallankas*. According to Garcilaso de la Vega, *kallankas* were public buildings where ceremonies were held during the

Figure 4.2. The monumental center of Espíritu Pampa is defined by a large plaza flanked by several compounds of impressive buildings. Foundations of other buildings continue in all directions (map by Axel Aráoz Silva and Gabriel E. Cantarutti).

rainy season. The northwestern side of the central plaza at Espíritu Pampa is defined by a *kallanka*. Measuring some 80 m long and 7.5 m wide, this is one of the largest buildings of the Inca Empire (Lee 1998). The Espíritu Pampa *kallanka* contains 12 doorways on each of its long sides, totaling 24. The double-sided dooring is a rather unusual feature for *kallankas*. There are two additional, although smaller, doorways on its southern corners, and perhaps two others once stood on its now poorly preserved northern corners. The building was first noted in 1911 by Bingham, who describes it

as "a long rectangular building . . . with twelve doors in front and twelve behind, the doors being about 3.5 feet in width. The building was in a ruinous condition, none of the roof remaining, much of the walls being almost totally destroyed, and none of the stone lintels of the doorways being in place. One section of the wall appeared to have been plastered with mud" (Bingham 1914a:186).[8]

In 2003 José Pilares Daza conducted a series of four excavations within the *kallanka*. These units yielded a moderate number of ceramics sherds (n = 458), which

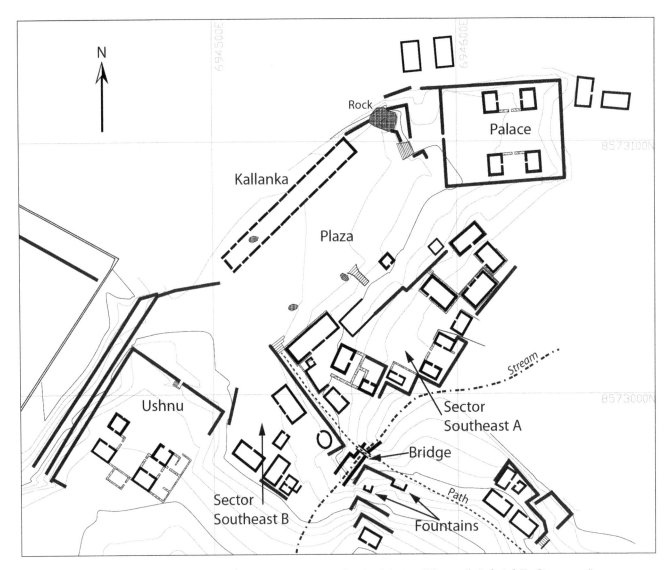

Figure 4.3. The monumental core of Espíritu Pampa (map by Axel Aráoz Silva and Gabriel E. Cantarutti).

included fragments from large storage vessels, cooking vessels, plates, jars, drinking vessels, and lids. There was also clear evidence that the building had been burned. One additional excavation unit was placed in the Kallanka by Bauer and Aráoz Silva in 2010, and is described in this volume. The excavation revealed that the Kallanka had been completely cleared sometime after 2003 and now contains few materials dating to the time of the Incas.

The Ushnu

At the southern end of the plaza is a large, multitiered platform currently called the Ushnu (Figure 4.4). (An *ushnu* is a terraced, platform structure.) This name is largely a misnomer, as the complex is strikingly dissimilar to other central-plaza terraced platforms found elsewhere in the empire. An impressive L-shaped stairway

leads from the plaza to the top of the Ushnu. This platform is about the size of the Palace Compound, which is located at the opposite end of the plaza, and like the Palace Compound, the Ushnu originally contained two pairs of symmetrically placed buildings on its summit. Although the quality of these buildings is slightly inferior to that of the buildings in the Palace Compound, their corners and doorways are made of carved stone blocks. During a second construction phase, a series of adjacent walls, rooms, and patios was added to the original four buildings on the Ushnu, making a more complex architectural arrangement. During this second construction phase, a doorway of one of the original buildings was sealed and a small, two-stepped interior platform was built against the sealed door.

The Ushnu was first described by Savoy (1970:103) and was excavated by Juan Samaniego in 2005. His excavations revealed various fallen lintels within the four original buildings, indicating that these structures previously had interior niches. The walls of the original four structures were once covered with red plaster, and their floors were made with yellow clay mixed with gravel. Each of the buildings on the Ushnu contained a small number of decorated and undecorated ceramic vessels. Among the reported vessels were aryballoi, a range of cooking vessels, plates, and perhaps drinking vessels (*keros*). A small number of metal objects, mostly copper pins (*tupus*), were also recovered. The original four buildings, as well as the subsequent structures built on the Ushnu, all showed evidence of having been burned. No European-style objects are reported as being recovered, with the exception of one iron nail.

The Southeastern Sectors

The southeastern side of the plaza contains a sprawling set of buildings, terraces, and patios. Most of the build-

ings in the southeastern sector were excavated by the Ministerio de Cultura in 2004, 2005, and 2007. Unfortunately, there are no reports on file describing these excavations. One additional building in this area of the site was excavated in 2008 under the direction of Javier Fonseca Santa Cruz. The results of his excavations are described in this report. (See Chapter 6.)

For this discussion, the southeastern ruins will be divided into two sectors, A and B, by the road that leads to the central plaza. The sector nearest the Ushnu, A, contains five rectangular buildings that vary in size and a single circular building.[9] The largest (13 x 6.4 m) of the rectangular buildings contains two doorways. It was excavated by José Pilares Daza in 2003. The large amount of carbon and crushed ceramic vessels found on the floor of the building indicates that it was burned while still occupied. Excavations revealed the remains of more than 60 unfired clay bases used to support large storage vessels (*rakis* and *urpus*). A substantial number

Figure 4.4. The largest terraces of the site are found on the northwestern side of the Ushnu (photograph by Brian S. Bauer and Miriam Aráoz Silva).

of ceramic fragments (n = 13,628) were also recovered within the building; most of them came from large storage vessels. Other identified vessel forms included plates, drinking vessels (*keros*), jugs, and lids. A copper pin (*tupu*) and copper knife (*tumi*) were also recovered. The two most unusual objects found in the building included a small pot with two puma-paw handles (Figure 4.5) and a drinking vessel with a human face (Figure 4.6). The latter most likely dates to colonial times and may depict a person of African descent. With its numerous storage vessels, there is little doubt that this building was used for the large-scale production of *chicha*, which was most likely consumed during celebrations on the nearby plaza. This building has been reconstructed (Figure 4.7).

Figure 4.5. A bowl with two puma-paw handles recovered by José Pilares Daza in 2003. The vessel is currently housed in the Museo de Garcilaso de la Vega in Cusco (photograph by Brian S. Bauer).

The other side of the road contains about 14 buildings, several of which were built on wide foundation bases. This area of ruins was first recorded by Savoy, in his breathless narrative style, during his first days at the site:

> Across from this group we fall into a depression and discover we have accidentally stumbled into a sunken group of Inca buildings under a mass of twisting vines and growth. It is below street level, completely walled. An hour of exploring the colossal group reveals inner streets, stairways and eighteen independent rooms. The group measures a stupendous 297 feet long! A canal with flowing water runs on one side. Tons of dead vegetation top the old ruins. One Inca house measuring 40 feet long by 18 feet wide is graced with thirteen niches and a broken doorway [Savoy 1970:101–102].

In this sector are four rather large, well-made rectangular structures grouped around a courtyard. There is also a series of smaller buildings and platforms clustered around an irregularly shaped courtyard. Several of these smaller buildings were built during a second construction phase at the site. The largest structure of this sector is most likely the building mentioned by Sa-

Figure 4.6. A drinking vessel with a human face found by José Pilares Daza in 2003. The vessel is currently housed in the Museo de Garcilaso de la Vega in Cusco (photograph by Brian S. Bauer).

Figure 4.7. The modern entrance to Espíritu Pampa. The large rectangular building was excavated by José Pilares Daza in 2003. When the city fell to the Spaniards, it was being used to produce *chicha* (photograph by Brian S. Bauer and Miriam Aráoz Silva).

Figure 4.8. The largest building on the east side of the plaza. This building may have once held as many as 13 interior niches. Note that this building, like many others in the sector, is built on a wide foundation (photograph by Brian S. Bauer and Miriam Aráoz Silva).

voy as containing 13 niches (Figure 4.8). However, the niches are no longer visible.

The sector also contains a series of smaller, poorly built walls that abut several of the buildings. These architectural modifications represent a second construction phase of the city. Similar modifications have been found on the structures on the Ushnu and in the Palace Compound.

The Central Rock of Espíritu Pampa

One of the many interesting features of the site of Espíritu Pampa is a large, isolated, unworked boulder near the north end of the plaza. Vestiges of possible walls suggest that a slightly raised platform may have been built around this impressive glacier-age remnant. Bingham may not have seen the rock during his brief time at

the site, but it was noted by Savoy (1970:102–103), who writes, "We found a huge boulder weighing hundreds of tons. It is topped by a great matapalo tree whose bole is 12 feet in diameter and covered with layers of moss and tropical vegetation. The buttress roots of the great rock enclose the boulder in a tenacious grip like arms of an octopus." The massive matapalo tree that once stood on top of this rock has long since been cut. The boulder now stands alone at the far end of the plaza.

Visitors to Espíritu Pampa have long assumed that this isolated boulder was a *huaca* (shrine) during Inca times, and the following passage by Murúa, describing the brief 1570 stay of Fathers Marcos and Ortiz in the region, is often referenced to support this classification: "When they arrived at the town, [Titu Cusi Yupanqui] did not want [the clerics] to lodge within it, so that they would not see the *huacas* [shrines] and *mochaderos* [holy places] he had there, nor reprimand him for the rites

Figure 4.9. A large, isolated, unworked boulder at the north end of the plaza may have been worshipped as a shrine by the Inca (photograph by Brian S. Bauer and Miriam Aráoz Silva).

and ceremonies that he held [there]" (Murúa 1987:270; translation by authors).[10] While certainly impressive, the fact that this stone has not been carved makes it difficult to assess with full certainty that it held special importance for the inhabitants of the town (Figure 4.9).

The Stone Bridge

A small stream runs through the site of Espíritu Pampa, and there is a well-preserved stone bridge near the center of the ruins. The bridge abutments are made of rough stones, and the span is composed of long schist slabs. Bingham (1922:296) noted this bridge during his visit and had his picture taken on it (Figures 4.10 and 4.11).

There are two fountains on the hillslope above the bridge (Figure 4.12). The lower of the two fountains has three spouts, while the upper fountain has one.

Bingham (1914a:186) saw the three-spouted fountain during his brief stay at the ruins. The bridge and its nearby fountains were also among the first features of the site noted by Savoy when he visited decades later. He writes, "Looking down through the darkened shadows we discover that our expert trail guide [Benjamin Cobos] had guided us to an Inca stone bridge. Not far away he shows us a fountain with three spouts" (Savoy 1970:98, 101). The next day, while clearing the forest, Savoy and his crew came upon the second fountain.

Summary

The city of Vilcabamba (the site of Espíritu Pampa) continued to be occupied for some 40 years after the Spanish first entered the Andes. Thus it offers us a unique opportunity to examine issues of cultural contact, indigenous resistance, and European colonization.

Figure 4.10. Bingham stands on top of the central bridge leading into Espíritu Pampa. The other man may be Juan Cancio Saavedra. (National Geographic Image Collection: negative 785908, photograph by Harry Ward Foote).

Figure 4.11. The stone bridge of Espíritu Pampa (photograph by Brian S. Bauer and Miriam Aráoz Silva).

Starting in 2008, we began conducting research in the Inca city of Vilcabamba to better understand its important history. More specially, Javier Fonseca Santa Cruz conducted excavations in various sectors in 2008 and 2009. His excavations were supported by the former Institutio National de Cultura. Brian S. Bauer and Miriam Aráoz Silva supervised excavations within the Inca ruins in 2010. We are please to be able to present the results of our work at the site in the following three chapters.

Endnotes

1   Wall thickness varies, but it averages around 70 to 80 cm for the rectangular structures.

2   It is worth noting that one building in the Tendi Pampa compound and another building in the New Sector have very narrow and tall trapezoidal niches, a style that is not common at other Inca sites.

3   Also see Howell and Morrison (1967:30, 35)

4   For a discussion of the Machiguenga of the lower Urubamba region at the time of the Bingham expedition, see Bowman (1916:36–45).

5   In 2011 Bauer and Aráoz Silva received permission to excavate several circular buildings. However, they canceled their project due to political unrest in the region.

6   For three months during 2005 and 2006, researchers from the University of Yamagata (Japan) directed a mapping project at Espíritu Pampa, which included the removal of many large trees from the central core of the site (Sakai 2009:144).

7   Information on Pilares's excavations comes from his 2003 report, which is on file in the Ministerio de Cultura in Cusco.

8   Savoy (1970) and Santander Caselli (in Pardo 1972:117) also describe the Kallanka.

9   The circular building is built with thick walls and worked stones. It is architecturally different from the large number of less-substantial circular structures scattered across the valley.

10 Murúa (1987:270) writes, "Llegados al pueblo, no quiso se aposentasen dentro del, porque no vieran las huacas y mochaderos que allí tenia, y los ritos y ceremonias que hacía, porque no se lo reprendiesen.

Figure 4.12. The three-spouted fountain at Espíritu Pampa (photograph by Brian S. Bauer and Miriam Aráoz Silva).

Chapter 5

Excavations at Tendi Pampa (Espíritu Pampa) in 2008 and 2009

Javier Fonseca Santa Cruz and Brian S. Bauer

THIS CHAPTER DESCRIBES excavations conducted by Javier Fonseca Santa Cruz in the architectural compound called Tendi Pampa at the site of Espíritu Pampa during 2008 and 2009.[1] The excavations were part of a long-term research project designed and supported by the former Institutio National de Cultura Region Cusco (sub direccion de investigación y catastro arqueologico). Much of the following is based on information provided in two final annual reports titled *Informe: Proyecto de investigación arqueológica de Espíritu Pampa—Vilcabamba* (2008) and *Informe final: Proyecto de investigación arqueológica en el complejo arqueológico de Espíritu Pampa—Segunda Temporada* (2009), written and submitted to the institute by Fonseca Santa Cruz. These reports are on file in the Ministerio de Cultura Dirección Desconcentrada de Cultura Cusco.

Early Descriptions of Tendi Pampa

Bingham arrived in Espíritu Pampa in late August of 1911. One of the first places he visited within the site was a set of ruins that the Campas called Tendi Pampa. Bingham writes:

> About 200 yards away [from the central plaza] was the most important group of the Espíritu Pampa

ruins. These were all, with one exception, rectangular. All except one or two had gable ends.[2] One of the buildings stood apart and was rounded at one end, having a single door at the other end...

> Most of these buildings resemble those at Choqquequirau in being built of rough blocks of stone, not squared or otherwise fashioned, expect occasionally on the corners and in the doorways. The stones were laid in mud. The lintels of the doors were not monolithic, but were made of three or long narrow stone blocks [Bingham 1914b:188, 190].

Bingham provided additional details on this group of buildings in later publications. Since these are among the earliest descriptions of Tendi Pampa, they are worth quoting in full:

> Two hundred yards beyond . . . hidden behind a curtain of hanging vines and thickets so dense we could not see more than a few feet in any direction, the savages showed us the ruins of a group of stone houses whose walls were still standing in fine condition.

> One of the buildings was rounded at one end. Another standing by itself at the south end of a little pampa, had neither doors nor windows. It was

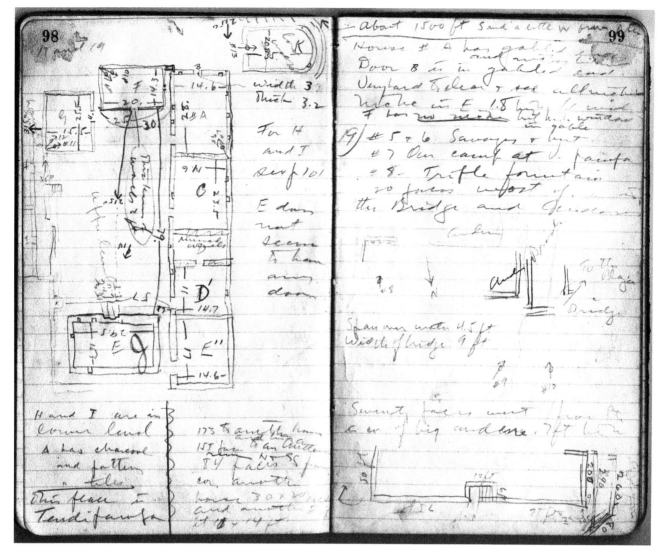

Figure 5.1. Bingham's field notes for 1911, showing his measures and notes on Tendi Pampa (Yale Peruvian Expedition Papers, Manuscript 664. Manuscripts and Archives, Yale University Library).

rectangular. Its four or five niches were arranged with unique irregularity. Furthermore, they were two feet deep, an unusual dimension. Probably this was a storehouse. On the east side of the pampa was a structure, 120 feet long by 21 feet wide, divided into five rooms of unequal size. The walls were of rough stones laid in adobe. Like some of the Inca buildings at Ollantaytambo, the lintels of the doors were made of three or four narrow uncut ashlars. Some of the rooms had niches. On the north side of the pampa was another rectangular building. On the west side was the edge of a stone-faced terrace. Below it was a partially enclosed fountain or bathhouse, with a stone spout and a stone-lined basin. The shapes of the houses, their general arrangement, the niches, stone roof-pegs and lintels, all point to Inca builders. In the buildings we picked up several fragments of Inca pottery. . . .

The next day the savages and our carriers con-

tinued to clear away as much as possible of the tangled growth near the best ruins. In this process, to the intense surprise not only of ourselves, but also of the savages, they discovered, just below the "bathhouse" where we had stood the day before, the well-preserved ruins of two buildings of superior construction, well fitted with stone-pegs and numerous niches, very symmetrically arranged. These houses stood by themselves on a little artificial terrace. Fragments of characteristic Inca pottery were found on the floor, including pieces of a large aryballus [Bingham 1922:293–295, 296].

Bingham also provides a list of measurements for each of the buildings at Tendi Pampa, a remarkably accurate map, and several photographs of individual buildings (Figures 5.1 and 5.2). Furthermore, he notes that the buildings contained the remains of ceramic

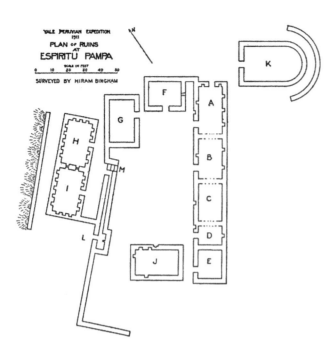

Figure 5.2. Bingham's (1914b:188) published map of the ruins of Tendi Pampa.

vessels and charcoal: "Nearly all of the houses have potsherds and some have charcoal remains. . . . In and around the houses were remains of water-jugs, numerous potsherds, and pieces of several fine Inca aryballos" (Bingham 1914b:192, 195). Perhaps most intriguingly, Bingham recorded that there were fragments of Spanish-style roof tiles in several of the buildings and in the patio (Bingham 1914b:196–197).

Bingham wrote several articles and book chapters that centered on his finds at Espíritu Pampa. However, he never returned to the site. Over the next five decades, there was almost no mention of the site in scholarly or popular literature. Researchers, both Peruvian nationals and foreigners alike, focused on other ruins and other research questions. The public focused on the spectacular remains of Machu Picchu, as it began to emerge as an iconic symbol for the Inca, Cusco, and Peru in general. However, in July of 1964, the adventurist Gene Savoy, drawn by the idea that Espíritu Pampa represented the "lost" Inca city of Vilcabamba, organized an expedition to the site.

At the time of Savoy's visit, Julio Cobos owned most of the pampa. He and his family were living near the ruins, converting the area from sugar to coffee production. On the first day of Savoy's stay, Benjamin Cobos, a son of Julio, took him to the ruins that had been mapped by Bingham more than 50 years before. Like Bingham, Savoy noted that fragments of Inca pottery

and Spanish-style roof tiles were scattered across the surface of the site. Savoy wrote the following description of the Tendi Pampa compound after he had seen the lower two buildings and moved on to the central group:

> Atop the platform are a series of galleries so overgrown with vegetation I cannot estimate their size or importance. When I had the buildings cleared, a task that took three precious days out of our schedule, the two-story platform group was found to consist of twelve rooms graced with niches and doorways, including a semicircular room, inner and outer courtyards, a fountain, hallway and stairways, the whole surrounded by high walls decorated with roof pegs [Savoy 1970:96].

Working with Savoy's field notes, Emilio Harth-Terré drafted a map of the compound in 1964. However, it is less accurate than Bingham's original map (Figure 5.3).

Many other individuals visited the compound in the years that followed. Most importantly, Vincent Lee (2000:414–415, 502–503) spent many weeks at the site during the 1990s and produced a map of the compound. The Tendi Pampa compound was also cleared and mapped in 2005–2006 as part of a much larger mapping project (Sakai 2009). While these two mapping projects described various architectural details about the compound, they did not include excavations.

An Overview of the Tendi Pampa Compound

The Tendi Pampa compound is located on a low ridge, about 10 m higher than and 300 m to the southwest of the central plaza of Espíritu Pampa. One modern trail arrives at the northeastern edge of the Tendi Pampa compound and another trail arrives at its northwestern corner, but it is not clear if these follow original Inca trails. The compound is relatively isolated, with only a few terraces and structures scattered across the surrounding slopes.

The site of Tendi Pampa contains 11 rooms built on two rectangular platforms. The higher and larger platform holds a suite of eight rooms organized around a central patio (or *cancha*). The southeastern edge of the patio is defined by a single long building with five adjacent rooms. This type of building, with numerous internal divisions, is rare in Inca architecture. Each of the rooms has a unique internal layout, although the exact number and size of the internal niches and windows are difficult to determine. The southwestern side of the patio contains a single rectangular building. This building is the only structure in the compound and one of the few buildings in the site of Espíritu Pampa that contains external double niches. This building also contains two corner doors, an architectural feature that is unusual at other Inca sites but that is relatively common at Espíritu Pampa. The northeastern side of the patio contains two buildings, while the northwestern edge is defined by a terrace.[3] The smaller, lower terrace holds two adjoined, nearly identical rectangular structures, which each contain 14 internal niches. There is also an L-shaped stairway and a U-shaped, walk-in basin in the terrace that divides the two platforms. Finally, a U-shaped structure is located to the east of the other buildings (Figure 5.4).

The walls of the buildings are composed of schist, granite, and a limited range of other stones. The corners, doorways, and niches of the buildings show slightly better craftsmanship that the other parts. The stones are held together with a weak clay mortar, and the walls are slightly inclined. Excavations revealed patches of red clay on the interior walls of all the buildings.

Early visitors to the site noted the remains of gables on several of the buildings and described how cylindrical stones protruded from the gables. The cylindrical stones were used as pegs to help hold down thatch roofs. While numerous fallen roof pegs were found during the excavations, none of the gables has survived.

The 2008 and 2009 Excavations

Since 2006, employees of the former Institutio National de Culture Region Cusco, who both guard the site and attempt to hold back the relentless tropical growth, have cleared the Tendi Pampa compound annually. Nevertheless, at the time of the 2008 and 2009 excavations, a number of large trees stood in the compound; some of their roots had become intertwined with the walls of the structures. Several of these trees were removed during the investigation

in an attempt to stabilize the buildings.

During the 2008 and 2009 investigations, the complete interiors of all 11 structures at Tendi Pampa were excavated. The U-shaped fountain and the L-shaped stairway were also cleared of wall fall and eroded ma-

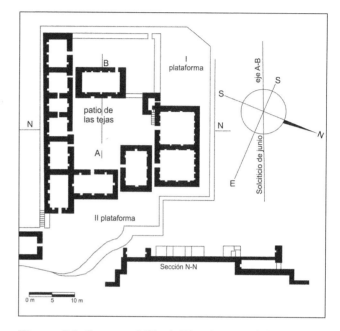

Figure 5.3. Savoy and Harth-Terré's map of the Tendi Pampa compound (Savoy 1964b:4).

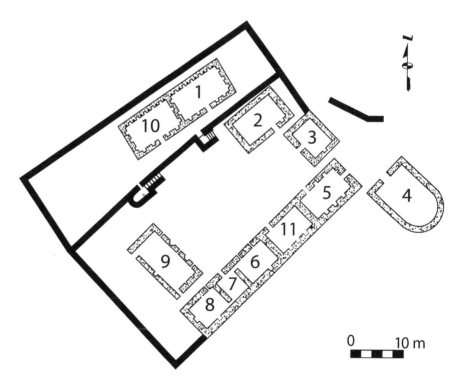

Figure 5.4. The Tendi Pampa compound with building numbers used in this report. Buildings 1 through 9 were excavated in 2009, while Buildings 10 and 11 were excavated in 2008 (map by Brian S. Bauer).

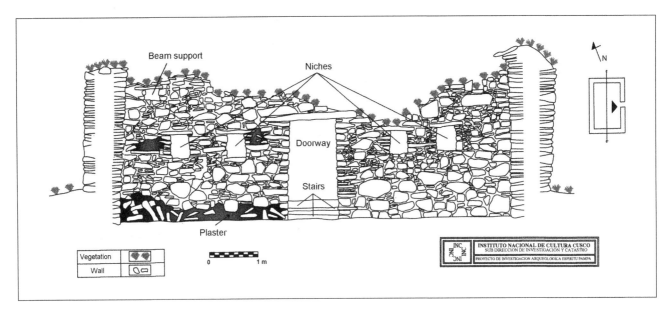

Figure 5.5. Profile of Building 1, interior east wall, showing doorway and niches (Ministerio de Cultura, redrawn by Gabriel E. Cantarutti).

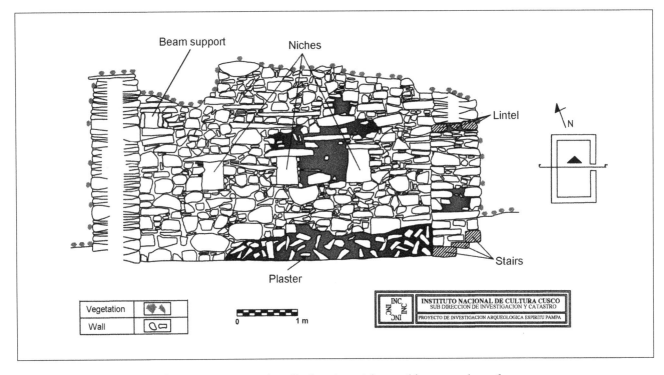

Figure 5.6. Profile of Building 1, interior north wall, showing niches and large patches of plaster (Ministerio de Cultura, redrawn by Gabriel E. Cantarutti).

terials. The excavations were conducted in natural levels. Excavation tools included picks, shovels, trowels, and brushes. The first excavation level was largely composed of dense organic materials. This humus level was the result of several centuries of organic buildup from the subtropical forest. The second excavation level contained a semicompact soil, as well as many roots from surface plants, fallen wall stones, and eroded mortar from the collapsed walls. The third level included the original floors of the structures along with numerous artifacts that were left in the buildings when the site was abandoned. The excavations provided an extraordinary number of ceramic vessels, all of which were classic Inca in style, as well as many other stone, metal, glass, and wooden objects.

At the conclusion of the 2008 and 2009 investigations, many of the reconstructable and intact vessels, the most important metal and glass objects, and various stone artifacts were taken to Cusco and submitted to the former Institutio National de Cultura Region Cusco. All other recovered artifacts were bagged, labeled, and placed in a storage room near the site. This storage room also holds the artifacts from all the other archaeological projects conducted at Espíritu Pampa. In 2012 most of the complete artifacts that had been excavated at Tendi Pampa during 2008 and stored in Cusco were transported to Quillabamba for storage in the newly constructed Museo Amazónico Andino Qhapaq Ñan de Quillabamba. In contrast, most of the complete artifacts excavated in 2009 were not moved to Quillabamba but are currently held in various locations, including the Ministerio de Cultura Dirección Desconcentrada de Cultura Cusco in Cusco, the Garcilaso de la Vega Museum in Cusco, and an official storage space in the town of Quispecancha.

BUILDING 1

Buildings 1 and 11 are nearly identical, abutting buildings located on the lower terrace of Tendi Pampa. These two buildings are among the best-preserved structures at Espíritu Pampa. Each has a single entrance with stone steps, facing the large terrace wall of the site. Each building also has 14 internal niches.[4] Their east walls contain four niches, two on each side of the doorways. The opposite walls contain five niches, and the end walls contain three niches each. The wall that adjoins the two buildings contains two irregularly spaced niches on both of its sides.[5] Several small holes

Figure 5.7. Interior of Building 1, circa 1980 (photograph by David Drew).

that once supported second-story crossbeams have survived (Figures 5.5 and 5.6).

Bingham (1914b) was especially interested in Buildings 1 and 11 and provides several photographs taken within them.[6] His descriptions are important, since some of the structural features, most notably the gabled ends of the buildings, have not survived. Bingham writes:

> The two most important buildings of this group were carefully constructed, and were well provided with niches symmetrically arranged. . . . The gabled ends of the houses were ornamented by roughly cylindrical blocks protruding at the point where the wooden rafters had once been. The two houses were situated on an artificial terrace, but their entrances faced the hillside. . . . In these two rooms we found fragments of better pottery than in other buildings. This may have been due to the fact that [they] appeared to be unknown to the Indians, as they had been covered with very dense vines and heavy jungle [Bingham 1914b:190–193].

Building 1 measures approximately 8 x 5 m, with walls that reached up to 3 m high (Figure 5.7).[7] Excavations within the building were conducted using a grid system of eight units. At the time of the excavation, the interior of the building was covered with thick vegetation, and a large yanay tree was growing near the center of the building. Fallen stones from the two gables were notable at both ends of the building, and a number of roof pegs could be identified on the ground. A few roof tile and aryballos fragments were recovered as the humus was cleared from Building 1. With the removal of the second excavation level, the remains of a crushed cooking vessel were found near the northwestern corner of the building, and several ceramic vessels and tiles were identified within the northern wall fall area (Figure 5.8).[8]

The central area of Building 1, dominated by the roots of a large yanay tree, yielded a small piece of sheet copper,[9] which rested above a fragmented ceramic vessel lid and near the base of a pedestal pot. A large round piece of red-and-white quartz of undetermined use, measuring 9 cm in diameter, and a copper nail were also found. A few roof tile fragments and a shattered cooking vessel were recovered south of the yanay tree among a line of fallen slabs. The southern end of the building also contained a large area of wall fall, much of which came from the central gable. Roof tile fragments and concentrations of ceramics were found near the southeastern corner of the building (Figure 5.9).

DISCUSSION OF BUILDING 1

The excavation of Building 1 yielded around 360 ceramic fragments, a small piece of sheet copper, a copper nail, and several quartz nuclei. No complete ceramic vessels were found. The majority of the ceramic fragments were from large storage vessels (*urpus/rakis*[10] and aryballoi [n = 321; 89 percent]). However, a small number of plate (n = 12; .03 percent), drinking vessel (n = 17; .05 percent), cooking vessel (n = 8; .02 percent), and roof tile fragments (n = 8) were also recovered. Thus the building contained a relatively small number but a wide range of ceramic vessels. The function of the building is not known.

BUILDING 2

Building 2 is a rectangular structure that measures about 7.5 x 4.5 m. This building, along with Building 3, forms the north side of the central patio. The structure contains one slightly off-center doorway, which opens onto the patio. The walls of Building 2 are narrower in width (75 cm) than

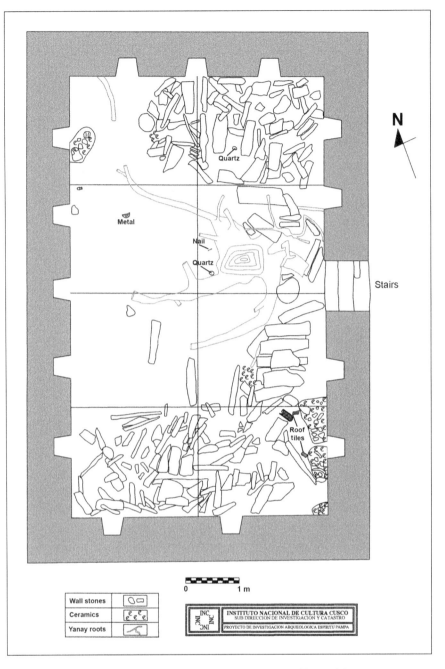

Figure 5.8. Final plan view of Building 1. Note the fallen gables at either end of the building (Ministerio de Cultura, redrawn by Gabriel E. Cantarutti).

those of most others at the site (about 80 cm), and its walls now stand less than 1.5 m high. The remains of one interior niche can be seen on the south wall, and a second niche once stood between the doorway and the northeastern corner of the building. The building may have contained other niches, but the poor preservation of its walls prevents their identification (Figure 5.10).

Excavations in Building 2 were conducted using a six-unit grid system. At the time of the investigation, the structure was covered with vegetation and wall fall.

A large tree had grown in its northeastern corner, and several large roots from other nearby trees crossed the interior of the building. The removal of the first level revealed a modern offering, which was approximately 50 cm in diameter and was located in the southwestern corner of the building. The offering included a concentration of burnt maize as well as fragments of ceramics, including parts of an aryballos. A stake-like stone was found standing upright in the center of the offering. The excavation of the second level yielded numer-

Figure 5.9. The south end of Building 1. Note the materials from a fallen gable and the irregularly spaced niches on the end wall (Ministerio de Cultura; photograph by Javier Fonseca Santa Cruz).

ous ceramic sherds, including a concentration of *urpu/raki* sherds in the southeastern corner of the building and a few plate, cooking pot, and possible jug fragments in the northern half.[11] The removal of the second level exposed a well-preserved, packed-earth floor with numerous concentrations of ceramics, various carbonized remains, and other artifacts.

The northwestern end of the building contained an area of unfired clay mixed with grass, as well as the shattered remains of large storage vessels (*urpus/rakis* and aryballoi) and cooking pots. The northeastern corner of the building held a small platform made of stone slabs and clay, which stood about 25 cm high.

The center of Building 2 also contained a dense concentration of shattered ceramic vessels and other cultural remains. A small platform near the door, made of stone slabs and clay, was found abutting the east interior wall. The platform was 31 cm high and was once covered with plaster. Three small grinding stones (*mus-*

cas) were identified on top of this platform. Fragments of cooking vessels were recovered near the platform, and there were two large concentrations of unburnt clay and grass adjacent to it. Furthermore, several mica fragments were recovered in the doorway.

A large concentration of cultural objects was found about 2 m from the northern wall and 1.5 m from the door. This concentration included fragments from *urpus/rakis*, plates, a miniature plate, and one of the two iron nails found in the building. Iron nails have been recovered in other buildings of Espíritu Pampa and at other post-contact Inca sites such as Vitcos and Huánuco Pampa (Morris et al. 2011). The nails are especially interesting since they are highly portable objects that were brought into the region and are linked to Spanish influence (Figure 5.11).

The remains of several other vessels were recovered on the Inca floor on the central-west side of the building. For example, the remains of a large cooking vessel and a plate were identified about 1 m from the west wall. A large concentration of burnt corn (a type locally known as *chuncho*), as well as carbonized potatoes, beans and peanuts, was found just south of these vessels. This area of the building also yielded fragments of a miniature plate and the remains of cooking vessels.

Part of the southeastern wall of the structure had collapsed, which made the excavations in this area of the building more difficult. Perhaps most importantly, a large (55 cm long, 32 cm wide, and 2 cm thick) vermilion-painted roof tile was recovered. The roof tile is sharply concave, with an arch approximately 17 cm high. A third platform made of stone slabs and clay was found abutting the south wall. The exterior of this platform still held patches of clay plaster. Fragments of a plate were recovered on the floor, directly in front of the platform. In this area was a large section of earth and ash, representing a possible hearth. A number of aryballos, *urpu/raki*, and roof tile fragments were also recovered in this area. Additional fragments from plates, cooking pots, and a vessel lid were found across the south end of the building. The southwestern corner of the building contained an area of burnt clay and a small line of stone that may have served as a bench.

DISCUSSION OF BUILDING 2

Excavations in Building 2 yielded approximately 342 ceramic fragments. The majority of the fragments (n = 290; 74 percent) were from large storage vessels (*urpus/rakis* and aryballoi). However, sherds from two miniature plates, a number of normal plates (n = 20; .06 percent), a cooking pot (n = 25; .07 percent), a lid, and a pedestal pot were also recovered. In addition, roof tile fragments (n = 32) were also found. Items of Western manufacture included two iron nails. Enough charcoal was found scattered across the interior of the building to indicate that the roof had burned. Food preparation in the building is

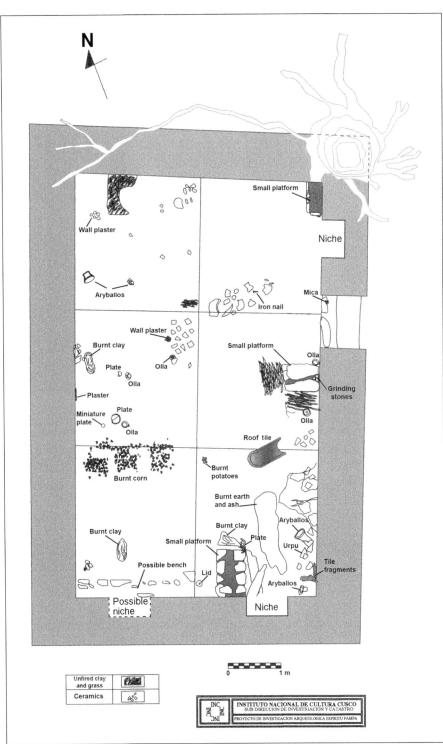

Figure 5.10. Final plan of Building 2 (Ministerio de Cultura; redrawn by Gabriel E. Cantarutti).

Figure 5.11. One of two iron nails found in Building 2 (Museo Amazónico Andino Qhapaq Ñan de Quillabamba; photograph by Brian S. Bauer).

suggested by the presence of grinding stones on one of the interior platforms, a possible hearth area, and carbonized plant remains.

BUILDING 3

Building 3, a rectangular structure measuring approximately 6 x 4.4 m, defines the north end of the Tendi Pampa compound. This building is frequently photographed because a massive matapalo tree has engulfed its southeastern corner (e.g., Lee 2000:346; Savoy 1978a:155). The building contains a single patio-facing door with a well-preserved stone lintel. The walls average 90 cm in thickness and still stands to a height of nearly 2 m. There is a single small interior niche near the center of the east wall.

Excavations within the structure took place using a grid of six units. At the time of the excavation, the interior of the structure was covered with dense vegetation and fallen wall remains. There was also a looter's pit, measuring approximately 1.3 m in diameter, near the center of the building. The looter's pit cuts through the Inca floor, well into the natural alluvial deposit that lies under the site.

During the removal of the first excavation level, a modern offering was found near the northeastern corner of the building. This *pago* (payment) consisted of a scallop shell,[12] six quartz crystals, and five small polished stones. The second excavation level included semicompacted soil, fallen lithic materials, and a continuation of roots from the surface vegetation. A few scattered ceramic fragments were recovered across the building, perhaps churned up during the looting process, as the level was removed.

The third level included the original floor and several ceramic concentrations (Figure 5.12). Fragments

included pieces from plates, ollas (cooking pots), aryballoi, and a few roof tiles. Bits of charcoal were found on the floor level, but no large concentrations were noted. Just west of the door, a complete but fragmented plate was recovered. The plate is painted with a central band of white-and-red geometric designs and a handle adorned with a human head (Figure 5.13).[13]

DISCUSSION OF BUILDING 3

Building 3 is the smallest freestanding structure in the Tendi Pampa compound. The building is generally well preserved, with high walls and a complete doorway. However, its southeastern corner is now covered by a large tree. The structure contained a looter's pit in its center and a small modern offering near one side. It yielded relatively few ceramic vessel fragments, approximately 100 in total. These fragments represented a small number of vessel types, including plates (n = 19; 20 percent), cooking vessels (n = 65; 69 percent), and a large storage vessel (n = 10; 11 percent). A small number (n = 12) of roof tile fragments were also found. The building also yielded one well-preserved plate. No metal items or objects of Western manufacture were found in the building. Its function remains unknown.

BUILDING 4

Since first described, the unusual shape of the easternmost building at Tendi Pampa has received considerable attention. The building is oval at one end and has a single door in the center of the other end. Such oval-ended buildings are rare within Inca sites, which are generally dominated by rectangular structures grouped around small patios (Gasparini and Margolies 1980). Bingham (1914b:188) highlighted this building in his first description of the compound, writing, "One of the buildings stood apart and was rounded at one end, having a single door at the other end." Later in his article, Bingham notes that the walls of this building were in extremely poor condition, suggesting that it may not have been contemporaneous with the other buildings in the compound. He also proposed a possible function, writing, "There is no reason why it should not have been a primitive chapel, built by the missionaries near the old Inca settlement. The fact that the walls have not stood as well as those of the other structures might be taken to indicate a later and more hasty construction" (Bingham 1914b:194). When Savoy (1970:98) visited Espíritu Pampa many years later, he also commented on the unusual shape of this

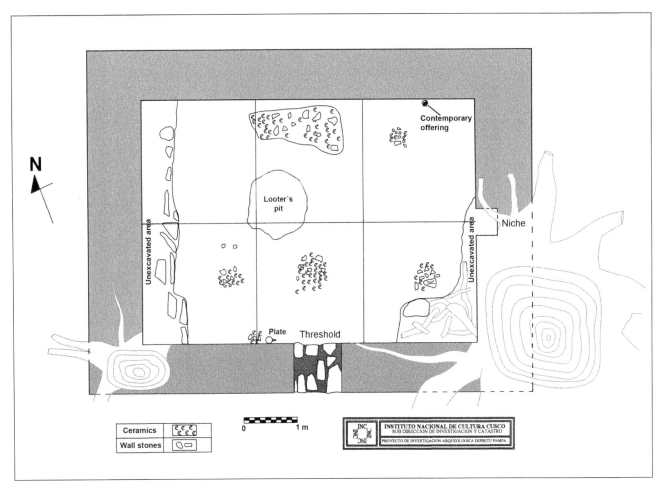

Figure 5.12. (above) Plan view of the floor of Building 3 (Ministerio de Cultura; redrawn by Gabriel E. Cantarutti).

Figure 5.13. (left) Plate with a handle in the shape of a human head from near the door of Building 3 (Museo Amazónico Andino Qhapaq Ñan de Quillabamba; photograph by Brian S. Bauer).

oval-ended building (also see Lee 2000). Other visitors to the site, including Sakai (2009), have noted that the position of the oval-ended building within the Tendi compound is similar to that of the famous curved wall within the Coricancha complex in Cusco (see Gasparini and Margolies 1980:224).

Building 4 measures some 6 m wide and is a little more than 10 m long. The wall averages 80 cm in width. During its excavation, the building was divided into 15 units, with the final 3 on the east side varying in size on account of the curved end of the structure. The walls, like those of the other structures of the compound, are composed of flat slabs and river cobbles. They are, as observed by Bingham, less well constructed than others at the compound and are now poorly preserved. The tallest wall remnant stands less than 1 m

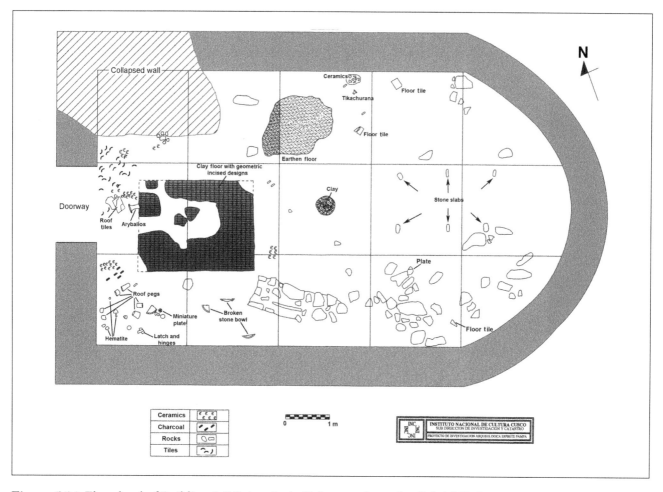

Figure 5.14. Floor level of Building 4 (Ministerio de Cultura; redrawn by Gabriel E. Cantarutti).

above the original floor level. Excavations revealed that the interior walls of Building 4, like most other buildings in Espíritu Pampa, were covered with clay plaster.

At the time of the excavation, the root mass of a fallen tree had disturbed the northwestern corner of Building 4, and there were several smaller trees growing within the structure. The removal of the first excavation level revealed a light scatter of pottery and roof tiles in the units near the door. Small amounts of fallen wall plaster and a fragmented piece of inscribed floor plaster were also recovered (see below). The remains of a curved wall, apparently postdating the primary occupation of the building, were found along the south side of the structure.

The removal of the second excavation level exposed a number of interesting features (Figure 5.14). A shattered aryballos and additional roof tile fragments were found near the doorway, and a broken stone bowl was found along the west wall. The southwestern area of the building held several stone roof peg fragments, four hematite polishing stones, and a shattered miniature plate. Furthermore, the remains of a copper latch and two

copper hinges, complete with their accompanying nails, were recovered near the southwestern corner. These were most certainly the hardware of a small wooden chest that has long since decomposed (Figure 5.15).

Of special interest on the west side of the building was an elaborately decorated rectangular clay floor area (2.65 x 2 x .05 m). The surface of this floor was inscribed with rectangles, measuring approximately 10 cm x 7 cm, clearly imitating European floor tiles. This is a remarkable find, since no other Inca building with an inscribed clay floor has been reported. Furthermore, a small patch (around 1.4 m in diameter) of a packed earthen floor was identified along the north wall. A P-shaped copper object and an L-shaped iron object, inlaid at one end with what appears to be seashell, were also recovered within this area.

Several fragments of rectangular clay floor tiles were also recovered along the north wall. The best-preserved floor tile is nearly complete, missing only a small chip on one of its corners. This well-fired floor tile, measuring 20 x 16.5 x 2.5 cm, is a remarkable find. The clay appears to be different from the roof tiles, suggesting that it may have been imported into the area (Figure 5.16). The neck of a small *tikachurana* (see Julien 1989:8, Form 1b; Pardo 1938) was also recovered along the north wall of the building.

Near the center of Building 4 was a mass of un-

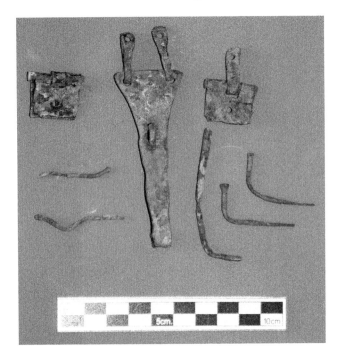

Figure 5.15. A copper latch, two hinges, and five nails were recovered from Building 4 (Museo Amazónico Andino Qhapaq Ñan de Quillabamba; photograph by Brian S. Bauer).

Figure 5.16. A nearly intact clay floor tile was found along the north wall of Building 4 (Museo Amazónico Andino Qhapaq Ñan de Quillabamba; photograph by Brian S. Bauer).

fired clay. The function of this feature has not been determined. Finally, a notable arrangement of six stones, placed vertically into the floor, was found in the east end of the structure. Together these six stones form a rectangle, approximately 3 m long and 1.5 m wide. Based on modern analogies, they were used as supports for a wooden platform. The location of the stones (and the presumed wooden platform) at the far east end of the building, directly opposite the west entrance, is intriguing, since any object that was placed on the platform would have been visible through the doorway.

DISCUSSION OF BUILDING 4

In comparison with the other buildings of this area, Building 4 is not especially large and it contains poorly constructed walls. Nevertheless, because of its unusual form, several researchers who have studied Tendi Pampa suggest that this building was of unique importance. The 2009 excavations, which recovered several unusual artifacts and architectural features within Building 4, support the impression that it was a special venue.

The excavations yielded a relatively small number of roof tile (n = 23) and ceramic vessel (n = 110) fragments. The vast majority of the vessel fragments came from a single aryballos (n = 108; 98 percent) found near the doorway. The small number of vessels within the building suggests that it was not used for cooking, serving, or fermenting. In contrast, the building contained several unusual artifacts suggesting that elite or ritual-related activities occurred within it. For example, a copper latch and hinges to a small box and a small iron pin-like object with inlaid shell, both of European origin, were found within the building.[14] In addition, the east end of the building once held a wooden platform, supported by stone slabs, which was visible through the west doorway. Most importantly, the building contained a clay floor that was incised to imitate European floor tiles, as well as a few actual rectangular floor tiles. Together with the unusual shape of the building, these findings support the suggestion that special activities took place within it. We will discuss the possible function of Building 4 in the conclusion to this chapter.

BUILDING 5

A single long rectangular structure, divided into five rooms, defines the east side of the Tendi Pampa compound. Building 5 is the northernmost room within that long structure. The room is rectangular, measuring approximately 8 x 4.8 m. The walls are 80 to 90 cm thick and stand at various heights, from 2.17 m to only 29 cm. The building may have had two doorways. One clearly defined door leads to the north, out of the compound and toward the semicircular building. There are unusually narrow niches on either side of this doorway. Bingham took several pictures of this doorway, which show that the building contained a northern gable (Figures 5.17–5.19).

There may also have been a doorway that led into the plaza near the southwestern corner of Building 5 (See Bingham 1914b; Lee 2000:502). Confirmation of this doorway is difficult, since this section of the building is now poorly preserved and damaged by tree growth. There were two, perhaps three, internal niches along the east side of the building and three along the west side. It is possible that the south end of the building also contained two additional niches, but this is less clear.

At the time of excavation, the massive matapalo tree that covered the southeastern corner of Building 4 had also grown over much of the west wall of Building 5. A

Figure 5.17. The north end of Building 5. Note the gable end, which has since fallen, and the two narrow niches on either side of the doorway. The man standing next to the doorway is one of the Campas, who were living near Espíritu Pampa when Bingham visited the ruins (National Geographic Image Collection: negative 785760, photograph by Hiram Bingham).

second matapalo tree had grown on the east wall, and several smaller trees were within the building. The extensive root system of these various trees crossed the interior of Building 5 and complicated the excavation process.

Before the excavation began, a six-unit grid system was placed within the building. The first excavation level revealed a burnt area, approximately 60 cm in diameter, near the center of the building. Although fragments of roof tiles and ceramics were found in the ashes, the shallowness of this feature suggests that the burning occurred long after the building was abandoned. The narrow neck of an aryballos and various aryballos body fragments were found near the southeastern corner of the structure, and a few additional aryballos and plate sherds were recovered across its interior. The second excavation level produced a large number of ceramic vessel fragments, including the remains of aryballoi, *urpus/rakis*, jugs, plates, ollas, pedestal pots, and roof tiles. There was also a large amount of charcoal across

Figure 5.18. Building 5 in 1983. Parts of the gable can still be seen above the doorway (photograph by David Drew).

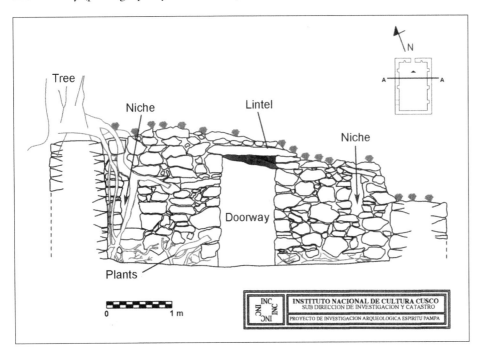

Figure 5.19. Profile of the north wall of Building 5 in 2009. The wall had the remains of a gable when it was photographed by Bingham in 1911 (Ministerio de Cultura; redrawn by Gabriel E. Cantarutti).

ner continued various large roof tile fragments. Some of the roof tiles were painted vermilion, and one was decorated with a pair of snakes. Rather than having fallen as the roof burned, these roof tiles were in a pile on the floor of the building. A grinding stone (*batan*; 35 x 17 x 7 cm) was recovered near the roof tiles, along with the base of a miniature polished black-ware plate with a llama-head handle.[15]

Most importantly, the badly fragmented remains of a large serving vessel, with two pairs of small handles on each side, were recovered near the north door of Building 5. The exterior of the vessel is painted a dark red, and it is covered with a wide range of figures and designs of different colors. The images include animals (for example, rainbow-snakes, bees, butterflies, llamas/alpacas, and large felines) as well as humans. Among the human images are Europeans riding horses and carrying lances. More interesting still, the Europeans are shown being attacked by Andeans with arrows and spears. Native prisoners with ropes tied around their necks are also shown; there are also dead warriors. The same battle scene is painted on both sides of this amazing vessel. The fact that the vessel was recovered within Espíritu Pampa, the

last capital of the Inca, and that it appears to have been shattered during the final assault on the town makes the vessel even more remarkable (Figure 5.21).

The central section of Building 5 contained a wide range of shattered ceramic objects, including plates, ollas, and many vermilion-painted roof tiles (Figure

the interior, indicating that the building had burned. The third excavation level, which included the original floor of the building, was covered with cultural materials (Figure 5.20).

The north end of Building 5 provided several interesting objects. For example, the northwestern cor-

5.22). There were also the burnt remains of two roof supports, concentrations of burnt maize ears, and a few carbonized potatoes. The position of these food remains suggests that the maize and potatoes were in a second-floor storage area when the building burned and collapsed. Small bone fragments were also found in patches on the original floor. The south end of the building was penetrated by a large matapalo root and was difficult to excavate because of extensive wall fall. However, like other parts of the building, the south end contained a large number of crushed vessels, broken roof tiles, burnt maize and potatoes, and burnt roof elements. Among the more notable finds were various aryballos fragments and the remains of a polished, black-ware plate.

DISCUSSION OF BUILDING 5

Building 5 contained many artifacts. Although no complete ceramic vessels were found, about 2,040 fragments were recovered. They represent the remains of a wide range of vessel types, including large storage vessels (n = 1,407; 69 percent), cooking vessels (n = 423; 21 percent), plates (n = 92; .05 percent),[16] jugs (n = 86; .04 percent), lids (n = 23; .01 percent), and drinking vessels (*keros;* n = 4; less than .01 percent). A large number of roof tile

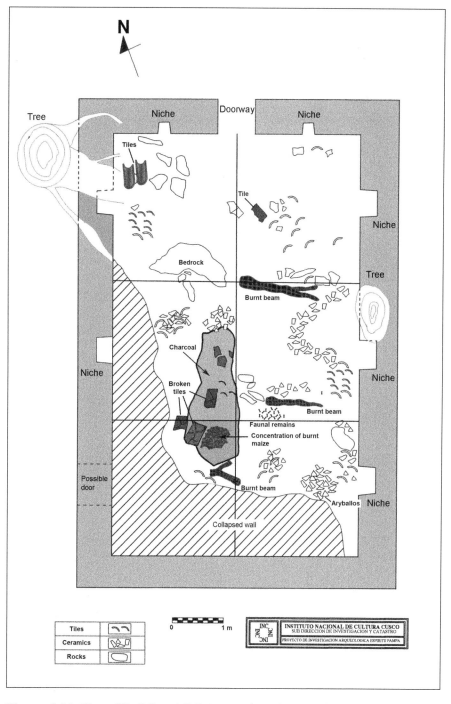

Figure 5.20. Plan of Building 5 (Ministerio de Cultura; redrawn by Gabriel E. Cantarutti).

fragments (n = 947) were also recovered. Many of them were painted vermilion; one of these was decorated with two snakes. Furthermore, the shattered remains of a large ceramic vessel with a spectacularly complex arrangement of figures, including fighting Spaniards and Andeans, were recovered. It should be noted that the buildings on the east side of Tendi Pampa (Buildings 6, 7, 8, and 11) all contained a large number of intact vessels. The crushed remains in Building 5 suggest that the

vessels in this building were purposely smashed. This smash event could have happened as the Incas were fleeing the compound or when the Spaniards took over the town.

Building 5 also yielded a great quantity of organic materials. Various charred roof supports were identified; one of these was more than 2 m long. In total, more than 230 burnt ears of maize, many still containing their husks, and at least 12 burnt potatoes were recovered. Two samples of carbon from this building were submitted for dating. The first sample was taken from burnt maize from the floor of the structure. This sample yielded a radiocarbon age of 357 ± 35 B.P. [A.D. 1593 ± 35], a date consistent with the timing of the final Spanish raid (A.D. 1572) into the Vilcabamba region.[17] The second sample was taken from the outside of a burnt roof support. Not surprisingly, the roof-support sample provided a slightly earlier radiocarbon age of 392 ± 35 B.P. [A.D. 1558 ± 35].[18] Since this carbon was derived from the outside of a major roof support, its date may reflect when the complex was built.

Building 5, with its high density and great range of ceramic vessels, both domestic and elite, appears to have been a multifunctional room. For example, it is clear that both food and beverages were stored and prepared within it. The recovery of a uniquely decorated vessel within the building also indicated that meals prepared within the building were related to impor-

tant events. Furthermore, the numerous painted roof tiles, many of which were stacked in a corner, seem to suggest that tile decoration was taking place within the building at the time of its destruction.

BUILDING 6

Building 6 is located within the long series of connected rooms that defines the east side of the Tendi Pampa compound. This room does not have direct access to the central patio; rather it is a side room off Building 7. The room contains two narrow windows in its west wall that face the patio and a single niche on its east wall. The room is rectangular, measuring approximately 6 x 4.5 m. The interior was divided into six units before excavations began. No artifacts were recovered in the first level. The second level contained fragments from plates, cooking vessels, arybolloi, *urpus/rakis*, drinking vessels (*keros*), and roof tiles. The northwest-

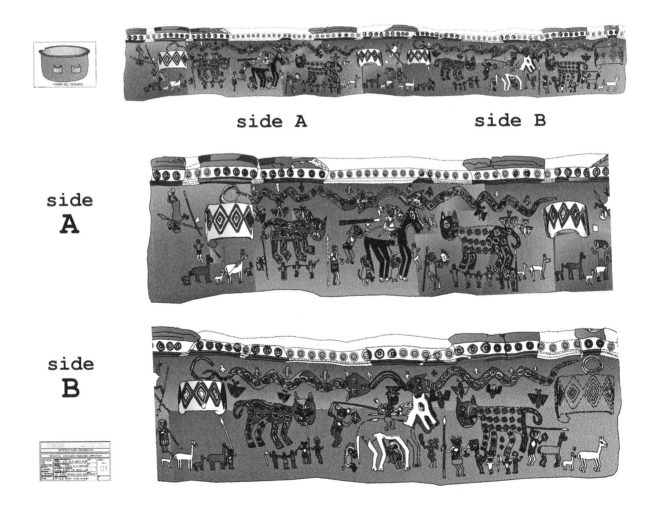

Figure 5.21. A reconstruction of a shattered vessel showing Europeans and Andeans fighting that was recovered on the floor of Building 5. Note that the same battle scene is painted on both side of the vessel (Ministerio de Cultura).

ern corner of the building contained some fallen wall plaster and a concentration of aryballos fragments. There was also a circular stain of dark earth directly in the center of the building—perhaps the remains of a shallow looter's pit (Figure 5.23).

The third excavation level included the original floor of the building, which held a massive amount of shattered ceramic vessels and numerous complete vessels. There was also a large amount of charcoal scattered across the floor, indicating that the roof of the structure had burned and then collapsed. The northwestern corner of the structure contained a small, 1.95 x .70 m, platform that stood .35 cm above the floor. Nearby were four nearly identical stacked plates with pairs of side nubbins (Figure 5.24). A crushed pedestal pot and the burnt remains of a large roof support, nearly 2 m long and 14 cm in diameter, were found nearby. Slightly farther toward the center of the building were the badly crushed remains of an *urpu/raki* and an aryballos.

The northeastern corner of the building contained the remains of two aryballoi, both of which had clay bases so that the vessels would stand upright. This

Figure 5.22. Building 5 during excavations (Ministerio de Cultura; photograph by Javier Fonseca Santa Cruz).

corner also held the remains of a cooking vessel, an asymmetrical pot (Figure 5.25), a lid, fragments from other domestic vessels, and pieces of roof tiles.

The central section of the building also contained a large array of ceramic vessels. On the central-west side, the remains of at least two large aryballoi and one small aryballos were identified. The larger aryballoi were supported by clay bases and small stones, so that they could stand upright. The remains of a pedestal pot, several small cooking vessels (one of which was intact), and a lid were also recovered in this area (Figures 5.26 and 5.27). A stack of three identical plates with strap handles was found on the floor near the center of the building (Figure 5.28).

The central-east side of the building was also covered in a dense deposit of cultural materials. The shattered remains of at least four large storage vessels were included within this deposit.[19] Large amounts of charcoal from burnt roof supports were preserved in this area of the building, as well as the remains of a vessel lid (Figure 5.29), pedestal pots, and various small cooking vessels (Figure 5.30). Perhaps most notable is that this area of the building also yielded the remains of at least nine small drinking vessels, which varied in height from 9 to 12 cm (Figure 5.31). While the remains of drinking vessels were found in a few other buildings of Tendi Pampa, Building 6 contained the largest number, all of them concentrated in one area.

The south end of Building 6 contained far fewer artifacts. Two broken, stacked plates and a concentration of burnt maize were found along the south wall. Furthermore, the neck of a large aryballos, two copper pins with rounded heads (*tupus*), one copper nail, and a grinding stone were recovered in this area of the building. A rectangular stone slab with a hole in its center was found in the doorway of the building. This stone and its hole served to hold the pointed end of a rotating door into the room.

DISCUSSION OF BUILDING 6

Building 6 contained an unusually large amount of cultural materials. In total, more than 3,140 ceramic fragments were recovered. They came from a wide range of vessels, including large storage vessels (n = 2,591; 82 percent), cooking pots (n = 440; 14 percent), jugs (n = 40; 1 percent), plates (n = 24; 1 percent), lids (n = 22; 1 percent), and drinking vessels (n = 19; less than 1 percent). Numerous roof tile fragments (n = 82) were also found. In addition, many complete or reconstructable vessels were recovered. These included nine drinking vessels, seven plates, four cooking vessels, two lids, and one pedestal pot. Most of these objects were found on the floor of the building; many were crushed when the roof of the building burned and collapsed. Large fragments of burnt roof supports and scattered pieces of charcoal were found across the building. A concentration of burnt corn, a copper nail, and two copper pins was also found on the floor of the structure. Apart from the roof tiles, no European-influenced items were recovered in this building.

Building 6 was a multifunctional room. The remains of corn, a grinding stone, the small work platform, and the cooking vessels indicate that food preparation, and

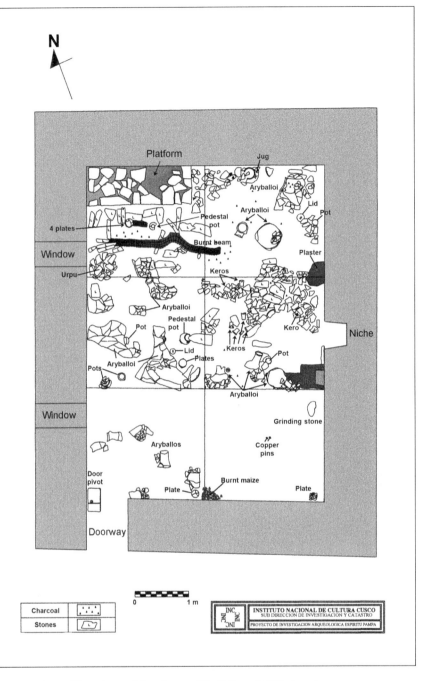

Figure 5.23. Plan view of the floor of Building 6 (Ministerio de Cultura; redrawn by Gabriel E. Cantarutti).

perhaps consumption, occurred in the building. The stacked plates were being stored in the room and may suggest that food was being served there as well. The numerous large storage vessels and the drinking vessels (*keros*) indicate that *chicha* was being fermented and perhaps was consumed in the room. However, the room's lack of direct access to the patio, the evidence for a door, and the fact that most of the cultural materials were placed at the far end of the room suggest to us that the room was largely used for storage.

BUILDING 7

Building 7 is located near the end of the multiroom structure that forms the east side of the Tendi Pampa compound. The room is rectangular, measuring 3.6

Figure 5.24. One of four nearly identical plates found stacked near the northwestern corner of Building 6 (Museo Amazónico Andino Qhapaq Ñan de Quillabamba; photograph by Brian S. Bauer).

Figure 5.25. An asymmetrical pot was found along the north wall of Building 6 (Museo Amazónico Andino Qhapaq Ñan de Quillabamba; photograph by Brian S. Bauer).

x 4.5 m. The interior walls stand between 1 and 2 m high. The west side of the building has a doorway with a preserved lintel that opens onto the central patio of the compound. Building 7 provides access to two other rooms: Building 6 to the north and Building 8 to the south (Figure 5.32).

The interior of Building 7 was divided into four units before the excavations began. The first excavation level yielded no cultural items. The second level contained charcoal from the burning of the building and

Figure 5.26. A pedestal pot from Building 6 (Museo Amazónico Andino Qhapaq Ñan de Quillabamba; photograph by Brian S. Bauer).

Figure 5.27. One of the small cooking vessels recovered in Building 6 (Museo Amazónico Andino Qhapaq Ñan de Quillabamba; photograph by Brian S. Bauer).

Figure 5.28. One of three plates found stacked on top of each other near the center of Building 6. This plate is missing one of its strap handles (Museo Amazónico Andino Qhapaq Ñan de Quillabamba; photograph by Brian S. Bauer).

Figure 5.29. A vessel lid from the central-east area of Building 6 (Museo Amazónico Andino Qhapaq Ñan de Quillabamba; photograph by Brian S. Bauer).

Figure 5.30. A fragmented cooking vessel from the central-east area of Building 6 (Museo Amazónico Andino Qhapaq Ñan de Quillabamba; photograph by Brian S. Bauer).

Figure 5.31. A drinking vessel (*kero*) found in Building 6 (Museo Amazónico Andino Qhapaq Ñan de Quillabamba; photograph by Brian S. Bauer).

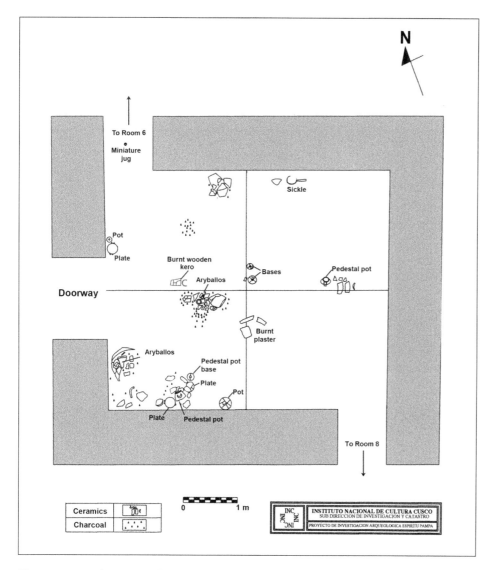

Figure 5.32. Plan view of Inca floor in Building 7 (Ministerio de Cultura; redrawn by Gabriel E. Cantarutti).

the exterior of this vessel contains geometric figures (Figure 3.35). Fragments from two cooking pots were also identified near the center of the building, and a broken pedestal vessel was found toward the eastern wall. A miniature jug was also recovered in the passageway between Buildings 6 and 7. Most intriguing, a large sickle-like iron tool was found on the Inca floor next to the northern wall (Figure 5.36).

DISCUSSION OF BUILDING 7

This small room yielded approximately 1,100 ceramic vessel fragments as well as other important cultural materials. The fragmented vessels included several large storage vessels (n = 942; 87 percent), cooking/pedestal pots (n = 138; 12 percent), a plate (n = 12; less than .01 percent), and a jug (n = 15; less than .01 percent). Complete vessels included two plates, a small cooking vessel, and a miniature jug. The building also contained a wooden *kero* and a sickle-like iron tool. The iron tool was found resting directly on the floor, which also held Inca-style vessels, so there is little doubt that this object of Western origins was used by the inhabitants of the compound. Because of the wide range of materials found in the building, no single function can be assigned to it.

BUILDING 8

Building 8 is the final of five adjacent rooms that form the east side of the Tendi Pampa compound. The building is rectangular, measuring about 5.3 x 4.5 m. The east and south walls contain single niches, and the west wall has a narrow window to the patio of the compound. The building also has an internal passageway that connects with Building 7 to the north.

various ceramic vessel fragments. These included the remains of two aryballoi, one located near the center of the room and the other in its southwestern corner. A broken pedestal vessel, a plate, and various ceramic fragments were found near the southwestern corner. Bits of burnt plaster and a few roof tile fragments were recovered in this level, scattered across the building.

The third excavation level included the materials on the original Inca floor. A complete plate and the base of a small cooking vessel were recovered next to the wall just north of the entrance to the patio. Another complete plate, similar to the set of four stacked plates with side nubbins found in Building 6, and a cooking vessel were found next to the south wall of the building (Figures 5.33 and 3.34). A carbonized wooden drinking vessel (*kero*) was found near the center of the room. Like many other Inca *keros* recovered in the Cusco region,

Figure 5.33. A complete plate with pairs of side nubbins was found near the west door of Building 7. This plate is similar to several other plates recovered in the Tendi Pampa compound (Museo Amazónico Andino Qhapaq Ñan de Quillabamba; photograph by Brian S. Bauer).

Figure 5.34. One of the small cooking pots found in Building 7. This vessel was found beside the south wall (Museo Amazónico Andino Qhapaq Ñan de Quillabamba; photograph by Brian S. Bauer).

Figure 5.35. A wooden drinking vessel (*kero*) was found near the center of Building 7 (Ministerio de Cultura; photograph by Javier Fonseca Santa Cruz).

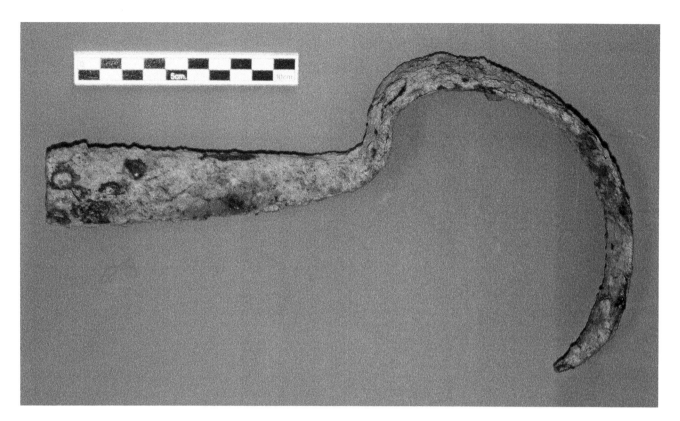

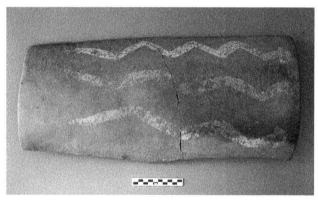

Figure 5.37. A large roof tile painted with three white snakes was recovered in Building 8 (Museo Amazónico Andino Qhapaq Ñan de Quillabamba; photograph by Brian S. Bauer).

Figure 5.36. (above) A large sickle-like iron tool was found on the floor of Building 7. It is one of several European artifacts recovered at Tendi Pampa (Museo Amazónico Andino Qhapaq Ñan de Quillabamba; photograph by Brian S. Bauer).

Excavations in Building 8 were conducted using six units. The excavations revealed the original Inca floor with a large number of in situ vessels and other objects. Scattered across the floor was much charcoal, including several large remains of roof supports, indicating that the roof of this structure, like so many others in the compound, had burned and then collapsed.

The northwestern corner of the building contained several large burnt clay plaster fragments and a complete roof tile, measuring 56 cm x 26 cm. The exterior surface of the roof tile was painted with three white snakes. Beneath this tile was a broken plate with a bird-head handle. Fragments of at least three other plates and several small cooking vessels were also found in this area of the building (Figure 5.37)

The northeastern corner of Building 8 contains a passageway into Building 7 (Figure 5.38). There was an intact small cooking vessel, a round cobble, and various roof tile and vessel fragments adjacent to the north wall. A large roof tile fragment was found associated with much charcoal along the east wall. Nearby was an impressive copper lid (22.6 cm in diameter) with a single strap (Figures 5.39 and 5.40). Fragments of roof support were found beside and on top of the lid, indicating that the lid was on the floor of the building when the roof burned.

The remains of a large aryballos were found about 1 m from the north wall. Although this aryballos was badly shattered, its base was still standing upright on the Inca floor. The north end of Building 8 also contained a cluster of shattered vessels, including two large pedestal vessels, a small polychrome aryballos with geometric decorations on one side (Figure 5.41), a large cooking/storage vessel (Figure 5.42), an *urpu/raki*, and a lid.

The central area of Building 8 also contained a large

concentration of ceramics and vessels. Along the west wall was a shattered *urpu/raki* and the remains of a large burnt roof support. A stack of four plates was found near the center of the unit. The first and third plates had two side strap handles (Figure 5.43). The second plate contained a bird-head handle and two nubbins on the opposite side, and the fourth plate contained two nubbins and a broken handle (Figures 5.44 and 5.45). Two additional plates with side strap handles were found on the floor near this stack. Also found nearby was a miniature *urpu/raki*, 17.4 x 14.5 cm, with two side handles and two modeled ears of corn (Figures 5.46 and 5.47). Slightly farther east were the remains of at least two large aryballoi, a medium-sized aryballos, two pedestal pots, two tripod vessels, three ceramic lids, and an asymmetrical vessel (Figure 5.48).

The southwestern corner of the building contained a small platform covered in plaster. The remains of a shattered tripod colander were found on the platform along with other ceramic sherds. The southeastern corner of the building also contained a concentration of ceramics, including the remains of a small aryballos, a pedestal vessel, and roof tiles. Shattered *urpu/raki* fragments were also recovered near the south wall of the building.

Various stone flakes, used as scrapers or knives, were also recovered in this area of the building. Most of the flakes contained fire spalls, which form when lithic materials are quickly heated to a high temperature. They were also darkened by the fire that destroyed the building (Figure 5.49).

DISCUSSION OF BUILDING 8

Building 8 contained a wide range of vessels. About 1,307 ceramic vessel fragments were recovered. Among these fragments were the remains of large storage vessels (n = 1,016; 78 percent), cooking pots (n = 191; 15 percent), plates (n = 20; less than 1 percent), tripod col-

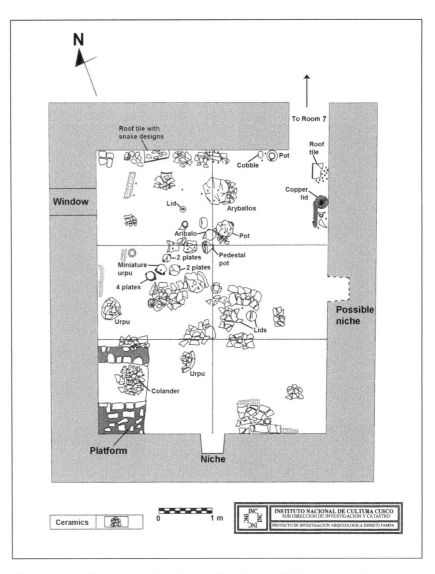

Figure 5.38. Plan view of the floor of Building 8 (Ministerio de Cultura; redrawn by Gabriel E. Cantarutti).

Figure 5.39. A large copper lid was found adjacent to the east wall during excavations in Building 8. (Ministerio de Cultura; photograph by Javier Fonseca Santa Cruz).

Figure 5.40. Copper lid with a strap handle recovered in Building 8 (Museo Amazónico Andino Qhapaq Ñan de Quillabamba; photograph by Brian S. Bauer).

Figure 5.42. A large cooking/storage vessel recovered from Building 8 (Museo Amazónico Andino Qhapaq Ñan de Quillabamba; photograph by Brian S. Bauer).

Figure 5.41. A small polychrome aryballos with geometric decorations was found with several other vessels in Building 8 (Museo Amazónico Andino Qhapaq Ñan de Quillabamba; photograph by Brian S. Bauer).

Figure 5.43. The first of four plates found stacked in Building 8 (Museo Amazónico Andino Qhapaq Ñan de Quillabamba; photograph by Brian S. Bauer).

anders (n = 53; 4 percent), lids (n = 19; less than 1 percent), and pedestal pots (n = 5; less than 1 percent), Complete or reconstructable vessels included a miniature *urpu/raki* decorated with maize ears, seven plates, two pedestal pots, a large cooking vessel, and a decorated medium-sized aryballos. Approximately 46 roof tile fragments were recovered, as well as a complete roof tile decorated with three white snakes. Building 8 also

113

Figure 5.44. The second of four stacked plates found in Building 8 (Museo Amazónico Andino Qhapaq Ñan de Quillabamba; photograph by Brian S. Bauer).

contained several stone knives. Perhaps most notable, however, was a large copper lid.[20]

The great variety of vessels found in Building 8 indicates that it served as a storage space for vessels and an area of food preparation. In particular, the platform in its southwestern corner may have served for food preparation, since a strainer was found on it. The absence of *keros* suggests that drinking did not occur in the room, although *chicha* was certainly fermented in some of the large storage vessels. Like all the connected rooms that define the east side of Tendi Pampa, Building 8 contained many high-quality artifacts, probably related to the ritual or elite function of the complex.

BUILDING 9

Building 9 is a large rectangular (9 x 4.5 m) structure that defines the south side of the Tendi Pampa patio. There are two double-jamb niches on the exterior wall that faces the patio. These are the only exterior niches in the compound, and as Lee notes (2000:415), such features are rare at Espíritu Pampa in general. There are also three small windows that connect the interior of Building 9 with the plaza. The east wall of Building 9 contains two narrow interior niches. A large mata-palo tree currently covers its west wall. The south wall contains a larger central niche. The structure has two entrances, one in the southwestern corner and the other in the southeastern corner; neither of these entrances led to the patio of the compound (Figures 5.50 and 5.51).

The interior of Building 9 was divided into eight units for excavation (Figure 5.52). The final two units

Figure 5.45. The final of four stacked plates found in Building 8 (Museo Amazónico Andino Qhapaq Ñan de Quillabamba; photograph by Brian S. Bauer).

Figure 5.46. A miniature *urpu/raki* with sculpted corn ears recovered in Building 8. Note the two aryballoi painted on the vessel (Museo Amazónico Andino Qhapaq Ñan de Quillabamba, photograph by Brian S. Bauer).

on the west side were not excavated because of the large matapalo tree. The excavations revealed that the east side of the building contained two slabs with Y-shaped tops, which had been placed vertically into the floor. Two similar stones, which have been pulled from their original vertical positions, were found nearby on the floor. It is likely that these four stones supported a wooden table within the building.[21] A concentration of artifacts, including four miniature plates, a miniature

Figure 5.47. Building 8 during excavations. Note the stack of plates and the miniature vessel near the center of the photograph (Ministerio de Cultura; photograph by Javier Fonseca Santa Cruz).

Figure 5.48. A asymmetrical vessel was found near the center of Building 8 (Museo Amazónico Andino Qhapaq Ñan de Quillabamba; photograph by Brian S. Bauer).

Figure 5.49. Lithic items showing fire spalls caused by the burning of Building 8 (Museo Amazónico Andino Qhapaq Ñan de Quillabamba; photograph by Brian S. Bauer).

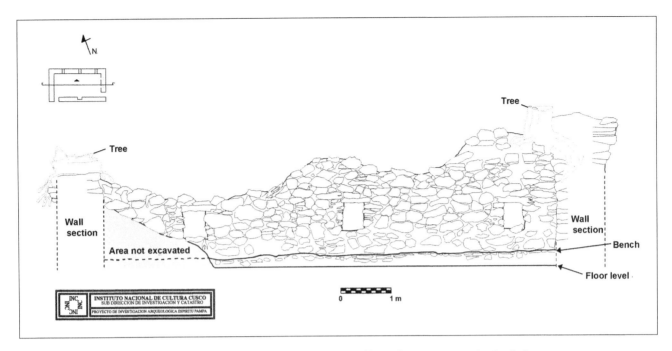

Figure 5.50. North profile of Building 9 showing the three small windows (Ministerio de Cultura; photograph by Javier Fonseca Santa Cruz).

Figure 5.51. One of two external niches of Building 10 in 1983 (photograph by David Drew).

aryballos, a miniature *urpu/raki*, a miniature jug, the base of a pedestal pot, and an iron nail, was found near the standing stones. Given the location of these objects, it is possible that they once were on the wooden structure supported by the vertical stones.

Nine chevron glass beads were recovered in the northeastern corner of the building. Multicolored beads such as these are made by dipping a glass cane (white in this case) into other colors to form a multilayered rod (in this case white, green, white, red, white, and blue). The rod is then cut into equally sized pieces, the ends of which are beveled and sanded (Heather Christie, personal communication 2012). The beveling of the ends reveals multiple levels of different colors. Chevron beads were common trade items found across Spanish-controlled areas of the Americas (Deagon 1987:164–167).[22] The Vilcabamba chevron beads are irregular and do not represent the high end of glass production for their time. Nevertheless, chevron beads have been rarely reported in colonial settings in Peru (Figure 5.53).

The midsection of the building also contained a number of interesting artifacts. A badly fragmented but largely complete polychrome aryballos was found in the niche on the south side of the building, and there was a very large concentration of roof tiles just west of the niche. These tiles appear to have been stacked on the floor of the building. A single complete roof tile was also found on the floor of the building, along with

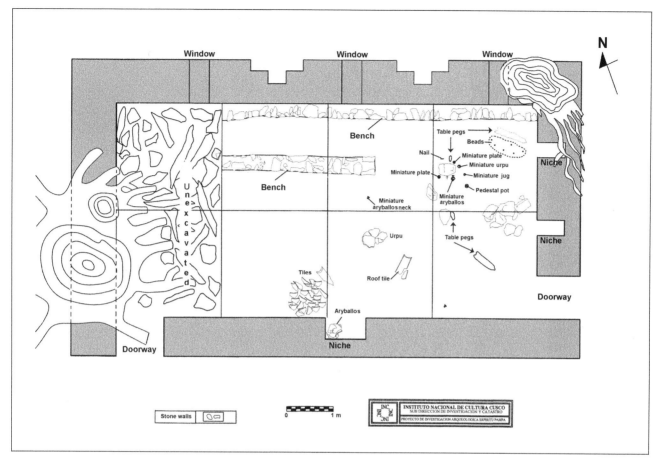

Figure 5.52. Plan view of the floor level of Building 9 (Ministerio de Cultura; redrawn by Gabriel E. Cantarutti).

an *urpu/raki* base and an aryballos neck.

The excavations also revealed a low-standing bench running the length of, and adjacent to, the north wall of the building. A second, shorter bench, or internal wall, was found running parallel to the first, but it extends across only half of the interior (Figure 5.54).

Unlike so many of the buildings in Tendi Pampa, Building 9 did not contain a host of different pots. The absence of cooking and serving vessels in Building 9 suggests that it was not a center of domestic activities. The collection of miniature vessels implies that rituals may have taken place within the building, and the bench along the building's north wall indicates that large groups of people were expected to attend. It is possible that this building served as place where rituals were held, perhaps during the region's long rainy months.

BUILDING 10

Building 10 is one of two abutting, nearly identical buildings on the lower terrace of Tendi Pampa.[23] The walls of the building are well preserved, with sections

standing nearly 3 m high. Holes for the second-story crossbeams can still been seen in the best-preserved sections of the wall. The building contains a central door and 14 internal niches. Because this structure once had gabled ends, there was a large amount of collapsed materials within it.

Before excavations began, in 2008, the interior of the building was divided into six equally sized units.

Figure 5.53. Nine chevron glass trade beads found within Building 9 (Museo Amazónico Andino Qhapaq Ñan de Quillabamba; photograph by Brian S. Bauer).

The removal of the surface vegetation yielded a few scattered pieces of pottery and some evidence of recent fires. The excavation of the first and second levels exposed a broad scatter of pottery and charcoal across the interior of the building. The north side of Building 10 contained various concentrations of ceramics, including fragments from a large storage vessel, a pedestal pot, a jug, a medium-sized aryballos, and a plate. The central area of the building contained a miniature ceramic drinking vessel (*kero*), a plate, and a few roof tile fragments. This area of the building also contained a badly broken but finely made vessel with two puma-head handles, a 7 cm copper *tupu*, a bola stone,

and several stone pestles. The south side of the building yielded the scattered remains of a wide range of objects, including fragments from plates, jugs, cooking vessels, roof tiles, and a 6 cm copper pin (perhaps the lower end of a *tupu*), and a stone pestle with a copper nail.

DISCUSSION OF BUILDING 10

The excavations in Building 10 yielded around 1,037 ceramic fragments. The quantity of fragments recovered in this building is very different from that recovered in Building 1, which yielded 360 vessel fragments, suggesting that although Buildings 1 and 10 are architecturally identical, different activities occurred within them. No complete vessels were found in Building 10. The majority of the ceramic fragments were from large storage vessels (*urpus/rakis* and aryballoi). However, the remains of plates, jugs, and cooking vessels were also identified. The building also contained several grinding stones. A range of special objects was also retrieved. These included a *tupu*, a possible *tupu* fragment, a miniature drinking vessel, a bola stone, and a finely made vessel with puma handles. Fragments from ceramic roof tiles were also recovered. From these remains it appears that the building supported a relatively wide range of activities. From the concentrations of charcoal found on the floor, it appears that this building, like the others at the site, was burned.

Figure 5.54. The interior of Building 9, looking west. The possible benches can be seen on the right, the pile of roof tiles on the left, and a stone table support in the foreground (Ministerio de Cultura; photograph by Javier Fonseca Santa Cruz).

BUILDING 11

Building 11 is the second of five adjacent buildings that form the east side of the Tendi Pampa compound.[24] It is rectangular, measuring about 7 x 4.35 m, with walls standing up to 1.8 m high. The room contains an off-center door on its west wall and three narrow windows that open onto the patio. The east wall contains three trapezoidal niches, while the north wall has two narrow trapezoidal niches.

The 2008 excavations in Building 11 began with the division of its interior into six equally sized units. While the first level yielded no cultural materials, the second and third levels provided an impressive variety of vessel fragments. There was also a large amount of charcoal and broken roof tiles scattered across the interior of the building, indicating that the roof had burned and collapsed. The density of the artifacts and the range of items are so great that they will be described in this report according to units in which they were recovered (Figure 5.55).

Unit A1, the southwestern corner of the building near the doorway, contained a square stone slab with a hole bored through it. This stone once served to hold the pointed end of a rotating door. The shattered remains of two aryballoi and an asymmetrical pot were recovered in the unit. There were also two clusters of serving vessels, including four lids, five plates with two pairs of nubbins (Figure 5.56), 16 plates with strap handles (Figure 5.57), seven nearly identical plates with llama-head handles (Figure 5.58), and two jugs (Figure 5.59). Unit B1 (the southeastern corner of the building) contained two large storage vessels. Beside one of these vessels were four stacked plates, including two plates with paired strap handles, one with two pairs of nubbins, and one polychrome plate with a pair of nubbins on one edge and a broken lip on the opposite edge. Another plate with strap handles and a small jug were also recovered in Unit B1.

Units A2 and B2 included the middle area of the building. Unit A2 contained at least one broken aryballos, a lid, a jug, and a pedestal vessel. It also contained two metal objects: a copper bell (Figures 5.60) and a copper celt (Figure 5.61). Unit B2 held the remains of at least one broken aryballos, two pedestal pots, five lids, a straight-sided bowl, a cluster of seven plates (each with two pairs of nubbins), a polychrome plate with two pairs of nubbins (Figure 5.62), and one plate

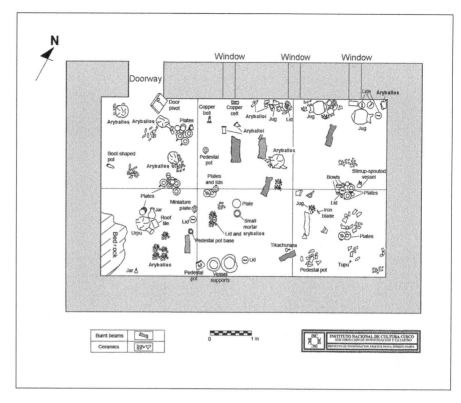

Figure 5.55. Final Plan of Building 11 (Ministerio de Cultura; redrawn by Gabriel E. Cantarutti).

Figure 5.56. A plate with two pairs of nubbins found in Building 11 (Museo Amazónico Andino Qhapaq Ñan de Quillabamba; photograph by Brian S. Bauer).

with two strap handles. Lithic items included a small pestle and mortar. The unit also held two especially fine *tikachuranas*, one of which had survived intact (Figure 5.63). Two unfired clay bases for large storage vessels were also found along the wall of the building.

Unit A3 included the northwestern corner of the

Figure 5.57. A plate with two strap handles found in Building 11 (Museo Amazónico Andino Qhapaq Ñan de Quillabamba; photograph by Brian S. Bauer).

Figure 5.58. A plate with a llama-head handle found in Building 11 (Museo Amazónico Andino Qhapaq Ñan de Quillabamba; photograph by Brian S. Bauer).

Figure 5.59. A large jug recovered in Building 11 (Museo Amazónico Andino Qhapaq Ñan de Quillabamba; photograph by Brian S. Bauer).

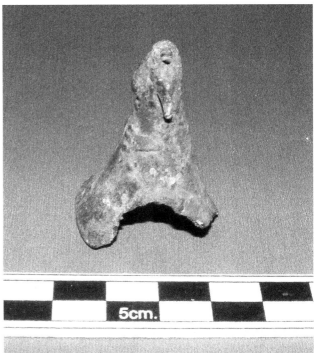

Figure 5.60. A copper bell recovered in Building 11 (Museo Amazónico Andino Qhapaq Ñan de Quillabamba; photograph by Brian S. Bauer).

structure, while Unit B3 incorporated the northeastern corner. Unit A3 included two jugs, one miniature *urpu/ raki*, one pedestal pot, one bowl, a shattered aryballos, and three lids. Unit B3 provided a large number of objects, most of which were found in a single group along

Figure 5.61. A copper celt recovered in Building 11 (Museo Amazónico Andino Qhapaq Ñan de Quillabamba; photograph by Brian S. Bauer).

Figure 5.62. One of two polychrome plates recovered in Building 11 (Museo Amazónico Andino Qhapaq Ñan de Quillabamba; photograph by Brian S. Bauer).

the A3 and B3 division. Vessels recovered from the unit included a jug, a pair of curved-sided polychrome bowls (Figure 5.64), a single curved-sided polychrome bowl with a different design, two straight-sided bowls with cream interiors, one straight-sided bowl with a fish (*suche*) (Figure 5.65), three plates with strap handles, a single plate with two pairs of nubbins, a lid, and a miniature *urpu/raki*. A single globular vessel with a stirrup spout, adorned with a bird, was also recovered (Figure

Figure 5.63. A fine *tikachurana* was recovered in Building 11 (Museo de Garcilaso de la Vega, Cusco; photograph by Brian S. Bauer).

Figure 5.64. One of two curved-sided polychrome bowls found in Building 11 (Museo Amazónico Andino Qhapaq Ñan de Quillabamba; photograph by Brian S. Bauer).

Figure 5.66. A globular vessel with a stirrup spout, adorned with a bird, was recovered in Building 11 (Ministerio de Cultura; photograph by Javier Fonseca Santa Cruz).

Figure 5.65. A large straight-sided bowl with a fish (*suche*) painted in the bottom, recovered in Building 10 (Museo Amazónico Andino Qhapaq Ñan de Quillabamba; photograph by Brian S. Bauer).

5.66). This is an especially interesting find, since this style of ceramics is generally associated with the north coast of Peru.[25] It is also important to note that a large (about 23 x 4 cm) iron blade was also recovered in this unit. This is an exceptionally rare item to find.

DISCUSSION OF BUILDING 11

Building 11 held the largest number of intact vessels of any building at Tendi Pampa. By the end of the excavation, an astounding collection had been recovered. It included 46 plates (many of them matching), 13 lids,

five jugs, four straight-sided bowls, three curved-sided bowls, two pedestal pots, two miniature *urpus/rakis*, two *tikachuranas*, one small jug, one asymmetrical pot, and one globular jug with a stirrup spout. Building 11 also yielded the largest sherd count (7,140 fragments) of any room in the complex, indicating that there were many other vessels in use when the building burned and the roof collapsed.[26] Field notes and sherd counts suggest that among the sherds there were about eight large storage vessels, perhaps as many as ten plates, and various additional vessels (Figures 5.67 and 5.68).

In short, at the time of its abandonment, Building 11 contained a vast number of ceramic vessels. The presence of many large storage vessels indicates that *chicha* was fermented in the room, and the various jugs hint that it may have been decanted there. Yet the complete absence of drinking vessels suggests that beverages were not drunk in the room. The astonishingly large number of plates, many found still stacked in sets, as well as a good number of bowls, suggests that vessel storage as well as the initial serving tasks were also carried out in the room. In other words, while some vessel storage, food cooking, and drink fermentation was conducted in the room, it appears that the building also served as an area for final meal preparation. Given

Figure 5.67. Some of the objects recovered from Building 11 (Ministerio de Cultura; photograph by Javier Fonseca Santa Cruz).

Figure 5.68. Some of the objects recovered from Building 11 (Ministerio de Cultura; photograph by Javier Fonseca Santa Cruz).

Figure 5.69. The stone basin after being cleared of debris (Ministerio de Cultura; photograph by Javier Fonseca Santa Cruz).

that the only doorway of this building opens onto the plaza, it is reasonable to assume that the meal preparation was for feasting events that most likely took place in the plaza.

THE L-SHAPED STAIRWAY AND THE U-SHAPED BASIN AT TENDI PAMPA

The Tendi Pampa complex is built on two terraces. The lower terrace contains two buildings while the upper terrace holds nine. The upper terrace stands some 2 m above the lower terrace. There is an L-shaped stairway leading from one terrace to the other and a U-shaped stone-lined basin (about 3 x 2 m) with a single green-slate spout between the terraces (Bingham 1922:295).

In 2009 the former Institutio National de Cultura Region Cusco conducted excavations at both the stairway and the fountain. Both spaces were filled with eroded earth, terrace collapse, and vegetation. The ex-

cavations revealed that the U-shaped basin has a well-constructed cobblestone floor and a small stairway leading into it. The excavation of the L-shaped stairway uncovered several fallen lintel stones (Figure 5.69). These lintels suggest that the stairway was the principal entrance to the upper terrace. Neither of these excavations yielded ceramic materials.

THE ROOF TILES OF ESPÍRITU PAMPA

Bingham noted the presence of Spanish-style roof tiles at Tendi Pampa. He specifically mentions them in his many articles and books that followed his visit (Figure 5.70). For example, within his first published description of the Tendi Pampa complex, Bingham writes, "With one exception, everything about the fragments of pottery and the architecture of the houses was unquestionably Inca. The exception was the presence of a dozen or fifteen roughly made Spanish roofing tiles of varying sizes" (Bingham 1914b:196). Bingham did not associate the tiles with the Inca occupation of the site, writing, "On account of the small number of them and of the great irregularity of their sizes . . . it seems to me possible that these tiles had been made experimentally by recent Peruvians or possibly early Spanish missionaries, who might have come to this place three centuries ago" (Bingham 1914b:196–197).

Nearly 50 years later, Savoy also noted the curious fact that roof tiles could be found at Tendi Pampa. However, he correctly associated the production of roof tiles with the European–Andean encounter:

I notice an unusual piece of orange-red ceramic protruding from the ground. I pick it up and discover that it is roofing tile, the kind used by the Spaniards during colonial times. Kicking up a pile of dead leaves with the heel of my boot, I find there are several layers of tile strewn about the floor. Many pieces are well preserved, colors still vivid. One piece is incised with serpentine lines. . . . From our findings it would appear that the Incas of Vilcabamba learned the art of manufacturing roofing tile and were utilizing it in their modern buildings; proof that they were experiencing a kind of transition, absorbing Spanish refinements while retaining their own (Savoy 1970:97–98).

Savoy also found within the Hall that many of the roof tiles at Tendi Pampa were painted red and that a smaller number were decorated with serpent designs. More recently the remains of roof tiles have been noted within the four buildings in the Palace Compound (Lee 2000; Pilares Daza 2003) and a few tiles were found also within the Hall of the Miniatures (Bauer and Aráoz Silva, this volume, Chapter 7).

The importance of the roof tiles to the identification of the site of Espíritu Pampa as the Inca town of Vilcabamba came into focus only under the careful eye of John Hemming in the 1970s. While reviewing Martín de Murúa's chronicle,[27] Hemming noted that Murúa mentions the presence of roof tiles within the town of Vilcabamba. Murúa (1987:298 [1611–1616:Chapter 82]) writes, "The house of the Inca had upper and lower floors covered in tiles, and the whole palace [was] painted with a great variety of paintings in their style, which was quite a sight to see."[28] Combining this refer-

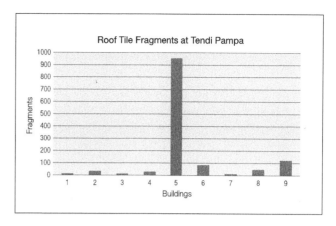

Figure 5.71. Number of roof tile fragments recovered in buildings at Tendi Pampa.

ence with many others concerning the location of the final Inca capital, Hemming (1970) was able to definitively link the ruins of Espíritu Pampa with the Inca town of Vilcabamba.

Recent excavations have shown that the distribution of roof tiles is very uneven, not only across the site but within specific sectors (Figure 5.71). For example, some buildings within Tendi Pampa contained large numbers of roof tile fragments while other buildings contained only a few.[29] It is also notable that, perhaps with the exception of Building 5, there were not enough tile fragments within any individual building to suggest that their roofs had been completely covered. This irregularity was also noted by Bingham (1914b:197), who writes, "Apparently none of the houses ever had tiled roofs, as the number of fragments is not enough to cover more than a few square feet, and nearly all were outside the buildings."

After reviewing the reports of earlier excavations at Espíritu Pampa and comparing those data with observations made at the site and the results of more recent excavations, we believe that the majority of the buildings at Espíritu Pampa did not have tiles and that the use of roof tiles was limited to Tendi Pampa, the Palace Compound, and a small number of other isolated buildings. Tiles may have completely covered the roofs of a few buildings, but in most cases tiles were placed only over doorways or along roof ridges. Their use in limited numbers also suggests that they were viewed as decorative or status-linked elements.

Overview of Tendi Pampa

Excavations at Tendi Pampa revealed large amounts of charcoal across many of the floors, indicating that the compound was burned. The long row of rooms that

Figure 5.70. Two roof tiles found in Tendi Pampa during Bingham's 1911 visit (National Geographic Photographic Archive: negative 785914, photograph by Hiram Bingham).

define the east side of the compound (Buildings 3–8 and Building 11), as well as Building 2, appear to have burned especially quickly; their roof supports collapsed inward during the fire. As the roofs of these buildings burned, harvested crops (primarily maize but also potatoes, beans, and peanuts) kept in their second-story storage areas fell to the ground.

The results of the excavations also suggest that the compound was abandoned quickly, with little time to collect valued objects. The rapid abandonment of the compound is illustrated by the large number and wide range of items left in the buildings. These include ceramic vessels of all sizes (portable and nonportable), types (storage, drinking, cooking, serving, and so on), and quality (fine, domestic, and miniature). Some, but certainly not all, of these vessels would have been considered valuable. The many upright standing vessels and the stacks of plates found in different buildings highlight the in situ nature of the artifacts. The most spectacular vessel of the compound (a large vessel with a battle scene painted on it) may have been dropped and shattered near the doorway of Building 5 during the abandonment chaos.

Various metal objects were also left in different rooms. Most notable are a sickle-like iron tool, a large iron blade, and a large copper lid. Other metal objects left behind when the occupants fled included a copper celt, a wooden box with a copper latch and hinges, a copper bell, several copper pins (*tupus*), and a variety of iron and copper nails. A set of nine glass beads was also left behind. Given the rarity of these objects, we can assume that they were valued and would not have been left had there been time to empty the buildings.

We suggest that the fire that destroyed the Tendi Pampa compound was set by the citizens themselves on the evening of June 23, 1572, in anticipation of the arrival of the colonial forces. The Spaniards and their allies had won the Battle of Huayna Pucará, two days before and had moved swiftly toward the town. The nobility had limited time to collect the most important items, which included the mummies of Manco Inca and Titu Cusi Yupanqui, the golden male-sun idol called Punchoa (daylight), and the female-earth idol called Pachamama (Earth Mother) (Toledo 1899). In addition, a large amount of fine cloth and a host of items made of gold and silver were collected before the inhabitants escaped in different directions into the mountains.[30] Nevertheless, it is clear that all items of value could not be removed and that the citizens surely hoped to return to the town after the Spaniards returned to Cusco. What food the Incas could not carry

they destroyed in an effort to limit the invading force's stores and thus reduce the time that the Spaniards and their allies could occupy the region. Murúa provides the following description of the town of Vilcabamba as the Spaniards and their Andean allies entered it on the morning of June 24:

> They marched into the town of Vilcabamba at ten o'clock in the morning, everyone on foot [as] the terrain is very rough and craggy and not suited in any way for horses. They found the entire town sacked, such that if the Spaniards and Indian allies had done it, it would have been no worse because the Indian men and women fled and went into mountains, taking as much as they could with them. The rest of the maize and food was [left] in the *buhíos* [huts] and storage houses, where they typically keep them. They burned and destroyed [the town] such that it was [still] smoldering when the army arrived. *The House of the Sun where they kept their major idol was also burnt.* [The Indians] believed that if the Spaniards did not find food or any sustenance quickly, they would soon turn around and leave the region rather than remain and settle it, because they had done this when Gonzalo Pizarro and [Francisco de] Villacastín entered.[31] The lack of sustenance forced [the Spaniards] to turn back and leave the land in their control. [It was] with this intention that the Indians fled, setting fire to everything they could not take [Murúa 1987:296–297 (1611–1616:Chapter 82); translation by the authors; emphasis added].[32]

In the days and weeks after the invading forces arrived in the town of Vilcabamba, both Europeans and Andeans would have walked across Tendi Pampa and perhaps even searched among its smoldering ruins for valuable objects. Some of the ceramic vessels that had miraculously survived the fire may have been shattered then, or they may have been broken as a result of indiscriminate actions over the following centuries. Nevertheless, given the size and importance of the compound, and the large number of items that remained in the buildings, it is surprising that there is only minor evidence of looting.[33] The floors of the buildings and the objects on them remained in remarkably good condition over the centuries.

DATING THE COMPOUND

Two charcoal samples taken from material collected at Tendi Pampa were submitted for AMS dating (Figure

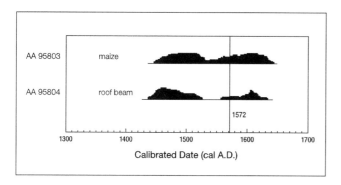

Figure 5.72. The two charcoal samples from Tendi Pampa were submitted for AMS dating.

5.72). One sample (AA 95803) was a maize kernel recovered on the floor of Building 2. The other sample (AA 95804) was taken from the outer layers of a burnt roof support in Building 5 (Appendix 1). The maize sample provided a date consistent with the early-colonial-period occupation of Tendi Pampa. The roof support suggests that the roof, and by inference the compound itself, was constructed sometime between A.D. 1430 and 1520.

FUNCTION OF THE COMPOUND

Insights into activities that occurred in Tendi Pampa are provided through a statistical analysis of the recovered ceramics. For statistical purposes, the many ceramic vessel types recovered at the site were reduced into five general-use classifications, including serving vessels (plates and bowls), cooking vessels (ollas, jugs, asymmetrical pots, colanders, pedestal vessels), drinking vessels (*keros*), large storage vessels (aryballoi and *urpus/rakis*), and miniature vessels. Our statistical tests were complicated by the fact that more than 100 complete ceramic vessels, as well as thousands of ceramic fragments, were recovered during the course of the excavation. On the other hand, the tests were aided by the extraordinary preservation of the rooms and the fact that most of the broken vessels were recovered in situ rather than in midden contexts. By reviewing the photographs, the excavation plans, and the vessel fragment counts (recorded by vessel type), we estimated the likely number of broken serving, cooking, drinking, storage, and miniature vessels that were contained within each room. Having developed these estimates, we then combined the complete-vessel count and the estimated broken-vessel counts and tested for correlations between the five general-use categories. A Spearman's rho shows that the presence of serving vessels correlated with cooking and storage vessels at a 99 percent confidence interval. In turn, cooking vessels are correlated with storage vessels at 95 percent. These results suggest that storing, cooking, and serving food were highly intermixed activities that occurred within different rooms of the complex. No other correlations were found.[34]

Before the 2008 and 2009 excavations at Tendi Pampa, several researchers had speculated on the possible function of this compound (e.g., Bingham 1914b; Lee 2000; Sakai 2009). Based on the research conducted at Tendi Pampa by Fonseca Santa Cruz, we propose that the Tendi Pampa compound served as a temple complex. That is, while a small number of individuals may have lived in the compound, perhaps in Building 1 or Building 10, it seems clear to us that large ritual and feasting events were also being hosted within its walls. Furthermore, it is clear that many of the buildings at the compound were dedicated to the preparation of food and the storage of ritual items, particularly those directly related to feasting.

Not surprisingly, different activities took place within the various rooms of the compound. For example, Building 2 appears to have been largely concerned with initial food preparation. From the many stacked plates found in Buildings 6 and 8 and the large numbers and types of ceramic vessels found in Buildings 5, 6, 7, 8, and 11, it is clear that the rooms that define the east side of the compound were all used in the preparation of food and/or the serving of meals. Furthermore, the copious number of large storage vessels indicates that *chicha* was also being fermented and served within these same buildings, especially within Building 6, which contained numerous drinking vessels (*keros*). Building 9, on the other hand, does not appear to have been related to food preparation. With its two doorways, its many miniature vessels, and its two internal benches, Building 9 may have been the focus of ritual events during the region's many long months of rain.

The function of Building 4 is perhaps the most difficult to determine. Both Bingham (1914b:194) and Lee (2000:414–415) suggest that this semioval structure may have been a chapel constructed by the Spaniards for their own use during their brief occupation of the town in 1572. This is possible, since we know that the Spaniards built a series of small churches farther down the Urubamba during their later colonization of the region. For example, in the following, Ocampo Conejeros (2013:46 [1611]) describes encounters between Christians and Andeans where churches were built farther down the Urubamba after the fall of Vilcabamba:

> The Indians showed themselves to be so affable and friendly, that the four Spaniards brought an image of Our Lady painted on a canvas. To entrust themselves to God, the soldiers instructed the Indians to construct a small chapel, which they built, where they hung her image. [They also erected] a large cross outside of the chapel on a stone pedestal and other small crosses inside the chapel.[35]

A reading of the little information we have concerning the post-1572 occupation of Espíritu Pampa also indicates that a few Spaniards, led by Francisco de Camargo y Aguilar (Maúrtua 1906:71–98), established an outpost at the site for at least a year following the Spanish invasion. In short, based on pre-excavation information, it was certainly possible to suggest that Spanish soldiers built Building 4 as a small chapel or that it was the result of unrecorded missionary efforts in the region.

The 2009 excavations within Building 4 revealed imitation floor tiles that further strengthen the idea that the structure once served as the locus of special events. However, the excavations also revealed enough charcoal within Building 4 to suggest that it was burned at the time of abandonment. This is an important observation since it raises the possibility that Building 4 was destroyed in the same fire that consumed other parts of Tendi Pampa on the eve of the Spanish arrival. If this is the case, then the construction of Building 4 would necessarily predate the 1572 raid. In other words, given that the U-shaped structure most likely burned at the same time as the other parts of Tendi Pampa, it seems unlikely that the building was built by the Spaniards after the fall of the town.

We believe that Building 4 is a relatively late addition to the Tendi Pampa compound but that it was made before the 1572 raid. The building is less substantial than the other structures at the site, and its position suggests that it was not part of the original layout. With its unusual shape and its tiled floor reflecting European influences, the building may have served as a special space for early colonial indigenous worship. Perhaps it may even mark the introduction of Christianity into the region.[36]

Knowing the general history of the site of Espíritu Pampa enables us to speculate more broadly on the function of Building 4. When the Inca nobility retreated into the Vilcabamba region, they transformed what was formerly a provincial installation into a new center for political activities and indigenous resistance. During this process, new buildings were certainly added to the already established town of Vilcabamba. Perhaps inspired by the U-shaped and clay-tiled floors of Christian chapels, the Incas may have constructed a new building beside the Tendi Pampa compound to hold religious icons they had removed from Cusco in 1536 or had crafted during their time in exile. Or they may have included Christian icons to match with the architectural style of the building.

In the above scenario, the interior platform built at the west end of Building 4 may have held an important religious icon (Andean or Christian) that was to be viewed by those who entered. What could that have been? One of the most concise descriptions of the various religious icons captured during the Vilcabamba campaign is provided by Viceroy Francisco de Toledo in a letter written to the king of Spain. Toledo writes the following:

> Túpac Amaru and Quispi Titu and all their brothers, relatives, wives and children and captains and people were taken prisoner. They also [captured] the bodies of Manco Inca and Titu Cusi, their fathers and brothers, and the golden idol named Punchao, or sun, which used to be kept in the House of the Sun in Cusco, who everyone in these kingdoms worshipped. It had been taken to the said province, in great disservice to God and the purpose of the teachings of the Holy Gospel. [They] had it nearly 40 years, sacrificing human beings, committing idolatry and apostasy. They made the Indians, who were already baptized, who went there or who they captured from [Spanish-controlled] areas commit apostasy with [it and] another idol they called Pachamama, Mother of the Earth, and many others that were burned and destroyed [Toledo 1899:126; translation by the authors].[37]

As detailed above, when the Spaniards entered the town of Vilcabamba in 1572, they seized the mummies of Manco Inca and Titu Cusi Yupanqui.[38] It was a strong Inca tradition to place the mummies of the past kings on semipublic display within structures. When the Spaniards first entered the city of Cusco in 1532, they saw various Inca mummies holding court or on display in different temples and elite households (Bauer 2004:159–189, Bauer and Coello Rodríguez 2007). Cobo, building on information found in Murúa (1987:262 [1611–1616]), suggests that the mummy of Manco Inca was transported to Vilcabamba and placed in the Temple of the Sun. He writes, "The Indians embalmed his body, and after carrying it to Vilcabamba, they put it in the temple of the Sun, where it was found by the Spaniards who conquered that province during the time of Viceroy Francisco Toledo (Cobo 1979:176 [1654])"[39] Likewise, testimonies dating to 1595 confirm that the body of Titu Cusi Yupanqui was taken after his death to Vilcabamba, where it was prepared for mummification (Bauer et al. 2014).

So it is possible that one or both of the royal mummies of Manco Inca and Titu Cusi Yupanqui were kept in the U-shaped structure in Tendi Pampa. Or, equally speculative, we know from Toledo (1899) that the Spaniards also captured the two most important religious icons of the Inca: the male image of the sun (Punchao) and its female counterpart (Pachamama).[40] One or both of these two icons could have been housed in the Tendi Pampa compound, perhaps in the U-shaped structure.

Alternatively, Christian icons may have been presented in the U-shaped building. Indeed, the size and the shape of the building closely mirror those of a Christian church. Furthermore excavations at other early churches in the Andes have shown similar layouts of doorways and altars (see Wernke 2010). If Building 4 was used as a chapel, it is even possible that it was built by Titu Cusi Yupanqui during his brief conversion to Christianity (around 1566–1570). We know that Titu Cusi Yupanqui, Marcos García, and Diego Ortiz built several small churches in the villages of the greater Vilcabamba region before 1570, including in Carco, Puquiura, and Huarancalla[41] and in three other villages located between Vilcabamba and Ayacucho (Titu Cusi Yupanqui 2005:134 [1570]). Crosses were raised in a number of others. In short, given Titu Cusi Yupanqui's interest in Christian customs, he may have ordered a small chapel built beside a larger indigenous religious center in Espíritu Pampa sometime during his rule.[42]

Endnotes

1   This area of the Espíritu Pampa has had many names. Bingham (1914b) reported that the Campas, who are Machiguenga speakers, called it Tendi Pampa. Savoy (1970) referred to it as Bingham's Group, the Spanish Palace, and the Two Story Group. Lee (2000) refers to it as Group 21 and the Two Story Group. During the course of the excavations described in this report, the former Institutio National de Cultura Region Cusco called it Sector V. It is locally known as 14 Windows. For this report, we have decided to return to the name used by the Campas, Tendi Pampa.

2   None of the gables seen by Bingham during his visit has survived.

3   The compound was constructed in a nearly a northwest–southeast orientation, making references to the different sides difficult.

4   The Tendi Pampa compound is currently called 14 Windows, a name that appears to derive from these buildings.

5   These niches are irregularly spaced; they are not back to back along the shared wall of the two buildings.

6   Savoy (1970:97) also included a photograph of the interior of one of these buildings.

7   All structure measurements presented in this book represent internal dimensions.

8   Because of their volume, the north and south wall fall areas within this building were left in situ.

9   Since no testing was conducted, some of the objects described in this work as being composed of copper may be composed of bronze.

10   *Urpus* and *rakis* are large vessels used for storing grain and fermenting *chicha*. *Urpus* tend to have straighter sides and wider mouths, but in archaeological contexts, the two types of vessels are at times difficult to distinguish, so we have used the joint term *urpus/rakis* in this work.

11   A modern bullet casing was also recovered in the first level of excavation.

12   Concha de abanico; genus *Argopectens*.

13   Similar although not identical plates with human heads have been recovered elsewhere at Espíritu Pampa and in a tomb in Sacsayhuaman (see Julien 1989; Valcárcel 1934).

14   A small piece of bent copper was also recovered.

15   Examples of miniature polished black-ware plates have also been recovered in excavations in Vitcos (Rosaspata).

16   This number includes the remains of two polished black-ware plates.

17   AA 95803; calibrated 1478 (95.4 percent) to 1644 cal A.D.

18   AA 95804; calibrated 1457 (95.4 percent) to 1628 cal A.D.

19   The base of these was found still standing upright and supported by clay.

20   It is currently not clear if this copper lid is of Andean or European manufacture.

21   Similar stone supports have been found elsewhere in Espíritu Pampa.

22   Most recently, a set of nearly identical beads was found at the Glass Site in the southeastern United States (Georgia), which is believed to have been visited by de

Soto in 1539 (Ohlson 2014)

23 In the original 2008 field report, this building was labeled "Sector V (14 ventanas) Recinto J."

24 This building was excavated in 2008. In the original field report it was designated "Sector V (14 windows) Enclosure D."

25 It is worth noting that Bingham also recovered a stirrup-spout vessel at Machu Picchu.

26 It is likely that some of these sherds were from roof tiles.

27 Murúa lived in the Mercedarian monastery in Cusco from 1585 to 1588, perhaps even longer, and he was the parish priest of Curawasi on the southern edge of the Vilcabamba region in 1595 (Ossio 2008). So although Murúa was not a member of the 1572 raid into Vilcabamba, he had plenty of opportunity to learn about it from eyewitnesses.

28 "Tenía la casa el Ynga con altos y bajos cubierta de tejas y todo el palacio pintado con grande diferencia de pinturas a su usanza que era cosa muy de ver" (Murúa 1987:298 [1611–1616:Chapter 82]).

29 Building 5 yielded by far the greatest number of roof tiles (n = 900+), followed by Building 9 (n = 100+). However, in both of these cases, most of the tiles were found stacked on the floor, perhaps awaiting decoration.

30 Several hoards of gold and silver items, as well as fine textiles, were collected by the Spaniards as they were hunting down members of the royal court after the fall of Vilcabamba. Some of those items could have been removed from the Tendi Pampa compound before it was set alight.

31 Gonzalo Pizarro and Francisco de Villacastín entered the Vilcabamba region in 1539. After taking Vitcos they moved on to Pampaconas, and they may have even entered the city of Vilcabamba. They remained in the region for about two months before returning to Cusco.

32 "Caminando entraron a las diez del día en el pueblo de Vilca Bamba, todos a pie, que es tierra asperísima y fragosa y no para caballos de ninguna manera. Hallóse todo el pueblo saqueado, de suerte que si los españoles e indios amigos lo hubieran hecho no estuviera peor, porque los indios e indias se huyeron todos y se metieron en la montaña, llevando todo lo que pudieron. Lo demás de maíz y comida que estaba en los buhíos y depósitos, donde ellos los suelen guardar, lo quemaron y abrasaron, de suerte que estaba cuando el campo llegó humeando, y la casa del Sol donde estaba su principal ídolo quemada. Porque cuando entraron Gonzalo Pizarro y Villacastín hicieron lo mismo, y la falta de mantenimiento les forzó a volverse y dejarles la tierra

en su poder, entendieron asimismo que al presente los españoles, no hallando comidas ni con que sustentarse, se tornarían a salir de la tierra y no se quedarían en ella ni la poblarían, y con este intento se huyeron los indios, pegando fuego a todo lo que no pudieron llevar" (Murúa 1987:296–297 [1611–1616:Chapter 82]).

33 One looter's pit was dug near the center of Building 3, and there were a few other disturbed areas in other buildings. Several modern offerings had also been left at the site, but these did little damage.

34 The recovered ceramic remains can also be used to compare the similarity between buildings and to divide the structures into a limited number of groups based on their contents. For example, Room 11 contained a massive number of intact and broken vessels, and it appears to be an area for final food preparation and the initial stages of serving. It stands out as uniquely different in the sheer number and variety of vessels recovered within it. Among the other buildings, Rooms 5, 6, and 8 form a group. Like Building 11, these three buildings are found within the long structure that defines the east side of the compound. Although Room 6 stands out for its uniquely large number of drinking vessels, all three of these rooms contained a wide range of ceramic vessels and appear to have been involved in storage as well as food and drink preparation. With very little ceramics, Rooms 1, 2, 3, 4, 7, 9, and 10 can be considered another group. However, the scarcity of artifacts recovered in these seven rooms makes their functional identifications difficult.

35 "Y se mostraron los indios tan afables y amigos, que los dichos cuatro españoles llevaron una imagen de Nuestra Señora en un lienzo, y para encomendarse a Dios, mandaron a los indios que les hiciesen una capilla pequeña; y la hicieron, y pusieron la imagen, y una cruz grande fuera de la capilla, sobre una peana de piedras, y otras cruces pequeñas en la dicha capilla" (Ocampo Conejeros 2013:46 [1611]).

36 While we suggest that the Tendi Pampa compound served as a temple, a historical passage may argue against this stance. Military orders written in Cusco in March of 1573 instructed the few troops stationed in the Inca town of Vilcabamba to use the former Houses of the Sun as a fort: "For its security, it was agreed that a town would be established in Vilcabamba, which is twelve leagues from the site of Vitcos, being on the route of the Manarí Indians and other warring Indians, who usually come to the site of Vilcabamba, [and] that a fort should be made in the Houses of the Sun, and that a garrison stay there. To do this, Francisco de Camargo was named captain and *alcalde*" (Para la seguri-

dad del, se acordó quen Vilcabamba, que es doze leguas del dicho asiento de Viticos, por ser paso para los yndios Manaríes é otros de guerra que suelen venir al dicho asiento de Vilcabamba, se hiziese un fuerte en las casas del sol, é quedase gente de guarnición; é para ellose nombró Capitán é Alcalde al dicho Francisco de Camargo) (Maúrtua 1906:90; translation by the authors). We believe that these orders were not followed and that the Spaniards established a garrison elsewhere in the ruins, perhaps near the central plaza.

37 "Fueron presos el dicho Inga Topa Amaro y Quispi Tito y todos sus hermanos, deudos mugeres y hijos y capitanes y gente, é habido los cuerpos de Manco Inca é Titocuxi, sus padres y hermanos, y el ídolo de oro llamado Punchao ó Sol que antiguamente estaba en la Casa del Sol del Cusco, en quien todos estos Reinos adoraban, y lo habían llevado á la dicha provincia con tanto desservicio de Dios y objeto de la predicación del Santo Evangelio, le tenían casi cuarenta años había, sacrificando criaturas humanas, idolatrando é apostatando é haciendo apostatar á los indios ya bautizados, que allá iban y ellos prendían y llevaban de la tierra de paz, con otro ídolo que llamaban Pachamama, Madre de la Tierra, é otros muchos que fueron quemados e destruidos, y que habiéndole yo proveído Gobernador de aquella provincia, dejando en Vilcabamba hecha una fortaleza, y en ella alcalde y gente competente" (Toledo 1899:125–126).

38 These were later destroyed by Viceroy Toledo in Cusco (Bauer and Coello Rodríguez 2007).

39 "Embalsamaron su cuerpo los indios, y llevado a Vilcabamba, lo pusieron en el templo del sol, adonde fue hallado por los españoles en el tiempo del virrey don Fráncico de Toledo, conquistada aquella provincial" (Cobo 1964:102 [1653]).

40 The capturing of the gold sun image by the Spanish is widely noted by chroniclers. However, the seizure of its silver female counterpart is almost never mentioned.

41 Also spelled Rayancalla.

42 Titu Cusi Yupanqui (2005:134 [1570]) reports that he did not let the Augustinians Marcos García and Diego Ortiz into the town of Vilcabamba when they visited the settlement in January and February of 1570 since indigenous rituals were still being carried out there, but this does not preclude the existence of a chapel near the Sun Temple. Furthermore, it should be noted that Murúa (1987:270 [1611–1616:Chapter 70]) states that Christianity was never introduced into the Inca city of Vilcabamba. We believe that Building 4 at Tendi Pampa, with its unusual shape and its tile floor, stands in contradiction to Murúa's statement.

Chapter 6

Other Excavations at Espíritu Pampa in 2008 and 2009

Javier Fonseca Santa Cruz and Brian S. Bauer

DURING THE 2008 AND 2009 archaeological field seasons at Espíritu Pampa, four other sectors of the site besides Tendi Pampa were sampled. The excavations, supported by the former Instituto Nacional de Cultura Region Cusco and directed by Javier Fonseca Santa Cruz, took place in five buildings in the New Sector, one building in the Southeast Sector, and two buildings in the Entrance Terrace. Lastly, four additional units were dug in the central plaza. The results of these excavations are outlined below.

Excavations in the New Sector

A walled compound with five associated buildings, approximately 250 m southwest of the central plaza, has been classified as the New Sector by the former Instituto Nacional de Cultura Region Cusco. The compound was first noted, and perhaps partially cleared, by Savoy (1970:103), who observed that one of the buildings (here marked Building E) was built with finely fitted stone blocks (Figure 6.1).[1]

The compound wall of the New Sector is rectangular in shape, with a small notch in its southern corner. An internal wall with a central doorway divides the compound into two roughly equal halves. This wall is newer than the other parts of the compound. Each of the five rooms associated with the compound has off-center doorways, and excavations revealed that several contain internal walls. This type of building construction is unusual for Inca settlements and may reflect a late, post-contact architectural style.

There is a pair of attached buildings on the southeastern side of the compound (Buildings A and B) and a single structure on the northwestern side (Building D). There is also a larger structure adjacent to the north corner of the compound (Building C). The compound wall and those of these four buildings are made with river and quarried stones held together with a weak clay mortar. The corners, doorways, and niches of the buildings are constructed of slightly better stone blocks than the other parts. The doorways are slightly trapezoidal.

A short distance downslope, to the northwest of the compound, is the most notable structure of the cluster. Its low foundation walls are constructed of finely crafted stone blocks set together without mortar (Building E). There are a few isolated buildings and terraces farther downslope, but these have not between cleared or investigated. Excavations in the New Sector were conducted in 2008 and 2009.

BUILDING A

The 2009 excavations began in the two adjacent buildings on the southeastern side of the compound. Build-

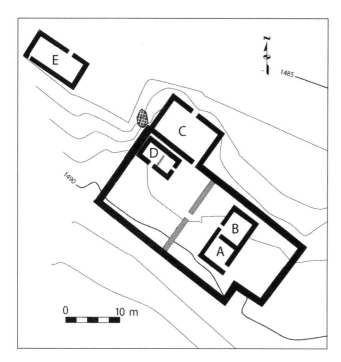

Figure 6.1. The five buildings of the New Sector (A–E) were excavated in 2008 and 2009 (map by Gabriel E. Cantarutti).

ing A measured some 7 x 6.8 m, with walls that stood up to 2.6 m high.[2] The structure has an external southeastern entrance and an internal passageway that connects it with the adjacent room. At the time of the investigation, a 1.5 m wide looter's pit could be seen in the room (Figure 6.2).

In preparation for the excavation, the interior of Building A was divided into six equally sized units. The first excavation level included the dark brown, organically rich soil that covers the site. No artifacts were found in this level. The second excavation level was composed of a more compact soil from melted adobes, eroded wall mortar, and fallen wall stones. The removal of this level revealed various interior features of the building, including a narrow (.3 m), long (4 m) wall, built to establish a hallway between Buildings A and B. A second narrower (.25 m), shorter (2.5 m), and less substantial division stands to the east of the hallway. A stone platform, once covered with clay plaster, was found abutting the south wall of the building, and a narrow bench was documented along the north wall.

A thick level of burnt material covered much of the floor, indicating that Building A had been burned. The shattered remains of an aryballos were found at the end of the hallway, and a nearly complete jug, resting upside down, was recovered near the center of the room. Fragments of both a large storage vessel (*urpu*) and an aryballos were noted smashed together in the southeastern corner of the room, perhaps reflecting an act of looting or post-abandonment vandalism. Part of a strainer

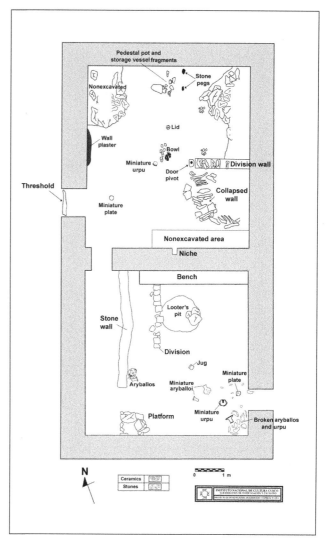

Figure 6.2. Buildings A and B in the New Sector at Espíritu Pampa (Ministerio de Cultura; redrawn by Gabriel E. Cantarutti).

(*colander*), a miniature plate, a miniature *urpu*, and two miniature aryballoi were also recovered on the floor of the building (Figures 6.3 and 6.4).

Given that Building A contained fragments of at least two storage vessels (n = 60; 92 percent), a fragment of a strainer (n = 1; 2 percent), and an intact jug, it appears that liquids (presumably *chicha*) were being prepared in the room. Furthermore, the narrow bench that runs along the north wall suggests that various individuals were expected to be in the room at the same time, perhaps being served. However, the recovery of four miniature vessels indicates that other activities also occurred in the room.

BUILDING B

Building B measures about 8 x 7 m and contains one slightly off-center exterior entrance along its west wall and an interior passageway leading into the adjacent

Figure 6.3. A nearly intact jug was recovered in Building A (Museo Amazónico Andino Qhapaq Ñan de Quillabamba; photograph by Brian S. Bauer).

Figure 6.4. Three miniature aryballoi from the New Sector at Espíritu Pampa. The left and central aryballoi were found in Building A. The right aryballos was recovered in Building D (Museo Amazónico Andino Qhapaq Ñan de Quillabamba; photograph by Brian S. Bauer).

room (Building A) along its south wall.[3] The south wall of Building B, which separates Buildings A and B, also contains an unusually narrow (15 cm at the base) and tall (90 cm) trapezoidal niche. This niche is reminiscent of the two niches that flank the doorway of Building 5 in the Tendi Pampa compound.

Before investigations began, Building B was divided into nine units. However, not all of these units were excavated, because several wall sections were unstable. After the removal of surface vegetation, some patches of plaster could still be seen on the interior walls. Additional wall plaster was noted still attached to parts of the west wall, which had collapsed into the building. The recovery of intact plaster on the collapsed wall indicates that it fell as a single unit.

The removal of the first excavation level revealed several small concentrations of ceramics and a short (1.65 m), narrow (.35 m) internal wall. Two upright-standing stone supports were found in the floor near the north wall. The ends of the slabs were worked into small protuberances, presumably to better fit a wooden crossbar.

The second excavation level revealed the original hard-packed earth floor and the remains of various ceramic vessels. A shattered short-necked, medium-sized storage vessel and a pedestal pot were found near the two standing stone slabs. A miniature *urpu* and a straight-sided bowl were found near the center of the room. The bowl, which is painted red, is especially striking, with cotton plants painted in cream and black in its interior and a pair of modeled snakes running along its rim (Figure 6.5). A miniature plate was also recovered on the floor near the entrance of the building, and a fragmented lid and plate were found elsewhere in the building (Figure 6.6). Other notable artifacts included a flat stone with a hole bored through its center, found at the end of the interior wall near the center of the room. A

Figure 6.5 A straight-sided bowl from Building B. This vessel has snakes on its rim and four cotton plants painted in its center (Museo Amazónico Andino Qhapaq Ñan de Quillabamba; photograph by Brian S. Bauer).

Figure 6.6. Two miniature plates from the New Sector. The plate on the left is from Building A. The plate on the right is from Building B (Museo Amazónico Andino Qhapaq Ñan de Quillabamba; photograph by Brian S. Bauer).

similar stone was recovered in the Tendi Pampa compound and is believed to have served as a door pivot. Enough carbon was found resting on the floor to indicate that the building had burned.

In all Building B contained a limited number and a rather unusual combination of vessels, with sherds from a medium-sized storage vessel (n = 36; 64 percent), a pedestal pot (n = 11; 21 percent), a plate (n = 9; 16 percent), a straight-sided bowl, and a lid. A miniature *urpu* and a miniature plate were also found. The function of the room is not easily determined from this eclectic assortment of artifacts.

BUILDING C

Building C is a relatively large building, measuring about 13.8 x 9 m, built adjacent to the compound wall.[4] The structure contains a slightly off-center door along

its north wall and a second door leading into the patio area in its southeastern corner. It is possible that there were several internal niches—perhaps three—along the south wall. However, the building's poor state of preservation makes this determination difficult.

Before excavations began, a grid of 18 equally sized units was set within the building.[5] However, the excavation results were very limited. A line of three looter's pits, each measuring about 60 cm in diameter, was found crossing the center of the building. Since all three of these pits were dug in areas of the building that lacked wall fall, they appear to have been dug after the walls collapsed (Figure 6.7). Building C also yielded a small number (n = 25) of ceramic fragments, which appear to have come from one or two cooking vessels and a plate. Although the large size of the building suggests that it was not a domestic structure, its function remains unknown.

Figure 6.7. Building C during excavations. Note the looter's pits running down the center of the building. Areas of the building that contained extensive wall fall were not excavated (Ministerio de Cultura; photograph by Javier Fonseca Santa Cruz).

BUILDING D

Building D measures about 9.6 x 5.8 m and is located on the west side of the walled compound. The walls of this building are poorly preserved, and a large tree stands near its southeastern corner. The building contains a slightly off-center doorway, which leads to the plaza. The interior of Building D was divided into eight equally sized units for excavation.

As surface vegetation was removed from the interior of the building, a looter's pit was noted near the north corner. It was also revealed that the upper portions of Building D were constructed with adobes made from a yellowish clay;[6] many of which had collapsed into the building's interior. Despite the heavy rains of the Vilcabamba region, individual adobe blocks could still be identified. Mounds of adobes and melted adobe were especially pronounced in the south and west corners and along the north wall of the building. Several long stone slabs were found on the floor of the building. The size and spacing of these slabs suggest that they were niche lintels that fell into the building as the adobe sections of the walls deteriorated.

The excavations within the building exposed a narrow (3 cm) internal wall that divided Building D into two rooms (Figures 6.8 and 6.9). This internal wall ended 40 cm before it met with the back wall of the structure, leaving a narrow passageway between the two rooms. Enough carbon was recovered from the floors of both rooms to suggest that the building had burned.

The room of the building that includes the entrance to the plaza contained a number of interesting features and artifacts. Two upright-standing stone supports were found placed vertically into the floor in the north corner. The ends of the slabs were worked into small protuberances and are believed to have supported a wooden crossbar. Notable artifacts that were recov-

Figure 6.8. Building D. Note the looter's pit, the division wall, and the fallen lintels. Preserved adobes can also be seen near the looter's pit and in the south corner (upper right) of the building (Ministerio de Cultura; photograph by Javier Fonseca Santa Cruz).

ered scattered across the floor included a lid, an iron nail, a rhombus-shaped clay whistle (Figure 6.10), and a small (5 x 2.5 cm) figurine of what appears to be a bird in flight (Figure 6.11). There was also a cluster of miniature vessels on the floor near the entrance. It included an *urpu*, two *urpus* with lids (Figure 6.12), a jar, a plate (Figure 6.13), a pot with a lid, and a polished black-ware pot.

The other side of Building D displayed patches of a well-prepared orange-clay floor. A fragmented miniature plate was recovered near the northeastern corner of the building. Most importantly, a straight-sided bowl (*caserola*) and a highly oxidized pair of scissors were

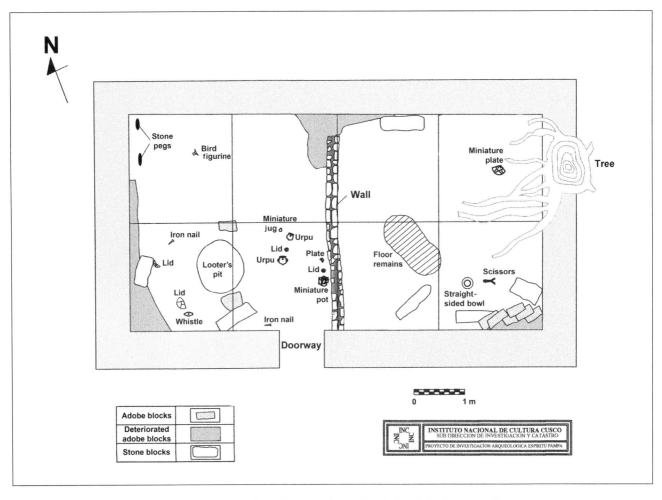

Figure 6.9. Plan of Building D (Ministerio de Cultura; redrawn by Gabriel E. Cantarutti).

Figure 6.10. A rhombus-shaped clay whistle from Building D (Museo Amazónico Andino Qhapaq Ñan de Quillabamba; photograph by Brian S. Bauer).

Figure 6.11. A bird-in-flight figurine from Building D (Museo Amazónico Andino Qhapaq Ñan de Quillabamba; photograph by Brian S. Bauer).

Figure 6.12. Two miniature *urpus* found in Building D (Museo Amazónico Andino Qhapaq Ñan de Quillabamba; photograph by Brian S. Bauer).

Figure 6.13. Miniature plates found in Building D (Museo Amazónico Andino Qhapaq Ñan de Quillabamba; photograph by Brian S. Bauer).

found on the floor near the center of the room (Figure 6.14). The recovery of scissors at the site of Espíritu Pampa is intriguing.[7] Garcilaso de la Vega (1966:55 [1609:Part 1, Book 1, Chapter 12]) singles out scissors as being especially valued by the Inca. He recalled that a schoolfellow jokingly stated, "If the Spaniards, your fathers, had done no more than bring us scissors, mirrors, and combs, we would have given them all the gold and silver we had in our land." We also know that scissors were traded into the Vilcabamba region, as Diego Rodríguez de Figueroa (1910 [1565]) specifically men-

tions that he brought three pairs into Vilcabamba to give to Titu Cusi Yupanqui.

In summary, the excavations in Building D of the New Sector provided a small number of ceramic fragments (n = 27), including a plate (n = 6; 22 percent), a straight-sided bowl (n = 12; 44 percent), and a lid (n = 9; 33 percent). Eight miniature vessels, two miniature lids, a ceramic bird-in-flight figurine, and a clay whistle were also recovered. Items of European import included an iron nail and a pair of iron scissors. There was no evidence of food storage or preparation. Although the function of the building is not clear, it is certain that this was not a domestic dwelling. The recovery of many miniature vessels, the whistle, the figurine, and the scissors mark the building as one of special use.

BUILDING E

Building E, which measures approximately 11.5 x 5.5 m, was excavated in 2008.[8] The building contains two doorways, both with stone thresholds. One door is built slightly off center, in the north wall, while the other is located near the southwestern corner of the building. The walls of Building E are made with mortarless cut-stone granite blocks. The foundation is low, standing between .2 m and 1.15 m high. Unlike the other rectangular buildings found at the site of Espíritu Pampa, the interior of Building E was not filled with a large quantity of stone from collapsed walls.

Building E was divided into 10 units before excavations began. The excavations revealed the remains of at least five large storage vessels and a small number of other vessels scattered across the floor. The low-standing walls and the lack of wall fall within the structure suggest that Building E was not complete when the city was abandoned (Figure 6.15). Alternatively, the walls of the building could have been completed with perishable materials or even adobe. However, this explanation seems at odds with the finely worked stones that make up the building's foundation. Furthermore, unlike the other buildings in the New Sector, no evidence of roof burning was noted when Building E was excavated. Because of the unfinished nature of this building, is worth noting that Túpac Amaru had held the title of Inca for less than two years before the 1572 Spanish raid on the city. While speculative, it possible that this unfinished building of fine stonework was related to his newly achieved position as Inca and its construction was cut short by the fall of Vilcabamba.

Excavations in the Central Plaza (2008 and 2009)

Like most Inca installations, Espíritu Pampa contains a large central plaza. One end of the plaza is defined by the walled Palace Compound, and the other end is delineated by the raised platform commonly called the Ushnu. The northwestern side of the central plaza is marked by the Kallanka, a building more than 80 m long with 12 doors on each side. The southeastern side of the plaza is delineated by a terrace and a steep bank that leads to the buildings of the Southeast Sector. The plaza was leveled by the Incas during the construction of the central core of Espíritu Pampa.

This large open space was a major feature of the city. Assemblies, celebrations, and ritual performances took place in the plaza during Inca times. Furthermore, Murúa mentions that the plaza was so large that horse races were held in it. It was in this plaza that Pedro Sarmiento de Gamboa (1977 [1572]) planted the Spanish flag on June 24, 1572, claiming the city for the Crown. It was also in this plaza that Martín

Figure 6.14. The remains of a straight-sided bowl (*caserola*) and a pair of scissors were found on the floor of Building D. Note the fallen lintel stones and the preserved adobe blocks in the corner of the building (Ministerio de Cultura; photograph by Javier Fonseca Santa Cruz).

Figure 6.15. Building E in 2010. Unlike the other rectangular buildings in the core area of Espíritu Pampa, the interior of Building E was free of wall collapse. We believe that the building was being constructed when the Spaniards entered the city (photograph by Brian S. Bauer and Miriam Aráoz Silva).

Hurtado de Arbieto held a meeting on August 8, 1572, to announce his governorship of the Vilcabamba region (Maúrtua 1906:218–220).

The plaza of Espíritu Pampa is so large and the tree cover was so dense that it may not have been recognized as a public gathering place when the site was first visited in the early twentieth century. In other words, while Bingham walked across the plaza and noted the many buildings that surrounded it, he may not have recognized that the plaza itself was an architectural feature of the former city.

To better understand the activities that once occurred within the plaza and to test for evidence of earlier occupations, Javier Fonseca Santa Cruz excavated four units within it in 2008 and 2009. In 2008 a trench measuring 2 x 10 m was dug near the midpoint of the plaza.[9] As the first excavation level, composed of a dark brown organically rich soil, was removed, several small boulders and large roots were exposed. The second excavation level included a semicompact dark yellow soil

with increasing amounts of gravel. Areas of bedrock and dense deposits of gravel were found across the unit, while the southeastern corner of the trench exposed the foundation of what appeared to be a circular structure. The foundation wall, built of two courses of stone, measured about 25 cm high and 30 cm wide. The interior of the structure contained a large number of small, round cobbles, ranging in size from 3 cm to 5 cm, and small pieces of slate. A few fragments of Inca-style pottery were recovered inside the building and across the unit. Although speculative, we suggest that the structure served as an expedient storage area for lithic materials, perhaps even for rocks meant to be used as sling stones as the Spanish forces approached the settlement.

In 2009, three additional 4 x 2 m excavations were dug in the plaza. One of these excavation units was placed alongside the 2008 trench, while the other two were situated elsewhere in the plaza. None of the units yielded ceramic materials. The excavation beside the 2008 trench confirmed the circular shape of the struc-

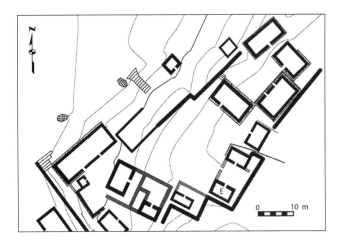

Figure 6.16. One building in the Southeast Sector was excavated in 2008 (map by Gabriel E. Cantarutti).

ture and revealed that the rest of its interior was also filled with small river stones and pieces of slate. As with other excavations described in this report, none of the plaza excavations provided evidence of any pre-Inca occupation at the site.

Excavations in the Southeast Sector (2008)

A structure in the Southeast Sector, labeled Building E, was excavated by Javier Fonseca Santa Cruz in 2008. It is one of a pair of structures built on a rectangular platform just above the stream (Figure 6.16). The building measures about 6.8 x 4 m and has a single doorway facing a small patio area. Its walls are poorly preserved, standing less than 1 m high.

Before research began, the building was divided into six equally sized units. With the removal of the surface vegetation, it became clear that the interior walls of the building had been covered with a clay plaster. There may also have been a prepared floor in the building, but this was more difficult to determine because of root damage.

Excavations revealed that a series of six upright-standing stone supports, forming a rectangle, were placed vertically into the floor at one end of the building. Some of these supports had been pulled from their settings, and the tops of others were broken. Nevertheless, it is clear that a wooden structure, perhaps a bed, once occupied that side of the room. A light scatter of domestic ceramics was recovered on the floor of the building. The excavation also found enough carbon on the floor to suggest that the building was burned. From the evidence recovered, it seems likely that this was a residential structure.

Excavations in the Entrance Terrace (2009)

As one approaches the center of Espíritu Pampa, there is small cluster of four buildings on an irregularly shaped terrace just below the modern trail. The terrace stands more than 2 m high, and a set of stairs leads to another, more rectangular terrace downslope. The buildings on the upper terrace are poorly preserved, with walls standing less than 1.5 m high. The two largest buildings are situated end to end and run parallel to the trail. They each contain single entrances. A smaller building runs perpendicular to these two larger buildings. There is also a much smaller building, with narrower walls, near the center of the terrace. This smaller structure is less substantial than the other buildings and may be a later construction. There are no previous descriptions of these terraces and buildings, although they do appear on Lee's (2000) and Sakai's (2009) Espíritu Pampa maps.

Two buildings in this cluster were excavated in 2009 under the direction of Javier Fonseca Santa Cruz (Figure 6.17). No carbon was found during the excavations, suggesting that this area of the site was spared the 1572 fire that destroyed many other buildings at the site. The first building excavated, identified here as Unit 15, was one of the larger structures along the trail. The building measures about 11.45 x 6.4 m, and it was divided into six equally sized units before research began. A few pieces of ceramics were visible in the humus at the time of the excavation. The first level, composed of an organically rich dark brown soil, contained several small

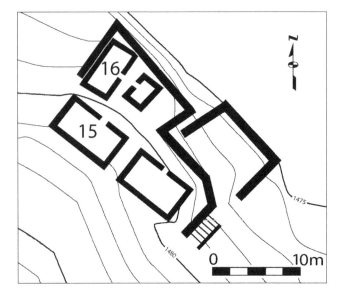

Figure 6.17 Two buildings within the Entrance Terrace were excavated in 2009.

Figure 6.18. A large jug recovered from Unit 15 in 2009. (Museo Amazónico Andino Qhapaq Ñan de Quillabamba; photograph by Brian S. Bauer).

clusters of ceramics, all of which continued into the following level. The second excavation level was composed of a harder-packed yellow-brown loam and debris from the collapsed structure that rested above the original floor of the building.

A series of large ceramic concentrations, totaling some 727 fragments, was found within the building. These concentrations contained a limited range and a relatively small number of vessels. The majority of the fragments came from large storage vessels (n = 681; 94 percent). A small number of cooking pot (n = 39; .05 percent) and jug (n = 8; .01 percent) fragments were also identified. From the distribution of the sherds, it appears that at least four of the large storage vessels (aryballoi or *urpus/rakis*) stood along the south wall of the building and that two more large storage vessels stood along the west wall. A nearly complete jug was also found along the south wall. This jug may have been used to decant *chicha* that was fermented and stored in the largest vessels (Figure 6.18). The poorly preserved remains of a wooden drinking vessel (*kero*) were found in the center of the building, near the doorway. Like the wooden drinking vessel recovered in the Tendi Pampa complex, it was decorated with geometric designs. No roof tile fragments were found.

The second building excavated in 2009 was on the west side of the terrace. Recorded as Unit 2009:16, the structure measures approximately 7.7 x 5 m. Before the excavation began, the interior of the building was divided into eight equally sized units. As the wall fall was being cleared, several large stone slabs were noted and removed. The recovery of these stones suggests that there were once interior niches in this building. The excavation proceeded in a single level and recovered a relatively small number of ceramic fragments (n = 140). These fragments were from one, perhaps two, large storage vessels (n = 125; 89 percent), a pedestal pot (n = 9; .06 percent), and a plate (n = 5; 4 percent). A small number of clay roof tile fragments (n = 5) were also noted.

In summary, it appears that at the time of site abandonment, the two excavated structures on the entrance terrace held several large storage vessels and a small number of cooking and serving vessels. The limited range of vessels implies that these buildings were not domestic cooking dwellings. It seems most likely that they were being used for storage and perhaps brewing.

Endnotes

1. The mortarless masonry of this building was also noted by Lee (2000:414).
2. In the 2009 Institutio National de Cultura report, this building is referred to as Unit 17.
3. In the 2009 Institutio National de Cultura report, this building is referred to as Unit 18.
4. In the 2009 Institutio National de Cultura report, this building is referred to as Unit 19.
5. Because of the instability of the walls, not all of these units were excavated completely.
6. This may have also been the case at other buildings at the site of Espíritu Pampa. However, the heavy rainy seasons in the region make this assessment difficult.
7. It is always possible that the scissors postdate the abandonment of the structure. However, given that they were found directly on the floor of the building alongside Inca ceramics, this seems unlikely.
8. In the 2008 Ministerio de Cultura report, this excavation is labeled UE 04.
9. The northeastern corner: 06945.46 E; 85739.54 N.

Chapter 7

Excavations Conducted at Espíritu Pampa in 2010

Brian S. Bauer and **Miriam Aráoz Silva**

I N 2010 WE CONDUCTED two months of archaeological research at the site of Espíritu Pampa. During the first part of the field season, we spent approximately three weeks making a map of the monumental core of the site with the use of a total station, and we documented the locations of a large number of outlying structures with the use of global positioning systems. (See Figure 4.1.) During the second part of the field season, approximately six weeks were spent conducting excavations within various buildings. The following year, 2011, we conducted our laboratory analysis in Cusco on the materials recovered during our 2010 fieldwork.[1] At that time, we also began working with Javier Fonseca Santa Cruz, who had already spent several field seasons at the site. During 2012 we continued our laboratory analysis in Cusco and visited several storage areas where Espíritu Pampa materials were held.

The 2010 excavation work at Espíritu Pampa focused on obtaining new information about the last capital of the Inca Empire and testing unknown areas within this historically important city. From the broadest perspective, we wanted to better our understanding of the everyday conditions that the people of the Vilcabamba region experienced during the first several decades of European–American contact. Earlier maps of the site of Espíritu Pampa indicated that it was composed of numerous buildings organized into various sectors. We wanted to test different areas of the city and compare the results with areas previously studied by the Ministerio de Cultura. As research by Javier Fonseca Santa Cruz had shown that the Tendi Pampa compound had burned in a single event and that the interiors of its buildings were exceptionally well preserved, we felt that there was a strong possibility that other areas of the town also remained in good condition. Such preservation would help us explore the impact that European influence and trade goods had had in different areas of the city.

We selected to excavate six closely spaced structures located just upslope from the principal trail leading to the center of the site. Three of these excavations (Units 1, 4, and 6) took place within a set of rectangular buildings grouped around a patio (*cancha*), while the other three excavations (Units 2, 3, and 5) were conducted within a nearby large multiroom building that we named the Hall of the Miniatures. One additional excavation (Unit 7) was placed within the Kallanka, beside the central plaza.

The buildings tested in Units 1 through 6 were first cleared of the small trees, ferns, brush, and other plants that had grown within them since the area had last been cleared, approximately three years before. No large trees were cut, although several large fallen logs were

Figure 7.1. In 2010 a 4 x 7.5 m unit was excavated near the northern end of the Kallanka. Note the small cluster of stones on the left side of the excavation unit. The large stone of the central plaza can be seen in the background (photograph by Brian S. Bauer and Miriam Aráoz Silva).

removed. The excavations took place with the use of trowels and brushes only. The excavations proceeded in 10-cm levels or until a natural soil change was detected. All earth removed during the excavations was screened through 1/4-inch wire mesh. Ten-liter flotation samples were collected from all features and floors as well as from each excavation level.[2] After the excavations were finished, profiles were drawn, final photographs were taken, and the units were backfilled. During our project, we left 50 percent or more of the interiors of the selected buildings unexcavated for future research. Our excavations have helped confirm that although the site is currently covered with dense vegetation, it is exceptionally well preserved. Most importantly, intact Inca floors were found within 30 cm of the modern ground surface in all sampled structures. These floors contained a wide range of artifacts that had remained largely undisturbed since the time of site abandonment (June 24, 1572).

During our work at the site of Espíritu Pampa, information for each level was recorded on standardized level forms. Separate forms were filled out for features, carbon samples, and flotation samples. The recovered artifacts from each level or feature were separated by type (ceramic, bone, lithic, carbon, and so on) and bagged in the field for transport to the laboratory. Each category of artifact was assigned a unique bag number, and the site, level, date, and artifact type were recorded. The bag numbering system was also used to designate bulk soil collections as well as unique items recovered in the course of the excavations. For example, metal objects and other uniquely important artifacts were placed in individual bags and their locations were plotted on the excavation drawings and forms. Identified but broken vessels were also bagged separately and given their own bag numbers. In the laboratory, the artifacts were washed, counted, weighed, cataloged, and coded with identifying numbers.

The bulk of the materials recovered during the excavations were placed in wooden boxes and deposited in the Ministerio de Cultura's storage facility near the site. Only a limited number of items were taken to

Cusco, since they needed to be transported four hours by horse from Espíritu Pampa to Azulmayo and then shipped some six hours by truck to Quillabamba and then on to Cusco. At the close of the project, the artifacts recovered during our fieldwork at Espíritu Pampa and taken to Cusco were deposited in the Ministerio de Cultura in specially constructed wooden containers for permanent storage.[3]

Our work at the site used the well-established pottery sequence and ceramic vessel types defined by researchers working in the Cusco region (e.g., Bauer 1999; Julien 1989; Rowe 1946). Vessel forms were linked to functional classifications and used to analyze activities that occurred at the site. This type of classification was first developed by Morris at the Inca site of Huánuco Pampa (1971; Morris et al. 2011) and is now

a widely used research tool. Carbon samples were collected during the excavation; a select number were sent to the University of Arizona for radiocarbon dating using accelerator mass spectrometry (AMS).

The 2010 Excavations in the Kallanka

During the 2010 field season, we placed one excavation unit within the structure commonly referred to as the Kallanka. This building, located on the edge of the central plaza, is approximately 80 m long and 7.5 m wide. With its great size, the building dominates the central core of the city. The building was cleared in the first decade of the 2000s. Pilares Daza dug four test excavations within it in 2004.

Our excavation (Unit 7) consisted of a 4-x-7.5-m excavation placed approximately 10.5 m from the north end of the Kallanka (Figure 7.1). The previous clearance of the building had removed much of the wall fall, so the floor of the building was found less than 15 cm beneath the modern ground level. The floor was especially well made, consisting of hard-packed earth and small stones. There were also areas of dark red clay and a dark red cement-like material made with gravel, sand, and a binding agent. It is possible that knowledge of the cement was acquired by the Incas from the Spaniards and that, when needed, areas of the floor were patched with this new material.

Only a few small ceramic fragments were recovered on the floor of the Kallanka, suggesting that a previous clearance of the building by the Ministerio de Cultura had removed its occupation level. Nevertheless, a small circle of stones was found tangent to the western wall and above the Inca floor. Within this circle was the neck of a small, elegant *tikachurana* made of a polished black-ware (Figure 7.2). As the *tikachurana* neck had been placed among the stones, like an offering, it is clear that this feature dates to after the site was abandoned. No other features or objects were found during the excavation.

Figure 7.2. The neck of a polished, black-ware *tikachurana* was found within the circle of stones in the Kallanka (photograph by Brian S. Bauer and Miriam Aráoz Silva).

Excavations in the Hall of the Miniatures

During our time at Espíritu Pampa, we conducted three excavations within the Hall of the Miniatures. This building is composed of twin rectangular galleries, set back to back, with an attached cluster of four much smaller rectangular rooms. The two largest rooms are unusually long and narrow, each measuring approxi-

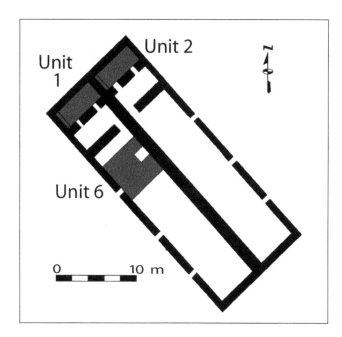

Figure 7.3. The Hall of the Miniatures at Espíritu Pampa; Units 1, 2, and 6 (map by Brian S. Bauer and Miriam Aráoz Silva).

mately 21 x 4.5 m. The exterior wall of the building is approximately .70 m wide, while the central wall, which divides the building into two symmetrical halves, measures about 1.5 m. Both of the two large rooms contain three slightly trapezoidal doorways on their exterior walls and narrower corner doors that led to the suite of smaller rooms. There is also a well-defined platform with a terrace wall near the building. Although double structures are common at Inca sites in general, the form of this building, with a suite of four adjacent rooms, is unusual. As a result, we placed three excavations units (Units 1, 2, and 6) within this structure to gain information on its original function (Figure 7.3).

RESULTS OF UNIT 1

Unit 1 consisted of one of the four relatively small (5 x 2.5 m) rectangular rooms attached to the northwestern end of the Hall of the Miniatures (Figure 7.4). The room contains two narrow doorways (70 cm) on one side and no evidence of internal niches. The walls are

Figure 7.4. Units 1 and 2 before excavation (photograph by Brian S. Bauer and Miriam Aráoz Silva).

poorly preserved, standing about 1 to 1.5 m high. At the time of the excavation, the room was covered with a thick layer of humus (Level 1), and the walls had fallen inward. With the removal of the wall collapse (Level 2), a narrow bench (approximately 40 cm high and 50 cm wide) was revealed along one end of the room. The bench and a few interior areas of the wall were still covered with a dark red plaster. While the southwestern half of the building yielded no artifacts, excavations in the northeastern half exposed a burnt floor area, which most likely resulted from an informal hearth. In this same area, four broken but largely complete ceramic vessels were recovered: a plate, a cooking pot, a straight-sided bowl, and a unique triangularly shaped vessel. The incidental nature of the floor burning and its location in front of one of the doorways suggest that the hearth was not an original feature of the room. We suspect that it, and the associated vessels, represents a brief reuse of the building after the site was abandoned (Figure 7.5).

RESULTS OF UNIT 2

Unit 2 encompassed the second of the four nearly identical rooms at the northwestern end of the Hall of the Miniatures. Like the work done in Unit 1, the excavation in this room revealed a narrow bench, covered with plaster, at one end of the room. The excavation also yielded a very limited although intriguing set of artifacts. A small nodule of worked clear glass was found near the interface of the wall fall and the floor (Figure 7.6). Although the context of the glass is somewhat problematic, it is important to note that glass objects were common trade items between Europeans and Andeans. For example, Diego Rodríguez (1910 [1565]) brought several glass objects into Vilcabamba as gifts. Given the rarity and special qualities of glass, even a fragment such as this might have held value for the Incas.

Two metal objects of European origin were also found on the floor of the room (Figures 7.7 and 7.8). The first was a small (1 cm), badly preserved piece of bent copper with a rivet. The second was a small (2 cm) copper hinge that still contained two copper nails (4 cm and 6 cm). Part of a cooking vessel and a fragment of a small, finely made straight-sided bowl were also found on the floor near the copper objects. No roof tile remains were recovered in either Units 1 or 2.

The dearth of artifacts recovered in Units 1 and 2 complicates our interpretation of these small rooms. Given the lack of storage vessels and the small number of cooking and serving vessels, we suggest that these rooms were not

Figure 7.5. Unit 1 after excavation. Note the bench at the far end of the room and the remains of a hearth in the foreground (photograph by Brian S. Bauer and Miriam Aráoz Silva).

Figure 7.6. A worked piece of clear glass was found in Unit 2 (photograph by Brian S. Bauer and Miriam Aráoz Silva).

Figure 7.7. A piece of bent copper with a rivet recovered in Unit 2 (photograph by Brian S. Bauer and Miriam Aráoz Silva).

used for the storage or preparation of food. In contrast, the three European items (a piece of clear glass and two copper objects) found in Unit 2 may suggest that at least one of the rooms was used to store valuable or rare objects.

RESULTS OF UNIT 5

Unit 5 was a 4 x 4.4 m excavation placed near the northwestern end of the western gallery of the Hall of the Miniatures.[4] At the time of the excavation, the exterior wall and much of the massive interior wall of the building had collapsed. Furthermore, several large matapalo roots crossed the interior of the building.

Figure 7.8. A copper hinge with nails recovered in Unit 2 (photograph by Brian S. Bauer and Miriam Aráoz Silva).

Nevertheless, with the removal of the humus layer, the original floor of the building was found less than 20 cm beneath the modern ground surface in the middle of the room (Figure 7.9). The removal of the humus and the areas of wall fall revealed several dense concentrations of shattered ceramic vessels near the center of the room and to a lesser extent along the west wall.

One complete, although broken, roof tile was found on the floor of the building, and the badly shattered remains of two or three other roof tiles were found scattered across the excavation area. While most of the ceramic vessels were badly crushed, we were able to estimate that the excavation area contained the remains of four or five large storage vessels (*urpus/rakis*), three plates (one with a pair of strap handles), and four cooking pots (Figures 7.10–7.12).

Unit 5 also exposed a large number of miniature vessels resting on the floor of the building (Figures 7.13–7.16). A cluster of nine intact miniature vessels was recovered on the floor in the northwestern corner of our excavation. Seven other miniature vessels were found within a mass of broken sherds near the center of the building. In total, we recovered at least six miniature plates, eight miniature lids, two miniature pedestal

Figure 7.9. (above) The northwestern end of the Hall of the Miniatures before excavations. The Inca floor was only 20 cm below the modern ground surface. Note the corner door, complete with lintel, in the upper-right corner of the room (photograph by Brian S. Bauer and Miriam Aráoz Silva).

Figure 7.10. (left) A complete but broken roof tile was recovered from the floor of the room (photograph by Brian S. Bauer and Miriam Aráoz Silva).

Figure 7.11. Unit 5 looking to the northwest. Note the dense concentration of ceramics in the foreground and the very thin soil profile at the back of the excavation (photograph by Brian S. Bauer and Miriam Aráoz Silva).

Figure 7.12. Unit 5 looking to the southeast. The complete but fragmented roof tile can be seen in the upper left (photograph by Brian S. Bauer and Miriam Aráoz Silva).

Figure 7.13. Two miniature pedestal vessels found in Unit 6 (photograph by Brian S. Bauer and Miriam Aráoz Silva).

Figure 7.14. Two miniature lids found in Unit 6 (photograph by Brian S. Bauer and Miriam Aráoz Silva).

Figure 7.15. A normal-sized plate recovered in Unit 4 and a miniature plate from Unit 6. (photograph by Brian S. Bauer and Miriam Aráoz Silva).

Figure 7.16. A normal-sized pedestal vessel from Unit 3 and a miniature pedestal vessel from Unit 6 (photograph by Brian S. Bauer and Miriam Aráoz Silva).

vessels, and two miniature storage vessels (*urpus*). Fragments of several other miniature vessels, mostly plates, were also recovered across the unit.[5] A charcoal sample (AA 95801), scraped from the exterior bottom of one of the pot sherds recovered in this building, yielded an AMS date of B.P. 352 ± 36 (1598 ± 36) and a calibrated range of A.D. 1481–1646 (95.4 percent). This date range is consistent with our presumed site abandonment date of 1572.

In summary, although our excavation unit represented less than 25 percent of the building, an impressive number and variety of vessels were recovered. These include a range of standard cooking, serving, and storage vessels as well as a host of miniature vessels. While isolated miniature vessels are occasionally found within Inca buildings, and groups of miniature vessels are commonly found within Inca offerings, it is unusual to find this many miniature vessels on the floor of a single structure. At this time, we can only suggest that a combination of food storage and meal preparation were occurring within the room, along with some other activities (ritual/play?) that required miniature vessels. Unfortunately, the exact nature of those activities remains unknown.

Excavations in the Lower Cancha

During the 2010 field season, we also conduct excavations (Units 3, 4, and 6) within three of the six structures grouped around what we call the Lower Cancha (Figure 7.17). The *cancha* is built on a platform constructed by the Incas by cutting into the gentle slope of the valley. There is a short set of stairs leading to the platform on the north side of the terrace, and its back wall is built along the slope cut on the south side. The two buildings on the east and west ends of the *cancha* are about the same size. There are two slightly larger buildings along the south side of the *cancha*, and there are two smaller buildings of differing size (4 x 6 m and 2 x 4 m) on the north side. All six of the buildings have single, slightly trapezoidal doors that open onto the patio.

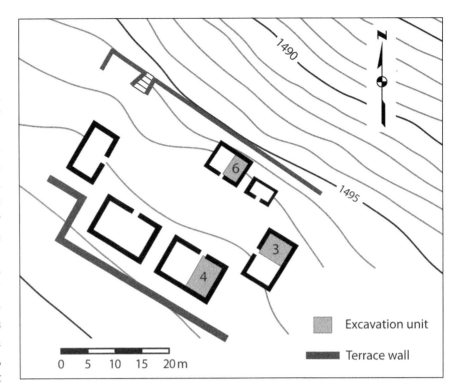

Figure 7.17. In 2010 three excavation units (3, 4, and 6) were placed in the Lower Cancha (map by Brian S. Bauer and Miriam Aráoz Silva).

RESULTS OF UNIT 3

Unit 3, measuring 4.6 x 4 m, covered half of the southeasternmost building of the Lower Cancha. At the time of our excavation, the west corner of the building was covered by a massive matapalo tree, and a medium-sized tree had grown near its east corner. The first excavation level included dense forest humus, 10 to 30 cm in depth, composed of fallen leaves, rotting branches, and roots. It lay directly above the collapsed interior walls of the building. As the humus was removed, small concentrations of ceramics were noted near the east and south corners of the unit. The second excavation level included the collapsed walls of the building. The west wall had fallen into the building. Its debris measured up to 70 cm in depth and covered much of the interior of the building. In contrast, the east wall had collapsed toward the exterior and had deposited far less material in the building. As the second level was removed, the remains of one, perhaps two, large storage vessels (*urpus/rakis*) were exposed in the north corner of the building. Fragments of other large and small vessels appeared among the roots of the medium-sized tree and within the wall fall near the south corner of the unit. The position of these fragments, resting above the floor and mixed within the matrix of the wall fall, suggests that they were moved from their original positions within the structure after it was abandoned, perhaps the result of minor looting activities or of being casually cast aside by curious intruders over the centuries.

With the removal of the wall collapse, several clusters of ceramics appeared in different areas of the building. A dense collection of fragments, including the necks and body fragments of two aryballoi, was found near the south corner of the excavation unit (Figure 7.18). A third aryballos neck was recorded near the west wall, and a number of fragments from a mixed variety of vessels were recovered spread across the unit.

The third level consisted of a 10- to 15-cm stratum of eroded mortar and wall plaster, which rested directly above the uneven, earthen floor of the structure. In some areas, the floor included a hard-packed, dark red clay (7.5 YR 4/6 strong brown), while in others it was composed of gravel and small stones. A large number of ceramic fragments were scattered across the floor. Although concentrations of ceramics marked the probable loci of a number of vessels, no intact vessels or complete but crushed vessels were recovered from the floor of the building, suggesting that its contents had been disturbed sometime after it was abandoned. Many of the small pot fragments contained the remains of car-

Figure 7.19. A pedestal vessel was buried as an offering in a corner of Unit 3 (photograph by Brian S. Bauer and Miriam Aráoz Silva).

bon on their outsides, indicating that they had been used in cooking.

An offering was also found in the northeastern corner of the building, where a small pit had been dug through the original floor. A pedestal vessel had been placed in the pit, and a fragment of a large storage jar, functioning like a top, had been placed over the mouth of the vessel (Figure 7.19).

In all, 970 ceramic fragments were recovered during the excavation of Unit 3. No roof tile remains were recovered. Although the crushed and shattered condition of the ceramic vessels makes estimation difficult, we suggest that the north half of the room contained the remains of at least four aryballoi, two large storage vessels (*urpus/rakis*), three lids, a tripod vessel, a pedestal vessel, and several small cooking pots. These items suggest that food and drink were being prepared and perhaps consumed in the room.

Two small rectangular pieces of bent silver lamina (3 x 4 cm and 5 x 2 cm) and a copper celt were also recovered from the floor of the building (Figures 7.20 and 7.21). The recovery of these items suggests that although domestic activities occurred in the room, they were associated with high-status individuals.

All areas of the floor contained flecks of carbon. However, there was no evidence of a formal hearth; nor was there evidence that the building had been destroyed by fire. A charcoal sample (AA 95799) taken from the exterior of a cooking vessel provided an AMS

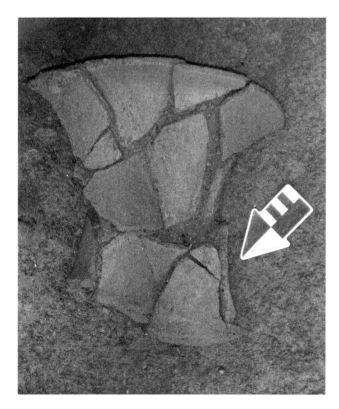

Figure 7.18. The crushed remains of the neck of an aryballos (Unit 3, south corner) (photograph by Brian S. Bauer and Miriam Aráoz Silva).

date of B.P. 327 ± 35 (1623 ± 35) and a calibrated range of A.D. 1495–1660 (95.4 percent). This date range is consistent with the assumed site abandonment date of 1572.

RESULTS OF UNIT 4

Unit 4 consisted of a 4.3 x 6.3 m excavation, placed in the southeastern side of one of the larger structures in the Lower Cancha. Before the excavation began, two large tree trunks on the ground were removed. The

Figure 7.20. One of two small pieces of bent silver lamina found on the floor of Unit 3 (photograph by Brian S. Bauer and Miriam Aráoz Silva).

walls of the structure were in a fair state of preservation, standing about 1.5 m high. The south corner of the building appeared unstable, so the area near it was left unexcavated. There were faint vestiges of niches on the interior walls of the building, but they were not pronounced enough for us to estimate the total number. The doorway, which opens onto the patio, was slightly trapezoidal in shape, and the walls had once been covered with a red clay plaster.

During the removal of the humus (Level 1), several ceramic fragments were recovered. The original floor of the building was later found less than 30 cm below the ground surface (Figures 7.22–7.30). Our excavations revealed a vast array of ceramic vessels within the building. Most of them were still in situ although badly crushed. Some of the vessels had been crushed as a result of wall fall. For example, a large pedestal vessel was found along the southeastern wall of the building beneath a fallen lintel. Other vessels, including several large storage vessels, were plastered flat on the floor, suggesting that they were broken when the roof of the building collapsed. One of these storage vessels even contained a small jug crushed inside it. The jug was presumably used to scoop out the contents of the storage vessel. A few of the smaller vessels, including a small cooking pot, a medium-sized cooking vessel, a jug, a small straight-sided bowl, a plate, and two miniature pots, remained intact.

There was ample evidence that cooking took place

Figure 7.21. (below) A copper celt was recovered on the floor of in Unit 3 (photograph by Brian S. Bauer and Miriam Aráoz Silva).

Figure 7.22.
Unit 4, looking
to the southwest
(photograph by
Brian S. Bauer
and Miriam
Aráoz Silva).

Figure 7.23.
Unit 4, looking
northeast
(photograph by
Brian S. Bauer
and Miriam
Aráoz Silva).

Figure 7.24. In the center of the building, the original floor was found less than 30 cm below the modern ground surface. Note the intact straight-sided bowl and broken cooking vessel in the profile (photograph by Brian S. Bauer and Miriam Aráoz Silva).

Figure 7.25. (right) A large pedestal vessel on the floor of Unit 4 was crushed by a lintel (photograph by Brian S. Bauer and Miriam Aráoz Silva).

Figure 7.26. Two large storage vessels in Unit 3. These vessels were crushed when the roof of the building collapsed (photograph by Brian S. Bauer and Miriam Aráoz Silva).

Figure 7.27. A jug was found standing upright on the floor of Unit 4 (photograph by Brian S. Bauer and Miriam Aráoz Silva).

Figure 7.28. An intact plate with strap handles was recovered on the floor of Unit 4 (photograph by Brian S. Bauer and Miriam Aráoz Silva).

Figure 7.30. A miniature vessel from Unit 4 (photograph by Brian S. Bauer and Miriam Aráoz Silva).

Figure 7.29. A small, straight-sided vessel from Unit 4 (photograph by Brian S. Bauer and Miriam Aráoz Silva).

in the building. The floor was rich in small flecks of carbon, and there were scatterings of minute burnt bone fragments in various locations. Four hearths, defined by areas of burnt clay, were recorded, and many of the cooking vessels contained thick coatings of carbonized materials on their exteriors (Figures 7.31–7.35). A number of lithic items, all known to be used in food processing, were also found on the floor of the building. These included six pestles and one mortar. A stone grinding platform and two grinding stones were also exposed in the profile of the unit. However, these were left in situ at the close of the research. It is also important to note that were was no evidence that the building

Figure 7.31. The southwestern end of the excavation profile of Unit 3. Note the grinding platform, the two grinding stones in situ beside it, and the edge of an intact cooking vessel within the profile (photo-graph by Brian S. Bauer and Miriam Aráoz Silva).

Figure 7.32. A stone mortar and a small crushed aryballos on the floor of the building (photograph by Brian S. Bauer and Miriam Aráoz Silva).

Figure 7.33. A small cooking vessel from Unit 4 (photograph by Brian S. Bauer and Miriam Aráoz Silva).

Figure 7.34. A medium-sized cooking vessel from Unit 4 (photograph by Brian S. Bauer and Miram Aráoz Silva).

Figure 7.35. One of the four hearths found within Unit 4. The hearths were defined by areas of burnt clay (photograph by Brian S. Bauer and Miriam Aráoz Silva).

was burned after its abandonment and no roof tile fragments were recovered. Metal objects included a copper needle and an iron nail. The latter was the only European object found within the building.

A charcoal sample (AA 95800) recovered from the floor of the building provided an AMS date of 369 ± 35 B.P. (1581 ± 35) and a calibrated range of A.D. 1446–1637. This date range is consistent with our presumed site abandonment date of 1572.

Although our excavations recovered more than 4,000 ceramic fragments from Unit 4, because most of the ceramic vessels were crushed—yet undisturbed—a probable vessel inventory could be established for the excavation area. It is likely that the exposed area of the building contained remains of the following ceramic vessels: nine large storage vessels (*urpus/rakis*), one large aryballos, nine small- to-medium-sized aryballoi, five medium-sized cooking vessels, four small cooking vessels, three pedestal vessels, three jugs, three plates,

two lids, one straight-sided bowl, and one large serving vessel with puma heads on its handles (Figures 7.36 and 7.37).[6]

RESULTS OF UNIT 6

Unit 6, a 3 x 4 m excavation, incorporated the east half of one of the smaller buildings constructed around the Lower Cancha. There was evidence of one small looter's pit in the building when we started to work, and the neck of a large aryballos had been set in one of the corners and covered up with loose stones. The excavation was conducted in three levels: the humus, the wall fall, and a thin level of deposited earth, which rested directly above the Inca floor.

In total, 1,320 ceramic fragments were recovered scattered across the floor. Although the vessels were badly crushed and scattered, a likely vessel count for the unit could be developed. We believe that the ex-

Figure 7.36. A vessel with puma-head handles was found standing on the floor of Unit 4. Also note the medium-sized aryballos neck (photograph by Brian S. Bauer and Miriam Aráoz Silva).

cavation area of the building contained parts for four aryballoi, three large storage vessels (*urpus/rakis*), one jug, one straight-sided bowl, a lid, a plate, a miniature plate, a pedestal vessel, and perhaps one or two small cooking vessels. A grinding stone was also recovered. No roof tile remains were found. The contents of this building, much like the others excavated around the Lower Cancha, suggest that it was used for storage, cooking, and meal preparation.

There were scattered flecks of charcoal across the floor but no areas of concentrated charcoal that suggested a hearth area or that the building had been burned. One carbon sample (AA 95802) was submitted for dating from this unit, but it proved to be an intrusive sample, yielding an AMS date range of B.P. 208 ± 35 (A.D. 1742 ± 35) and a calibrated range of A.D. 1649–1953 (95.4 percent). Given the shallowness of the excavation, it is not surprising that more recent carbon was recovered near the Inca floor level.

Figure 7.37. One of the puma-head handles recovered from Unit 3 (photograph by Brian S. Bauer and Miriam Aráoz Silva).

Endnotes

1   We initially planned to continue our excavations at the site of Espíritu Pampa in 2011. However, increased drug trafficking and political unrest in the region shifted our priorities to laboratory work.

2   Unfortunately, no carbonized cultigens were recovered in these samples.

3   Our project was supervised by the Ministerio de Cultura's Cusco office. At the end of the field season, the fieldwork was inspected and approved. At the close of the project, a final report, including copies of site maps, profiles, plan views, and forms, was submitted to the Ministerio de Cultura and approved. Most of the items recovered during our work were later sent by the Ministerio de Cultura from Cusco to Quillabamba. They are now housed at the Museo Amazónico Andino Qhapaq Ñan.

4   One area of this unit was left unexcavated because of an unstable section of wall.

5   Because of the sizes of these small fragments, we were not able to provide a minimum vessel estimate.

6   Earlier excavations at the site of Espíritu Pampa have recovered other examples of these types of vessels.

Appendix

The Results of Radiocarbon Tests Run on Charcoal Recovered in Inca Buildings at the Site of Espíritu Pampa

SAMPLE	SAMPLE ID	MATERIAL	d¹³C	F	¹⁴C age BP	A.D./B.C.		CALIBRATED
AA 95799	Espíritu Pampa 1 (Lower Cancha, Unit 3)	charcoal	-24.0	.9601 ± .0042	327 ± 35	1623 ± 35	68.2%	1510 (58.7%) 1576 cal A.D.
								612 (19.5%) 1645 cal A.D.
							95.4%	1495 (95.4%) 1660 cal A.D.
AA 95800	Espíritu Pampa 2 (Lower Cancha, Unit 4)	charcoal on pottery	-24.7	.9550 ± .0042	369 ± 35	1581 ± 35	68.2%	1499 (16.2%) 1525 cal A.D.
								1535 (41.1%) 1620 cal A.D.
								1609 (11.0%) 1626 cal A.D.
							95.4%	1446 (95.4%) 1637 cal A.D.
AA 95801	Espíritu Pampa 3 (Hall of the Miniatures)	charcoal on pottery	-21.2	.9571 ± .0043	352 ± 36	1598 ± 36	68.2%	1505 (57.6%) 1589 cal A.D.
								1617 (10.6%) 1633 cal A.D.
							95.4%	1481 (95.4%) 1646 cal A.D.
AA 95802	Espíritu Pampa 4 (Lower Cancha, Unit 5)	charcoal	-24.7	.9744 ± .0042	208 ± 35	1742 ± 35	68.2%	1660 (18.4%) 1696 cal A.D.
								1725 (49.8%) 1807 cal A.D.
							95.4%	1649 (24.4%) 1712 cal A.D.
								1718 (52.1%) 1814 cal A.D.
								1835 (11.6%) 1891 cal A.D.
								1922 (07.4%) 1953 cal A.D.
AA 95803	Espíritu Pampa 5 (Tendi Pampa, B5)	burnt corn	-9.9	.9565 ± .0042	357 ± 35	1593 ± 35	68.2%	1504 (58.7%) 1590 cal A.D.
								1616 (09.5%) 1630 cal A.D.
							95.4%	1478 (95.4%) 1644 cal A.D.
AA 95804	Espíritu Pampa 6 (Tendi Pampa, B5)	charcoal roof support	-25.1	.9524 ± .0043	392 ± 35	1558 ± 35	68.2%	1463 (32.6%) 1511 cal A.D.
								1553 (02.2%) 1557 cal A.D.
								574 (33.2%) 1621 cal A.D.
							95.4%	1457 (95.4%) 1628 cal A.D.

Bibliography

Angles Vargas, Víctor

1988   *Historia del Cuzco Incaico.* 3 vols. Industria Grafica, Lima.

Angrand, Léonce

2010   [1814–1838, 1847] *La Obra peruanista de Léonce Angrand,* edited by Edgardo Rivera Martínez, Ileana Vegas, and Bertha Martínez Castilla. Fundación Bustamante de la Fuente, Lima.

Aparicio López, Teófilo

1989   *Fray Diego Ortiz, misionero y mártir del Perú.* Ed Studio Agustiniano, Valladolid.

Arkush, Elizabeth N.

2011   *Hillforts of the Ancient Andes: Colla Warfare, Society, and Landscape.* University Press of Florida, Gainesville.

Bandelier, Adolph F. A.

1910   *The Islands of Titicaca and Koati.* Hispanic Society of America, New York.

Barraza Lescano, Sergio

2010   Redefiniendo una categoría arquitectónica Inca: la kallanka. *Bulletin de l'Institut Français d'Études Andines* 39(1):167–181.

Bauer, Brian S.

1999   *The Early Ceramics of the Inca Heartland.* Fieldiana Anthropology, New Series 31. Field Museum of Natural History, Chicago.

2002   *Las antiguas tradiciones alfareras de la región del Cuzco.* Centro de Estudios Regionales Andinos, "Bartolomé de Las Casas," Cusco.

2004   *Ancient Cuzco: Heartland of the Incas.* University of Texas Press, Austin.

Bauer, Brian S., Teofilo Aparicio, Jesús Galiano, Madeleine Halac-Higashimori, and Gabriel Cantarutti

2014   *Muerte, entierros y milagros de Fray Diego Ortiz: Política y religión en Vilcabamba, S. XVI.* Ceques editors, Cusco.

Bauer, Brian S., and Antonio Coello Rodríguez

2007   *The Hospital of San Andrés (Lima, Peru) and the Search for the Royal Mummies of the Incas.* Fieldiana Anthropology, New Series 31. Field Museum of Natural History, Chicago.

Bauer, Brian S., and R. Alan Covey

2002   State Development in the Inca Heartland (Cuzco, Peru). *American Anthropologist* 10(3):846–864.

Bauer, Brian S., Madeleine Halac-Higashimori, and Gabriel Cantarutti

2015   *Voices from Vilcabamba: Accounts Chronicling the Fall of the Inca Empire.* University of Colorado Press, Denver.

Bauer, Brian S., Lucas C. Kellett, and Miriam Aráoz Silva

2010   *The Chanka: Archaeological Research in Andahuaylas (Apurimac), Peru.* With contributions by Sabina Hyland and Carlo Socualaya Dávila. Cotsen Institute of Archaeology, University of California, Los Angeles.

Bauer, Brian S., Miriam Aráoz Silva, and George S. Burr

2012   The Destruction of the Yurak Rumi Shrine (Vilcabamba, Cuzco Department). *Andean Past* 10:195–212.Bauer, Brian S., and Charles Stanish.

2001   *Ritual and Pilgrimage in the Ancient Andes: The Islands of the Sun and the Moon.* University of Texas Press, Austin.

Beauclerk, John

1980   La Cordillera Vilcabamba: Ultimo refugio de los incas. *Boletín de Lima* 4/5:1–16.

Bingham, Alfred M.

1989   *Explorer of Machu Picchu: Portrait of Hiram Bingham.* Iowa State University Press, Ames.

Bingham, Hiram

1910   The Ruins of Choqquequirau. *American Anthropologist* 12:505–525.

1911 *Across South America: An Account of a Journey from Buenos Aires to Lima by Way of Potosí, with Notes on Brazil, Argentina, Bolivia, Chile, and Peru.* Houghton Mifflin, Boston.

1912a The Ascent of Coropuna. *Harper's Monthly Magazine.* March: 489–502.

1912b Preliminary Report of the Yale Peruvian Expedition. *Bulletin of the American Geographical Society* 44(1):20–26.

1912c A Search for the Last Inca Capital. *Harper's Monthly Magazine.* October: 695–705.

1912d Vitcos, the Last Inca Capital. *Proceedings of the American Antiquarian Society* 22 (April):135–196.

1913 In the Wonderlands of Peru: The Work Accomplished by the Peruvian Expedition of 1912. *National Geographic Magazine* 24:387–573.

1914a The Pampaconas River. *Geographical Journal* 44(2):211–214.

1914b The Ruins of Espíritu Pampa, Peru. *American Anthropologist* 16:185–199.

1915 The Story of Machu Picchu: The National Geographic Society–Yale University Explorations in Peru. *National Geographic Magazine* 27:172–186, 203–217.

1916 Further Explorations in the Land of the Incas. *National Geographic Magazine* 29:431–473.

1922 *Inca Land: Explorations in the Highlands of Peru.* Riverside Press, Cambridge, Massachusetts.

1930 *Machu Picchu: A Citadel of the Incas.* Memoirs of the National Geographic Society. Yale University Press, New Haven.

1948 *Lost City of the Incas: The Story of Machu Picchu and Its Builders.* Greenwood Press, Westport, Connecticut.

Bowman, Isaiah

1916 *The Andes of Southern Peru: Geographical Reconnaissance along the Seventy-third Meridian.* American Geographical Society, New York.

Buck, Daniel

1993 Fights of Machu Picchu. *South American Explorer* 32:22–32.

Bües, Christian

1989 [1935/1958] *El Señorío de Vilcabamba.* Instituto Nacional de Cultura, Cusco.

Burger, Richard L., and Lucy C. Salazar

2004 *Machu Picchu: Unveiling the Mystery of the Incas.* Yale University Press, New Haven.

Cabello de Balboa, Miguel

1951 [1586] *Miscelánea antártica, una historia del Perú antiguo.* Edited by L. E. Valcárcel. Universidad Nacional Mayor de San Marcos, Instituto de Etnología, Lima.

Calancha, Antonio de la

1981 [1638] *Corónica moralizada del Orden de San Agustín en el Perú.* Edited by Ignacio Prado Pastor. Universidad Nacional Mayor de San Marcos, Lima.

Cisneros, Carlos B.

1904 *Atlas del Perú: Político, minero, agrícola, industrial y comercial.* Librería e Imprenta Gil, Lima.

Clark, Simon

1959 *The Puma's Claw.* Little, Brown and Company, Boston.

Cobo, Bernabé

1964 [1653] Historia del Nuevo Mundo. In *Obras del P. Bernabe Cobo de la Compañía de Jesús,* vols. 91–92, edited by P. Francisco Mateos. Biblioteca de Autores Españoles, Madrid:

1979 [1653] *History of the Inca Empire: An Account of the Indians' Customs and Their Origin Together with a Treatise on Inca Legends, History, and Social Institutions,* translated and edited by Roland Hamilton. University of Texas Press, Austin.

Cosio, José Gabriel

1912 Machupiccho: Ciudad preincaica en el valle del Vilcanota. *Boletín de la Sociedad Geográfica de Lima* 28:147–161.

1924 *El Cuzco: Histórico y monumental.* Editorial Incaztec, Cusco.

1951 Vitcos: La última capital de los Incas. *Revista del Museo e Instituto Arqueológico* (Cusco) 13/14:7–17.

1961 Informe elevado al Ministerio de Instrucción por el doctor don Jose Cosio. *Revista del Museo e Instituto arqueológico* (Cusco) 19:326–364.

Covey, R. Alan

2006 *How the Incas Built Their Heartland: State Formation and the Innovation of Imperial Strategies in the Sacred Valley, Peru.* University of Michigan Press, Ann Arbor.

2008 Multiregional Perspectives on the Archaeology of the Andes during the Late Intermediate Period (ca. A.D. 1000–1400). *Journal of Archaeological Research* 16(3):287–338.

Covey, Alan, and Donato Amado Gonzales

2008   *Imperial Transformations in Sixteenth-Century Yucay, Peru*. Memoirs of the Museum of Anthropology (Studies in Latin American Ethnohistory and Archaeology) Vol. 6. University of Michigan Press, Ann Arbor.

Cruz Ccorimanya, Nicanor

2009   *Christian Bües: Biografía y recopilación de obras.* Centro Cultural José Pío Aza, Lima.

D'Altroy, Terence, and Christine A. Hastorf (editors)

2001   *Empire and Domestic Economy.* Plenum, New York.

Deagan, Kathleen

1987   *Artifacts of the Spanish Colonies of Florida and the Caribbean, 1500–1800*, vol. 1, *Ceramics, Glassware, and Beads.* Smithsonian Institution Press, Washington D.C.

Díaz Yampi, Ana María

2005   *Informe final de investigación arqueológica 2005, Sitio Arqueológico de Rosaspata Vitcos "Sector B."* Ministerio de Cultura Dirección Desconcentrada de Cultura, Cusco.

Drew, David

1984   The Cusichaca Project: Aspects of Archaeological Reconnaissance—the Lucumayo and Santa Teresa Valleys. In *Current Archaeological Projects in the Central Andes*, edited by Ann Kendall, pp. 345–375. BAR International Series 210. BAR, Oxford.

Fejos, Paul

1944   *Archaeological Explorations in the Cordillera Vilcabamba.* Viking Fund Publications in Anthropology, New York.

Flores Espinoza, Isabel, Rubén García Soto, and Lorenzo Huertas V.

1981   *Investigación Arqueológica-Histórica de la Casa Osambela (o de Oquendo).* Instituto Nacional de Cultura, Lima.

Fonseca Santa Cruz, Javier

2008   *Informe: Proyecto de investigación arqueológica de Espíritu Pampa—Vilcabamba (2008).* Ministerio de Cultura Dirección Desconcentrada de Cultura, Cusco.

2009   *Informe final: Proyecto de investigación arqueológica en el complejo arqueológico de Espíritu Pampa—Segunda Temporada (2009).* Ministerio de Cultura Dirección Desconcentrada de Cultura, Cusco.

2011   El rostro oculto de Espíritu Pampa, Vilcabamba, Cusco. *Arqueología Iberoamericana* 10:5–7. Electronic document, http://www.laiesken.net/arqueologia/.

Fonseca Santa Cruz, Javier and Brian S. Bauer

2013   Dating the Wari Remains at Espiritu Pampa (Vilcabamba, Cuzco). *Andean Past* 11:111–122.

García, José Uriel, and Albert Anthony Giesecke

1925   *Guía histórico-artística del Cuzco.* Imprenta Garcilaso, Lima.

Garcilaso de la Vega, Inca

1960   [1609] Comentarios reales de los incas. In *Obras completas del Inca Garcilaso de la Vega. Biblioteca de Autores Españoles*, vols. 132–135. Ediciones Atlas, Madrid.

1966   [1609] *Royal Commentaries of the Incas and General History of Peru*, parts 1 and 2, translated by H. V. Livermore. University of Texas Press, Austin.

Gasparini, Graziano, and Luise Margolies

1980   *Inca Architecture*, translated by P. J. Lyon. Indiana University Press, Bloomington.

Guillén Guillén, Edmundo

1977a   Documentos inéditos para la historia de los Incas de Vilcabamba: La capitulación del gobierno español con Titu Cusi Yupanqui. *Historia y Cultura* (Lima) 10:47–93.

1977b   Vilcabamba: La última capital del estado imperial inca. *Scientia et Praxis* (Lima) 10:126–155.

1978   Restauración geográfica del itinerario bélico seguido por los españoles, desde el puente de Chuquichaca a la ciudad de Vilcabamba. In *Etnohistoria y Antropología Andina*, edited by Marcia Koth Paredes and Amalia Castelli, pp. 45–150. Museo Nacional de Historia, Lima.

1979   *Visión Peruana de la conquista: La resistencia incaica a la invasión Española.* Editorial Milla Batres, Lima.

1980   El testimonio del Capitán Pedro Sarmiento de Gamboa y el itinerario de la campana española contra Thupa Amaro Inka: 1572. *Boletín de Lima* 9:22–40.

1981   Titu Cusi Yupanqui y su tiempo. *Revista de Historia y Cultura* (Lima) 13/14:61–99.

1994   *La guerra de reconquista Inka: historia* épica de cómo los Incas lucharon en defensa de la soberanía del Perú o Tawantinsuyo entre 1536 y 1572. R. A. Ediciones, Lima.

2005   *Ensayos de Historia Andina*, vols. 1 and 2. Universidad Alas Peruanas, Lima.

Hardy, Osgood

1918   The Incas. *The Mentor* 6(3):Serial 151.

Hemming, John

1970   *The Conquest of the Incas.* Harcourt Brace Jovanovich, New York.

Howell, Mark, and Tony Morrison

1967   *Steps to a Fortune.* Geofrey Bles, London.

Imhof, Eduard

1966   The Map of the Panta Group: Cordillera Vilcabamba, Peru. *Mountain World* 1964/1965:119–121.

Jamieson, Ross W.

2003   *De Tomebamba a Cuenca: Arquitectura y arqueología Colonial.* Ediciones Abya-Yala, Quito.

Julien, Catherine J.

1989   Las tumbas de Sacsahuaman y el estilo Cuzco-Inca. *Ñawpa Pacha* 25/27:1–126.

Kellett, Lucas C.

2010   Chanka Settlement Ecology: Hilltop Sites, Land Use, and Warfare in Late Prehispanic Andahuaylas, Peru. Ph.D. dissertation, University of New Mexico, Albuquerque.

Kendall, Anne

1984   Archaeological Investigations of the Late Intermediate and the Late Horizon Periods at Cusichaca, Peru. In *Current Archaeological Projects in the Central Andes,* edited by Anne Kendall, pp. 274–290. BAR International Series 210. Bar, Oxford.

Kosiba, Steve

2011   The Politics of Locality: Pre-Inka Social Landscapes of the Cusco Region. In *The Archaeology of Politics: The Materiality of Political Practice and Action in the Past,* edited by P. Johansen and A. Bauer, pp. 114–150. Cambridge Scholars Publishing, Newcastle-upon-Tyne.

2012   Emplacing Value, Cultivating Order: Places of Conversion and Practices of Subordination throughout Early Inka State Formation (Cusco, Peru). In *The Construction of Value in the Ancient World,* edited by John K. Papadopoulos and Gary Urton, pp. 99–127. Cotsen Institute of Archaeology Press, Los Angeles.

Kubler, George

1944   A Peruvian Chief State: Manco Inca (1515–1545). *Hispanic American Historical Review* 24(2):253–276.

1946   The Quechua in the Colonial World. In *Handbook of South American Indians,* vol. 2, *The Andean Civilizations,* edited by Julian Steward, pp. 331–410. Bureau of American Ethnology Bulletin 143. U.S. Government Printing Office, Washington, D.C.

1947   The Neo-Inca State (1537–1572). *Hispanic American Historical Review,* 27(2):189–203.

Larco, Rafael M

1934   *Cusco Histórico.* La Crónica y Variedades, Lima.

Lechtman, Heather

1996   El bronce y Horizonte Medio (Perú). *Boletín del Museo del Oro* (Colombia) 41:3–25.

Lee, Vincent R.

1998   Reconstructing the Great Hall at Inkallacta. *Andean Past* 5:35–71.

2000   Forgotten Vilcabamba: final stronghold of the Incas. Empire Publishing.

Levillier, Roberto

1935   *Don Francisco de Toledo, supremo organizador del Perú: su vida, su obra (1515–1582),* vol. 1. Años andanzas y de guerras. Biblioteca del Congreso Argentino, Buenos Aires.

Lister, Florence C., and Robert H. Lister

1974   Majolica in Colonial Spanish America. *Historical Archaeology* 8:17–52.

Llacsa Chuqui, Angelina

1916   [circa 1595] Testimony on the Martyrdom of Ortiz from Angelina Llacsa Chuqui in the Town of Lucma. In *Colección de libros y documentos referentes a la historia del Perú,* series 1, vol. 2, edited by Carlos A. Romero and Horacio H. Urteaga, pp. 133–137. Sanmartí, Lima.

MacQuarrie, Kim

2007   *The Last Days of the Incas.* Simon and Schuster, New York.

Mallet, Alain Manesson

1683   *Description de l'Univers.* D. Thierry, Paris.

Maúrtua, Victor M.

1906   *Juicio de límites entre el Perú y Bolivia. Tomo VII (Vilcabamba).* Henrich y Comp., Barcelona.

McCormac, F. G., A. G. Hogg, P. G. Blackwell, C. E. Buck, T. F. G. Higham, and P. J. Reimer

2004   SHCal04 Southern Hemisphere Calibration, 0–11.0 cal kyr BP. *Radiocarbon* 46(3):1087–1092.

Means, Philip Ainsworth

1931   *Ancient Civilizations of the Andes.* Charles Scribner's Sons, New York.

1932   *The Fall of the Inca Empire.* Charles Scribner's Sons, New York.

Merma Gomez, Luz Marina

2004   *Informe anual 2004. Investigación y restauración del sitio arqueológico Rosaspata—Vilcabamba.* Ministerio de Cultura Dirección Desconcentrada de Cultura, Cusco.

Morris, Craig

1971   The Identification of Function in Provincial Inca Architecture and Ceramics. In *Actas y Memorias del XXXIX Congresso Internacional de Americanistas* 3:135–144. Instituto de Estudios Peruanos, Lima.

Morris, Craig, R. Alan Covey, and Pat Stein

2011   *The Huánuco Pampa Archaeological Project*, vol. 1, *The Plaza and the Palace Complex.* American Museum of Natural History Anthropological Papers 96. American Museum of Natural History, New York.

Murúa, Martín de

1987   [1611–1616] *Historia General del Perú*, edited by Manuel Ballesteros Gaibrois. Crónicas de América 35. Historia 16, Madrid.

2008   [1616] *Historia General del Piru.* Getty Research Institute, Los Angeles.

Nowack, Kerstin

2004   Las provisiones de Titu Cusi Yupanqui. *Revista Andina* 38:139–179.

Ocampo Conejeros, Baltasar

2013   [1611] Descripción de la Provincia de San Francisco de la Victoria de Vilcabamba. In *Baltasar de Ocampo Conejeros y la Provincia de Vilcabamba*, transcribed and edited by Brian S. Bauer and Madeleine Halac-Higashimori. Ceques editorial, Cusco.

Ohlson, Kristin

2014   Searching for De Soto. Archaeological Conservancy. Electronic document, http://www.archaeologicalconservancy.org/searching-de-soto-kristin-ohlson/.

Olin, Jacqueline S., Garman Harbottle, and Edward Sayre

1978   Elemental Compositions of Spanish and Spanish-Colonial Majolica Ceramics in the Identification of Provenience. *Archaeological Chemistry* 2:200–229.

Oricain, Pablo José

2004   [1790] *Compendio breve de discursos varios sobre diferentes materias, y noticias geográficas, comprensivas a este obispado del Cuzco, que claman remedios espirituales.* Ministerio de Relaciones Exteriores del Perú, Lima.

Ossio, Juan M.

2008   Martín de Murúa. In *Guide to Documentary Sources for Andean Studies 1530–1900.* Edited by Joanne Pillsbury, pp. 3:436–441. University of Oklahoma Press, Norman.

Pardo, Luis A.

1938   Clasificación de la cerámica Cuzqueña (Época Incaica). *Revista del Instituto Arqueológico del Cuzco* 6(6–7):3–27.

1972   El imperio de Vilcabamba. *Revista del patronato Departamental de Arqueología del Cusco* 2(2):15–193.

Pérez Trujillo, Amelia

2002   *Informe final de la investigación arqueológica realizada en el sitio arqueológico de Rosaspata (Vilcabamba).* Ministerio de Cultura Dirección Desconcentrada de Cultura, Cusco.

Pilares Daza, José

2003   *Informe de investigación arqueológica Espíritu Pampa.* Ministerio de Cultura Dirección Desconcentrada de Cultura, Cusco.

Pizarro, Pedro

1921   [1571] *Relation of the Discovery and Conquest of the Kingdoms of Peru*, translated and edited by Philip Ainsworth Means. Cortés Society, New York.

1986   [1571] *Relación del descubrimiento y conquista de los reinos del Perú.* Pontificia Universidad Católica del Perú, Lima.

Polo de Ondegardo, Juan

1965   [1571] *A Report on the Basic Principles Explaining the Serious Harm Which Follows when the Traditional Rights of the Indians Are Not Respected*, translated by A. Brunel, John Murra, and Sidney Muirden, pp. 53–196. Human Relations Area Files, New Haven, Connecticut.

Protzen, Jean-Pierre

1993   *Inca Architecture and Construction at Ollantaytambo.* Oxford University Press, New York.

Quave, Kylie

2010   *Proyecto Yurac Rumi y Proyecto Vilcabamba: Ceramic Summary Report.* Department of Anthropology, University of Illinois, Chicago.

Raimondi, Antonio

1872   *El Perú: Historia de la geografía del Perú*, vol. 1. Imprenta del Estado, Lima.

Ramos Cóndori, Florencio Fidel

2007   *Los protagonistas de la resistencia Inka (1532–1572).* Imp. Edmundo Pantigozo, Cusco.

Regalado de Hurtado, Liliana

1992   *Religión y evangelización en Vilcabamba 1572–1602.* Fondo Editorial de PUCP, Lima.

Ridgeway, John

1987   *Road to Osambre.* Viking Penguin, New York.

Rodríguez de Figueroa, Diego

[1565]   Relación del camino e viaje que hizo desde la ciudad del Cuzco a la tierra de Guerra de Manco Inga. In *Nachrichten der Königlichen Gesellschaft der Wissenschaften zu Göttingen, Philologisch-historische Klasse aus dem Jahre Göttingen*, edited by R. Pietschmann, pp. 90–112. Commissionverglag der Dietrich'schen Verlagsbuchhandlung, Göttingen.

Romero, Carlos A.

1909   Informe sobre las ruinas de Choqquequirao. *Revista Histórica* (Lima) 4:87–103.

Rowe, John H.

1946   Inca Culture at the Time of the Spanish Conquest. In *Handbook of South American Indians*, vol. 2, *The Andean Civilizations*, edited by Julian Steward, pp. 183–330. Bureau of American Ethnology Bulletin 143. U.S. Government Printing Office, Washington, D.C.

1990   Machu Picchu a la luz de documentos del siglo XVI. *Histórica* 14(1)134–154.

Saintenoy, Thibault

2008   Choqek'iraw y el valle del Apurímac: Hábitat y paisajes prehispanicos tardíos. Una investigación en curso. *Bulletin de l'Institut Français d'Etudes Andines* 37:553–561.

2009   Ocupación prehispánica del curso medio del Apurímac. In *Visión de Apurímac*, edited by R. Carreño and S. Kalafatovich, p. 237. Fondo Italo-Peruano, Cusco.

2011   Choqek'iraw et la vallée de l'Apurimac: Paysages et Sociétés préhispaniques tardives. Ph.D. dissertation, Université Paris 1 Panthéon Sorbonne, Paris.

Sakai, Masato

2009   El Templo del Sol Coricancha en Cusco y Vilcabamba. In *Miradas al Tahuantinsuyo: Aproximaciones de peruanitas japoneses al imperio de los incas*, edited by Hidefuji Someda and Yuji Seki, pp. 133–158. Fondo Editorial, Lima.

Samanez, Roberto y Julinho Zapata

1996   El templo del sol en Vilcabamba. *Arkinka* 2:62–72.

Samanez y Ocampo, José B.

1980   *Exploración de los rios Peruanos: Apurímac, Eni, Tambo, Ucayali y Urubamba. Hecha por José B. Samanez y Ocampo en 1883 y 1884. Diario de la expedición y anexos*. Sesator, Lima.

Sarmiento de Gamboa, Pedro

1977   Acta de la toma de posesión real de la ciudad de Vilcabamba (24, June, 1572). *Scientia et praxis* 12:142–145.

Sartiges, Conde Eugène de

1851   *Voyage dans les Republiques de l'Amérique du Sud*. Written under the pseudonym of M. E de Lavandais. Revue des Deux Mondese, Paris.

Savoy, Gene

1964a   Discovery of the Ruins of Vilcabamba. *Peruvian Times*, 14 August.

1964b   Vilcabamba Grande: The Last Refuge of the Incas. *Peruvian Times*, 18 September.

1970   *Antisuyu: The Search for the Lost Cities of the Amazon*. Simon and Schuster, New York.

1978a   The Discovery of Vilcabamba. *Explorers Journal* 56 (1):32—37

1978b   Return to Vilcabamba: Discovery Confirmed and Surveyed. *Explorers Journal* 56(4):154–161.

Scarre, Chris, and Geoffrey Scarre (editors)

2006   *The Ethics of Archaeology: Philosophical Perspectives on Archaeological Practice*. Cambridge University Press, Cambridge.

Spiess, Ernst

1965   A Topographer in the Cordillera Vilcabamba (Peru). *Mountain World* 1964/1965:122–137.

Stuiver, Mince and Paula J. Reimer

1993   Extended 14C Data Base and Revised Calib 3.0 14C Age Calibration Program *Radiocarbon* 35(1):215–230.

Thomson, Hugh

2003   *The White Rock: An Exploration of the Inca Heartland*. Overlook Press. Woodstock, New York.

Titu Cusi Yupanqui, Inca Diego de Castro

2005   [1570] *An Inca Account of the Conquest of Peru by Titu Cusi Yupanqui*, translated, introduced, and annotated by Ralph Bauer. University of Colorado Press, Denver.

Toledo, Francisco de

1899   Situación de Gobernador Martín de Arbieto de 1000 pesos en los indios de Tinta y Moyna. *Revista de Archivos y Bibliotecas Nacionales* (Lima) 1:123–128.

Valcárcel, Luis

1934   Los trabajos arqueológicos del Cusco, Sajsawaman redescubierto I-II. *Revista del Museo Nacional* 3:3–36, 211–233.

1946   Cuzco Archaeology. In *Handbook of South American Indians*, vol. 2, *The Andean Civilizations*, edited by Julian Steward, pp. 179–182. Bureau of American Ethnology Bulletin 143. U.S. Government Printing Office, Washington, D.C.

von Hagen, Victor W.

1955   *Highway of the Sun.* Duell, Sloan and Pearce, New York.

von Kaupp, Roberto, and Octavio Fernandez Carrasco

2010   *Vilcabamba Desconocida.* Editorial Grafica Rivera, Cusco.

Wernke, Steven A.

2010   Convergences: Producing Early Colonial Hybridity at a *Doctrina* in Highland Peru. In *Enduring Conquests: Rethinking the Archaeology of Resistance to Spanish Colonialism in the Americas*, edited by Matthew Liebmann and Melissa S. Murphy, pp. 77–102. School for Advanced Research Press, Santa Fe, New Mexico.

White, Stuart

1984   Preliminary Survey of the Punkuyoq Range, Southern Peru. *Ñawpa Pacha* 22/23:127–160.

Wiener, Charles

1880   *Pérou et Bolivie. Récit de voyage suivi d'études archéologiques et ethnographiques et de notes sur l'écriture et les langues des populations indiennes.* Hachette et Cie, Paris.

Index

UCLA
COTSEN INSTITUTE OF ARCHAEOLOGY PRESS

MONOGRAPHS
Contributions in Field Research and Current Issues in
Archaeological Method and Theory

Monograph 81   *Vilcabamba and the Archaeology of Inca Resistance*, Brian S. Bauer,
Javier Fonseca Santa Cruz, and Miriam Aráoz Silva

Monograph 80   *An Archaic Mexican Shellmound and Its Entombed Floors*, Barbara Voorhies (ed.)

Monograph 79   *Archaeology of the Chinese Bronze Age: From Erlitou to Anyang*, Roderick B. Campbell

Monograph 78   *Visions of Tiwanaku*, Alexei Vranich and Charles Stanish (eds.)

Monograph 77   *Advances in Titicaca Basin Archaeology–2*, Alexei Vranich and Abigail R. Levine (eds.)

Monograph 76   *The Dead Tell Tales*, María Cecilia Lozada and Barra O'Donnabhain (eds.)

Monograph 75   *The Stones of Tiahuanaco*, Jean-Pierre Protzen and Stella Nair

Monograph 74   *Rock Art at Little Lake: An Ancient Crossroads in the California Desert*,
Jo Anne Van Tilburg, Gordon E. Hull, and John C. Bretney

Monograph 73   *The History of the Peoples of the Eastern Desert*, Hans Barnard and Kim Duistermaat (eds.)

Monograph 71   *Crucible of Pueblos: The Early Pueblo Period in the Northern Southwest*,
Richard H. Wilshusen, Gregson Schachner, and James R. Allison (eds.)

Monograph 70   *Chotuna and Chornancap: Excavating an Ancient Peruvian Legend*, Christopher B. Donnan

Monograph 69   *An Investigation into Early Desert Pastoralism: Excavations at the Camel Site, Negev*,
Steven A. Rosen

Monograph 68   *The Chanka: Archaeological Research in Andahuaylas (Apurimac), Peru*,
Brian S. Bauer, Lucas C. Kellett, and Miriam Aráoz Silva

Monograph 67   *Inca Rituals and Sacred Mountains: A Study of the World's Highest Archaeological Sites*,
Johan Reinhard and Maria Costanza Ceruti

Monograph 66   *Gallinazo: An Early Cultural Tradition on the Peruvian North Coast*,
Jean-François Millaire with Magali Morlion

Monograph 65   *Settlement and Subsistence in Early Formative Soconusco*, Richard G. Lesure (ed.)

Monograph 64   *The South American Camelids*, Duccio Bonavia

Monograph 63   *Andean Civilization: A Tribute to Michael E. Moseley*,
Joyce Marcus and Patrick Ryan Williams (eds.)

Monograph 62   *Excavations at Cerro Azul, Peru: The Architecture and Pottery*, Joyce Marcus

Monograph 61   *Chavín: Art, Architecture, and Culture*, William J Conklin and Jeffrey Quilter (eds.)

Monograph 60   *Rethinking Mycenaean Palaces II: Revised and Expanded Second Edition*,
Michael L. Galaty and William A. Parkinson (eds.)

Monograph 59   *Moche Tombs at Dos Cabezas*, Christopher B. Donnan

Monograph 58   *Moche Fineline Painting from San José de Moro*, Donna McClelland,
Donald McClelland, and Christopher B. Donnan

Monograph 57   *Kasapata and the Archaic Period of the Cuzco Valley*, Brian S. Bauer (ed.)

Monograph 56   *Berenike 1999/2000*, Steven E. Sidebotham and Willeke Wendrich (eds.)